DON'T PANIC

Don't PANIC

TAKING CONTROL OF ANXIETY ATTACKS

Revised Edition

R. Reid Wilson, Ph.D.

HarperPerennial
A Division of HarperCollins*Publishers*

HarperCollins books may be purchased for educational, business, or sales promotional use. For information please write: Special Markets Department, HarperCollins Publishers, Inc., 10 East 53rd Street, New York, NY 10022.

FIRST EDITION

Designed by Nancy Singer

ISBN 0-06-095160-5

96 97 98 99 00 ❖/RRD 10 9 8 7 6 5 4 3 2 1

To my parents, Robert and Ann Wilson

*And to my children, Joanna Foster Wilson and
Patrick Harrington Wilson*

Contents

Acknowledgments

Pursuing a career in clinical psychology fulfills two of my most cherished lifelong dreams: to continually explore the world of ideas as an eager and naive student and simultaneously to give to others in a way that makes a difference. This book is a reflection of a lifetime of learning, and I hope it in some small way honors those who have nourished and inspired me. Theoretically, it is a synthesis of the work of hundreds of dedicated professionals in a surprisingly broad spectrum of fields. Their names can be found in this book's bibliography.

Over the past twenty-five years I have had the distinct privilege of studying under the mentorship of seven professionals whose wisdom and example will remain powerful influences in my professional life: Takey Crist, M.D.; Ed Gurowitz, Ph.D.; Michio Kushi; Emily Ruppert, M.S.W.; Daniel Rutrick, M.D.; Stephen Lankton, M.S.W.; and David Hawkins, M.D. My four lifelong friends—Phillip Wilson, Leif Diamant, William "Bud" Garrison, and Alan Konell—have joined me in adventures that have opened my heart, expanded my perception of the potential of life, and given me the gift of self-love. Through his example, Robert Wilson taught me the value of determination, precision, and intellectual curiosity. My mother, Ann, and my sister, Karen Ann, have long been my steadfast, loving supporters. Bentha Newman continues to inspire me with her extraordinary blend of optimism, generosity, and assertiveness.

A number of people contributed directly to the existence of this book. Stephen Lankton, M.S.W., gave me endless encouragement, prodded me to address my self-doubts, and pointed me toward my creativity. Richard Bush, Ph.D., guided me through the logistics of book publishing and continually reminded me that I could succeed. I am indebted to Carol Houck Smith for her suggestions in redirecting the early drafts of the first edition of this book. John Ware, my agent and friend, arrived at just the right time with just the right support. I wish to express my appreciation to four dedicated and skilled physicians who reviewed and enhanced the medical information in this book: David Savitz, M.D., for material on the physical causes of paniclike symptoms; James Donohue, M.D., on panic within chronic obstructive lung diseases; James Harper, M.D., on panic within cardiac disorders; and James Ballenger, M.D., and Daniel Rutrick, M.D., on the use of medications. Kathie Ness and Margaret Wimberger gently presented significant editorial contributions in the final draft of the first edition. My close friends Annette Perot, Ph.D., and Susan Kanaan, M.S.W., offered their expert critiques for portions of the second edition. Special thanks to Melissa Mayo for processing the many drafts of this edition. I am grateful to the staff of the Countway Library at Harvard University Medical School and the Health Sciences Library at the University of North Carolina for the use of their valuable resources.

Foreword

Hope and guidance are often sought in the pages of books, and on occasion a volume generously rewards the seeker with a sense of comfort and direction. For people with symptoms of anxiety, Dr. Wilson's *Don't Panic* is one of those books. In preparing this volume, Dr. Wilson has drawn deeply both on his own experience in helping people with panic and on the scientific literature that deals with panic-related problems. He provides readers with the full understanding they need to begin to recover from debilitating and demoralizing anxiety disorders.

The highly successful first edition of this book became a forerunner in the field of anxiety by offering specific and powerfully effective self-help skills to those suffering from incapacitating symptoms. Now, in this revised edition, Dr. Wilson greatly expands his first work, with major additions throughout the book. He translates his pioneering clinical innovations into everyday language that adapt complex models of treatment into easily applied principles. In two of his new chapters he details compassionate advice for social anxieties and the fear of flying.

Dr. Wilson's book will help to dispel much of the fear and confusion that often accompany panic attacks. It is sensibly divided into three parts. Part 1 is packed with much-needed but hard-to-come-by information that will help the panic sufferer identify the components of his or her particular problem. In an invaluable first chapter, Dr. Wilson reviews the physical sensations that are commonly associated with panic and shows that these sensations are a part of the body's normal systems for dealing with emergencies. He explains how a number of factors—physical illness, dramatic or frightening events, current demands and responsibilities, psychological difficulties—can produce paniclike symptoms, and describes how fear of a repetition of these symptoms can lead to severe anxiety.

In the succeeding chapters of part 1, Dr. Wilson discusses the various psychological and medical problems to which panic symptoms may be related and the complications produced by such problems as premenstrual syndrome, hypoglycemia, depression, and alcoholism. He gives clear advice on how to sort the physical and psychological aspects of the problem. Perhaps most intriguing, he takes a look at the thoughts, beliefs, and behavior patterns he has observed in people with panic disorders and agoraphobia, and begins to suggest a plan for recovery.

In part 2, Dr. Wilson presents tools and techniques for overcoming panic disorders and phobias. Correctly emphasizing the loss of self-confidence that is so much a part of these problems, Dr. Wilson maps a path toward more independent functioning. The cornerstone of his pioneering theory is spelled out in chapter 13: to overcome your anxiety, you must change your attitude toward your symptoms. Here you will learn eight powerful shifts in perspective from a masterful teacher. You will be challenged by these provocative attitudes. But you will be well rewarded when you heed them.

The next chapters of part 2 build on this blueprint. An essential part of his plan is to help panic sufferers recognize the workings of the internal "observer"—that part of us that takes in information about a situation, assesses it, and decides what to do about it. When people have had repeated panic attacks, according to Dr. Wilson, they are likely to be listening to a "worried observer," a "hopeless observer," or a "critical observer," rather than an objective, patient inner voice. The antidote for those troublesome influences is to nourish and strengthen an "independent" or "supportive" internal observer. This inner friend sets reasonable goals and strives to meet them but grants the freedom to make a wide variety of choices at any given time. This observer recognizes negative thoughts and images but clears them from the mind, concentrating instead on facts, goals, or physical surroundings.

Don't Panic includes clear and complete instructions for a number of relaxation methods, including abdominal breathing, muscle relaxation and meditation. Dr. Wilson synthesizes the most practical skills from his recent book, *Stop Obsessing!*, to help during times of excessive worry. The concluding chapters of part 2 constructs the final stages of this well-organized plan, through step-by-step actions to confront fearful situations.

Part 3 provides clarity on three major issues. Chapter 19 offers the most comprehensive consumer guide available on medications for all anxiety disorders. Chapter 20 outlines the most effective ways to overcome fear of speaking and other social anxieties, based on well-researched treatment models. In chapter 21 Dr. Wilson employs his expertise in aviation psychology to outline the essential tools for conquering the fear of flying.

For years, people with panic attacks and agoraphobia have found reassurance and encouragement in the writings of Claire Weekes. *Don't Panic* continues in the tradition of Dr. Weekes, expanding her advice and integrating the experience of behavior therapists, cognitive therapists, and psychopharmacologists to design a time-tested strategy for recovery. This is a superb book from a well-respected expert.

Aaron T. Beck, M.D.
University Professor of Psychiatry
University of Pennsylvania

Part I

IDENTIFYING THE PROBLEM

1

Introduction

THE PANIC ATTACK

It is as though the symptoms jump you from behind. With little warning the heart begins its rapid pumping, a cold perspiration beads the forehead, trembling hands want to hide from view. The throat attempts in vain to swallow as any moisture remaining in the mouth disappears.

Your mind races to retain some semblance of control. "Just relax! Stay calm!" is the silent command. But you place little faith in such words. And why should you? They have always failed to relieve the anarchy of the body in the past.

The more you grip to keep control, the less control you feel. Panic! Seconds pass like minutes as your mind is pulled in two directions. First, to the past: "This is like last month, when I became so weak that I almost fainted." Then, to the body with a mind of its own: "I can't catch my breath. I'm trying. I can't!" The future rushes to the present: "What if this keeps up? I could pass out. If my heart beats any faster I could have a heart attack."

At that moment the fear of humiliation crowds the noise of the mind. "Everyone's going to see me collapse. I've got to get out of here." With the same suddenness that this attack started, you make your escape out of the door of the conference room or the movie theater, the doctor's office or the grocery store. The farther you get from the scene, the more comfortable you feel.

This scenario is what I call *the moment of panic:* an internal experience, supported by physical sensations, that one has immediately and dangerously lost control of one's circumstances. The changes in the body and mind take place so rapidly and unconsciously that they are experienced as an "attack" of panic or anxiety.

All of us have experienced the physical sensations of anxiety. We get butterflies in the stomach before we give a speech, or sore, tense muscles after driving for an hour through a rainstorm. But the experience of general anxiety is quite distinct from the overwhelming sensations of a panic attack.

An example may clarify the difference. Have you ever faced a physical emergency alone, one that you were ill prepared to deal with? Imagine opening your cellar door to the sound of water splashing onto the concrete floor. You run down the stairs, half guided by your feet, half carried by your arms pushing off the hand rails. How fast do you size up the situation? How many options do you rule out in the first thirty seconds? "Can I stop it with my hand? No . . . How about tying it with a rag? Is there a rag around? Won't work! Where's this pipe coming from? Where's the main valve?" Your eyes move rapidly, absorbing every detail that might play a role in reducing the damage caused by a flooding basement. "Grandma's chest of drawers, it's getting ruined! Should I move it? Stop the water first. Where is that valve?! There's the trash can. No use, it's spraying too broadly. Whom can I call?"

If you freeze the action of the scene at this precise moment, you would recognize in yourself many of the physical symptoms found in what we call a panic attack or anxiety attack. The muscles are tense, ready to respond immediately to any directions from the brain ("Get down those stairs—*now!*"). The blood is rushing to the brain to stimulate the thought processes. The heart and the respiration rates both rapidly increase to produce the shifting of blood throughout the body essential to energetic action.

Each of us should be thankful for the incredible ability of our minds instantly and automatically to respond in such an emergency. How many of us have been saved from injury or death on the highway because our right foot slammed on the brake while our hands pulled on the steering wheel—all this before we had time even to think the command "Watch out for that car!"

Brilliant as this built-in emergency system is, sometimes things can go awry. During panic, the body responds with many of the same psychological changes that take place during an emergency. However, panic is an exaggeration of our emergency response. Instead of taking advantage of the body's rapidly increased strength, the individual experiencing panic becomes overwhelmed by a variety of physical symptoms. The more he focuses his attention on these internal changes, the more anxious he becomes and the less able he is to reassure himself.

A panic attack causes the fastest and most complex reaction known within the human body. It immediately alters the functioning of the eyes, several major glands, the brain, heart, lungs, stomach, intestines, pancreas, kidneys and bladder, and the major muscle groups. Within the cardiovascular system, the heart increases its rates of contractions, the amount of blood it pumps with each contraction, and the pressure it exerts as blood is pumped into the arteries. The vessels that channel blood into the vital organs and skeletal muscles expand, increasing their blood flow, while the blood vessels in the arms, legs, and other less vital parts of the body begin to constrict, reducing blood flow in those areas.

While this is taking place, your rate of respiration increases. The pupils dilate to improve distance vision. Within the gastrointestinal system, all digestive activity is diminished. Metabolism, the conversion of foods into energy, is enhanced, and increased amounts of sugars and fatty acids are secreted into the bloodstream.

Your subjective experience during a panic attack can vary greatly. Certain sensations (such as noticing your heart rate) are directly related to the physiological changes I have just mentioned. Others (such as the fear that you are dying) are produced by your mental and emotional response to these sensations. Listed below are a variety of symptoms associated with different parts of the body during a panic attack. Generally speaking, the more symptoms you have during the attack and the greater the intensity of each symptom, the more devastated you feel by this assault.

The head. Decreased blood flow to the brain, caused by hyperventilation, may result in a feeling of lightheadedness or dizziness, as though your head is "swimming." You may feel faint.

The body. You begin to perspire, have hot and cold flashes, feel numb, or experience prickling or tingling. You feel as though you are whirling about (the sensation of vertigo). The whole body feels fatigued or depleted.

The mind. You feel disoriented, confused, or unable to concentrate. You feel cut off or far away from your surroundings (called "derealization"). Your body can feel unreal, as though you are in a dream ("depersonalization"). You become irritable or short-tempered.

Common fears are of fainting, going crazy, having a heart attack, dying, making a scene, or becoming trapped.

The eyes. Your eyes flicker or twitch, You may have difficulty focusing on objects, or objects might appear blurry. Figures such as numbers on a page "jump around" or appeared reversed.

The mouth and throat. Your mouth becomes dry. You have difficulty swallowing, feel as if there is a lump in your throat or as if you might choke. The muscles in your throat feel tight. As you speak, your voice trembles.

The heart. You may have noticed that your heart has increased its rate of contractions. The pumping of the heart feels quite strong and pounding, as though it could jump out of your chest. Your heart may seem to skip a beat or two. You experience pain or discomfort in your chest.

Respiration. Your rate of breathing increases and becomes more shallow, possibly leading to hyperventilation. You feel as though you cannot take a full, deep breath. You might have difficulty catching your breath, may painfully gasp for air or feel as if you will smother.

The stomach. Your stomach feels full of butterflies, or tied in knots. You might feel nauseated.

The muscles. The muscles throughout your body feel tense, especially in the neck and shoulders. If you are driving, you may notice that your hands are gripping the steering wheel so tightly that your knuckles are white and your arms are stiff. In another situation, you may be unconsciously squeezing your hands into fists. Or your muscles may feel weak, your legs unable to keep you standing. Your hands and legs tremble, feel cold, clammy, and sweaty, or feel numb.

In essence, your body, which has been fairly trustworthy over the years, begins to mutiny. And if you experience panic attacks with any frequency, this lack of control slowly erodes your self-confidence and your self-esteem. You begin to restrict your activities in order to ward off these attacks. Familiar situations become threatening.

- If panic hits you before or during speeches, you begin to turn down speaking engagements.
- If panic hits you while you are traveling, you begin to find excuses for canceling out-of-town business meetings and

become "just too busy" to take a vacation with the family.

- If panic hits you in groups of people, you begin turning down invitations to parties and other gatherings, preferring to stay at home.
- If panic hits you in stores or restaurants or at the hairdresser's, you begin to avoid those locations which might stimulate a recurrence of your symptoms.
- If panic hits you while you are involved in physical exertion, you begin to avoid any activity that exercises your respiratory or cardiovascular system.
- If panic hits you only while you are alone, you begin to cling to your husband or wife, friends, even your children, to ensure safety and protection from this assault by your body.

You make think that your panic attack came out of the blue the first time or continues to "jump you from behind." After you experience several panics, a certain doubt creeps into your mind: "What is wrong with me? Why is this happening? Am I crazy? Is this the beginning of a nervous breakdown? Are these job [marriage/new baby/house purchase] responsibilities too much for me to handle? Do I have a thyroid condition [heart problem/cancer/high blood pressure]?" For many people, these moments of high excitement or extreme anxiety, of dramatic and sudden changes in the body, are the most frightening and troublesome events of their lives.

It is difficult to pinpoint the causes of panic; complicating the situation is the fact that panic can be found in several psychological disorders and paniclike symptoms can be found in dozens of physical disorders. An exact diagnosis is often difficult to make, and the treatment approaches can differ greatly. Occasionally the symptoms elude a positive diagnosis in the context.

Panic can take place in several contexts.

PANIC IN CONTEXT OF PHYSICAL ILLNESS

There are a number of physical disorders that produce symptoms resembling extreme anxiety or panic. If an illness remains undiagnosed or misdiagnosed, the individual can grow fearful of these unexpected, dramatic changes in the body. This lack of understanding and the fearful anticipation that results lead to panic because the person becomes increasingly preoccupied with her body. However, once the illness is diagnosed and properly treated, the paniclike symptoms disappear.

Some patients with a diagnosed physical problem become susceptible to panic. For instance, patients who have suffered from a heart attack often are cautious of any activity that might place stress on their heart. If they feel their heart increase its pumping action or if they notice a shortness of breath, their worried thoughts can turn to panic: "Oh, no, I've overstressed my heart. Is there any tingling in my arm like before? My chest is beginning to feel tight." Soon, these fearful thoughts themselves can produce such strong symptoms that the patient rushes to the hospital emergency room for evaluation. Similar problems arise in those diagnosed with angina, stroke, mitral valve prolapse, asthma, and hypertension.

Such fears during or after a physical illness can have significant repercussions. It has been reported that 95 percent of patients who have had a heart attack begin to suffer from anxiety. Of those discharged from a coronary care unit, 70 percent are given medication to cope with anxiety. In one study of post–heart attack patients who never returned to work, 80 percent remained at home because of psychological causes. Similarly, a study of patients with chronic lung diseases such as emphysema and bronchitis found that 96 percent had disabling anxiety, 74 percent were seriously depressed, and 78 percent were overly preoccupied with their bodies. The fear of becoming breathless seemed to be at the root of most of their problems.

PANIC AND DRAMATIC, FRIGHTENING EVENTS

Imagine that twice in the course of one week at the local swimming pool with your young child you watch the lifeguards pull near-drowning children out of the pool. You might notice within yourself sensations of anxiety the next time you take your child swimming. This would be a normal response to such an event. Some people have a more extreme response to that same situation. Their minds become full of horrible fantasies about losing their children. They have strong physical reactions when they consider approaching a pool in the future. This is the type of panic that can arise after a person is involved in any traumatic or frightening event, such as the death of a loved one, a serious accident, the diagnosis of a serious illness, or an emergency such as a fire or a stuck elevator. When a person reacts with dread or panic in a harmless situation and begins to avoid all similar situations, it is defined as a phobia.

PANIC, CURRENT DEMANDS, AND FEARFULNESS OF THE FUTURE

Panic may result from fear of the future, regardless of what has actually happened in the past. For many people this occurs when they are faced with an increase in demands or responsibilities. They may believe that they are incapable of handling the pressures of their responsibilities, that they lack the strength, willpower, skill, intelligence, or emotional stability to cope with some future encounter or task. Their lack of confidence in their abilities is supported by their belief that their world is too demanding or their task too overwhelming. This fearful anticipation can be manifested physically through attacks of extreme anxiety or panic.

PANIC AND PSYCHOLOGICAL DISORDERS

Occasionally, severe anxiety is one part of a more complex psychological disorder. Panic attacks can occur in individuals suffering from such problems as depression, agoraphobia, post-traumatic stress disorder, alcoholism, or obsessive-compulsive disorder.

This book is designed to assist anyone who is suffering from panic attacks, whether they are produced by a fearful response to physical illness, a psychological disorder, some frightening event in the past or future, or the building up of stress from the pressures of daily living.

If you are experiencing some of the symptoms described in this chapter, your first obligation is to go to your family physician for a complete medical examination. (Chapter 2 presents the major symptoms of panic that might be caused by physical illness; under each of these symptom categories you will learn about the types of illnesses involved and any other signs that might indicate a physical problem.) Your doctor will identify any physical causes of your problem and will suggest a treatment approach or refer you to a specialist for further evaluation.

Once you understand the role—if any—of a physical illness in your symptoms, you can use this book to acquire understanding and skills necessary to overcome anxiety attacks at the moment they are taking place. You will learn how the mind may be triggering this emergency reaction in your body. I will describe and illustrate how altering what you think, what you believe, and what you do brings relief from the terror of panic. Your thoughts, beliefs, and actions will play powerful roles as you learn to conquer panic.

I will offer relaxation exercises, special breathing patterns, and specific behavioral strategies to use in controlling panic. But change will require more than techniques. You may need to find a new way of looking at old problems. You may discover that your attitudes about life will change as you open your mind to new ideas. And most likely you will learn more about the functions of your body, your mind, and your brain; many of my clients report that they began to feel relief as soon as they learned that there is a *reason* for these symptoms.

There are no simple, universal solutions to life's problems, no magic pills. Any real solution to a complex problem will include a broad and stable foundation from which to build greater strength. There is an old Japanese proverb that goes something like this: "You can give a person a fish and feed him for a day. You can teach a person to fish and feed him for a lifetime." This book will give you some specific tools to use during the moment of panic. However, to gain control of panic whenever it arises, you must also understand the complex interactions among your body, your mind, your beliefs, and your behavior. In addition, you will find it much easier to conquer these attacks of panic with the support of others, be they professionals, friends, or family.

2

Physical Causes of Paniclike Symptoms

Everyone experiences the symptoms of anxiety from time to time, caused by any number of things—changes in our lifestyle or undue stress or tension. These symptoms often reflect a normal response to problems arising in our daily lives. In some cases, however, they may be the symptoms of a psychological or physical illness. The diagnosis of a serious medical problem is not always a simple process.

A man may complain to his physician that this morning he noticed that his heart was racing, he had difficulty catching his breath, and he felt dizzy, with tingling around his mouth and in his hands. He is afraid he is going to die or have a heart attack. These symptoms could indicate cardiac arrhythmia, pulmonary embolism, a panic attack, or a hyperventilation episode.

Every day, people are rushed into emergency rooms with the distinct symptoms of a heart attack: a crushing pain in the chest, shortness of breath, sweating, rapid heartbeat, and elevated blood pressure. For some of these patients, after extensive monitoring and evaluation physicians diagnose the episode as an anxiety attack.

Because these symptoms are so difficult to assess, both patients and professionals can misdiagnose significant physical or emotional problems. Studies in recent years reveal that a number of physical disorders coexist in patients who have a psychological disorder, and some physical problem may cause 5–40 percent of psychological illnesses. In the majority of these cases the health professional fails to make the physical diagnosis.

Nowhere is this confusion more evident and diagnosis more difficult than with panic attacks. If the symptoms of panic are present, there are three possible diagnoses:

1. A physiological disorder is the sole cause of all the symptoms associated with panic. Treatment of the physical problem removes the symptoms.
2. A minor physical problem produces a few symptoms. The individual then becomes introspective and oversensitive to these physical sensations and uses them as a cue to become anxious. Her heightened awareness and unnecessary concern produce an increase in symptoms. If this continues, she can turn an insignificant physical problem into a major psychological distress.
3. There is no physical basis for the symptoms. Some combination of the following will help: education about the problem, reassurance, psychological treatment, and medication treatment.

This chapter identifies all the major physical problems that can produce paniclike symptoms. By no means should you use this chapter (or any other in this book) for self-diagnosis. Only a physician has the resources to determine whether any of these disorders is the cause of your discomfort and to advise you of your treatment options. Through a comprehensive evaluation, your physician can determine which, if any, of these physical problems is associated with your symptoms. In most cases, curing the physical illness or adjusting medication will eliminate the symptoms. In some disorders, the symptoms remain as part of a minor disturbance, and you must learn to cope with them.

When a person suffers from anxiety attacks, one of the greatest obstacles to recovery can be the fear that these attacks are the indication of a major physical illness—and in rare cases that is true. But most often, when a person continually worries about physical illness, that kind of worry intensifies or even *produces* panic attacks. In other words, the less you worry, the healthier you will become. For that reason, I strongly recommend that you adopt the following guidelines if you are experiencing anxiety attacks:

1. Find a physician whom you *trust*.
2. Explain your symptoms and your worries to him or her.

3. Let your physician conduct any evaluations or examinations necessary to determine the cause of your symptoms.

4. If your primary physician recommends that another medical specialist evaluate your problem, be certain to follow that advice. Make sure that your primary physician receives a report from the specialist.

5. If a physical problem is diagnosed, follow your physician's treatment advice.

6. If your doctor finds no physical cause for your anxiety attacks, use the methods presented in this book to take control of your symptoms. If your symptoms persist, consider the possible psychological disorder that can produce panic (see chapter 3). Ask your physician or some other source for a referral to a licensed mental health professional who specializes in these disorders.

The most destructive thing you can do when faced with panic attacks is to steadfastly believe that your symptoms mean that you have a serious physical illness, despite continued professional reassurance to the contrary. That is why it is essential that you work with a physician whom you can trust until he or she reaches a diagnosis. No matter how many consultations with other professionals you need, allow *one* professional to have primary charge of your case and receive all reports. Do not continually jump from doctor to doctor. If you remain fearfully convinced that you have a physical ailment, even when there is a consensus to the contrary among the professionals who have evaluated you, then you can be certain of one thing: your fear is directly contributing to your panic episodes. In part 2 you will learn how to control that fear and thereby take control of your symptoms.

Many physiological disorders produce paniclike symptoms; let us look at the symptoms themselves and their possible sources.

PHYSIOLOGICAL DISORDERS WITH PANICLIKE SYMPTOMS

Cardiovascular Disorders

Angina pectoris	Postural orthostatic hypotension
Arrhythmia	
Coronary artery disease	Pulmonary edema

Heart attack
Heart failure
Hypertension
Mitral valve prolapse
Mitral stenosis
Myocardial infarction
  (recovery from)

Pulmonary embolism
Stroke
Tachycardia
Transient ischemic
  attack

Respiratory Disorders

Asthma
Bronchitis
Collagen disease

Emphysema
Hypoxia
Pulmonary fibrosis

Endocrine/Hormonal Disorders

Carcinoid tumor
Hyperthyroidism
Hypoglycemia

Pheochromocytoma
Premenstrual syndrome
Pregnancy

Neurological/Muscular Disorders

Compression neuropathies
Guillain-Barré syndrome

Myasthenia gravis
Temporal lobe epilepsy

Ear Disorders

Benign positional vertigo
Labyrinthitis
Mastoiditis

Ménière's disease
Otitis media

Hematic (Kidney) Disorders

Anemia
B12 anemia
Folic acid anemia

Iron-deficiency anemia
Sickle cell anemia

Drug-related Disorders

Alcohol use or withdrawal
Illicit drug use
Medication withdrawal

Side effects of many med-
  ications
Stimulant use

Miscellaneous Disorders

Caffeinism
Head injury

RAPID OR IRREGULAR HEART RATE

Uncomfortable changes in heart rate are the most frequently reported symptoms of panic attacks. More than 80 percent of those experiencing panic cite a rapid or irregular heart rate as a symptom.

Three complaints are common among patients who seek a doctor's advice about their heart: "My heart feels like it's pounding violently in my chest," "My heart is racing," and "My heart feels like it skips a beat." An *arrhythmia* is any irregularity in the heart's rhythm. If the heart beats more rapidly than normal, this arrhythmia is called *tachycardia*. An unpleasant sensation in the heart, whether rapid or slow, regular or irregular, and of which one is consciously aware, is called a *palpitation*. Heart palpitation is typically an expected sensation when the force and rate of the heartbeat are considerably elevated. After strenuous exercise we are apt to notice the thumping of our heart against the chest wall. As we begin resting, that sensation may continue briefly until we recover from our exertion.

PHYSICAL CAUSES OF RAPID OR IRREGULAR HEART RATE

Arrhythmia	Post-myocardial infarction
Tachycardia	Organic heart disease
Palpitation	Heart failure
Extrasystole	Infections
Coronary artery disease	

People who are prone to anxiety may have palpitations more frequently when they find themselves in psychologically uncomfortable situations. In fact, the great majority of complaints about the heart presented to physicians indicate a psychological rather than a physical problem. An anxious person may turn her attention to her physical symptoms instead of learning to cope with the situation causing the symptoms. After several episodes in which she experiences her heart "pounding" or "beating too fast," she fears it is a sign of heart disease or some other physical disorder.

It is possible consciously to notice a few minor disturbances of the heart rhythm. For instance, some people describe sensations such as a "flop" of the heart, the heart "skipping a beat" or "turning a somersault." We call this sudden forceful beat of the heart followed by a longer than usual pause an *extrasystole.* These premature contractions of the heart are usually of no serious significance; in fact, because of several research findings, we now know that arrhythmias of all kinds are common in normal, healthy individuals. In a study published recently in the *New England Journal of Medicine,* Dr. Harold Kennedy found that healthy subjects with frequent and complex irregular heartbeats seem to be at no more risk of physical problems than is the normal population. In general, researchers are finding that the majority of even the healthiest people have some kind of rhythm disturbance such as skipped beats, palpitations, or pounding in the chest.

Tachycardia, or rapid heartbeat, is the most common complaint associated with the heart and is one of the typical reasons that patients seek medical attention. For many normal healthy individuals it is a daily occurrence in response to physical exercise or intense emotion. Any kind of excitement or trauma, even fatigue or exhaustion, can accelerate the action of the heart, especially in overly anxious individuals. Too many cigarettes, too much alcohol, and in particular, excessive amounts of caffeine can cause tachycardia on occasion. Infections such as pneumonia, as well as acute inflammatory diseases such as rheumatic fever, may also produce a rapid heartbeat.

Although most complaints of the sensation called palpitation reflect a minor cardiac problem or a sign of anxiety, it is possible that they involve some kind of coronary artery disease. A narrowing of the arteries to the heart causes such diseases. (See also "Chest Pain," below.)

Recovery and rehabilitation after a heart attack can be a difficult psychological challenge. Many people become afraid that too much activity or excitement might produce a second attack. It is no wonder, then, that post-myocardial infarction patients become fearfully preoccupied with the sensations of their hearts. Many will return to their doctor's office or hospital emergency room with complaints of palpitations. Fourteen percent of cardiac patients later suffer from panic disorder, which is the worried anticipation of having an anxiety attack or heart attack (discussed in more detail in chapter 3).

Chapter 6 describes the way in which panic complicates recovery from a myocardial infarction.

Complaints of a racing heart can signal certain kinds of organic heart disease and heart failure. More often, however, the symptom of these ailments will be breathlessness (see the following section on difficulty breathing). Infections, such as pneumonia and rheumatic fever, may also produce a rapid heartbeat.

CHEST PAIN

Almost 40 percent of people with panic attacks experience pain in their chests. The thought that this pain might be a serious heart problem sends many sufferers to the emergency room for help. The predominant complaint of those suffering from coronary artery disease is most likely to be a pain or pressure in the center of the chest. They may also feel such discomfort elsewhere in the chest or in the neck, jaw, or left arm, and occasionally may notice tachycardia, rapid heartbeat.

Angina pectoris is an acute pain in the chest caused by interference with the supply of oxygen to the heart. It is a distinct pain, usually concentrated on the left side and sometimes spreading (radiating) to the neck and down the left arm. The feeling is of tightness, strangling, heaviness or suffocation. It is not a disease, but a symptom of some underlying disorder that reduces the supply of oxygen to the heart. Coronary artery disease or hypertension are the most common causes, with aortic stenosis, anemia, or hyperthyroidism also possible causes.

PHYSICAL CAUSES OF CHEST PAIN

Coronary artery disease
Angina pectoris
Heart attack

A heart attack (myocardial infarction, coronary thrombosis) occurs when the blood supply to the heart is significantly blocked. The main symptom is usually a crushing pain in the center of the chest, which may continue into the neck, jaw, arms, and stomach. The pain may begin during exercise or a stressful event. Unlike angina, this pain does not stop when the exercise or event ends. A heart attack is a medical emergency. Medical help is needed immediately.

DIFFICULTY BREATHING

Dyspnea—difficult, labored, or uncomfortable breathing—can be a signal of a serious emergency or of a mysterious medical puzzle. Seek immediate professional evaluation if this problem has never been diagnosed. Most often a person will describe it as "not being able to catch my breath," or "not getting enough air," even while appearing to breathe normally. Certainly the inability to breathe properly can be alarming, and many persons will immediately react with anxiety, fear, or panic.

PHYSICAL CAUSES OF DYSPNEA
(DIFFICULT BREATHING)

Bronchitis	Pneumothorax
Emphysema	Hemothorax
Asthma	Pulmonary edema
Pneumoconiosis	Mitral stenosis
Collagen disease	Left ventricular failure
Pulmonary fibrosis	Aortic insufficiency
Myasthenia gravis	Pericardial effusion
Guillain-Barré syndrome	Cardiac arrhythmia
Pleural effusion	

Under normal circumstances, difficult breathing comes after any strenuous activity. If the degree of the problem seems out of proportion to the amount of exertion, concern is appropriate. Troubled breathing is sometimes experienced in pregnancy, since the uterus expands upward, reducing the possibility of a full inhalation. Severe obesity can also reduce the capacity of the lungs to inhale fully.

Most physical causes of dyspnea are associated with disorders of the respiratory and cardiac systems. Acute and chronic diseases of the lungs are the most common physical causes. Within the respiratory system, the problem usually stems from an obstruction of air flow (obstructive disorders) or the inability of the chest wall or lungs to expand freely (restrictive disorders). Each of these disorders makes the patient work harder to take each breath and decreases the amount of oxygen thats he can absorb with inhalation. The three major obstructive disorders are bronchitis, emphysema, and asthma. In these problems a second common symptom is "chest tightness" upon awakening, shortly after sitting up, or after physical exertion.

The primary symptom of bronchitis is a deep cough that brings up yellowish or grayish phlegm from the lungs. With emphysema, the shortness of breath gradually becomes worse over the years. The distinct symptoms of bronchitis and the gradual onset of emphysema will usually prevent these disorders from being misdiagnosed as severe anxiety or panic.

Those suffering from asthma complain of difficult breathing, a painless tightness in the chest, and periodic attacks of wheezing. Severe cases can cause sweating, increased pulse rate, and severe anxiety. The primary trigger of an asthma attack is an allergy to such things as pollen, dust, or the dander of cats or dogs. Attacks can also be caused by infections, exercise, or psychological stress or may occur for no apparent reason. Some asthma sufferers anxiously anticipate the next attack, since an acute attack of asthma can come suddenly out of the blue and last for an uncomfortably long time. This fear of an impending attack can actually increase the likelihood of the attack and can extend its length of each attack. Asthma is a good example of a physical disorder that can increase in severity because of anxiety or panic.

In chapter 6, the way panic can contribute to difficulties in patients with chronic obstructive pulmonary disease is described. Special attention is given to chronic bronchitis, emphysema, and asthma.

A number of restrictive disorders of the respiratory system cause difficult breathing. Some produce a rigidity of the lungs (pneumoconiosis, collagen disease, pulmonary fibrosis); others involve the interactions of muscles and nerves (myasthenia gravis, Guillain-Barré syndrome); and still others prevent the lungs from expanding to full volume (pleural effusion, pneumothorax, hemothorax). A restrictive deficit in pulmonary function can also be caused by pulmonary edema, which usually stems from heart failure or occasionally from toxic inhalants.

Dyspnea may occur in any of the various diseases of the heart and lungs, but it is more prominent in those associated with lung congestion. For example, *mitral stenosis* occurs when a small valve between the left upper chamber and left lower chamber of the heart (the left atrium and left ventricle) becomes abnormally narrow. As blood is forced through the heart, pressure backs up into the lungs and produces congestion, causing breathlessness.

Other possible cardiovascular problems that can lead to difficulty breathing include left ventricular failure, aortic insufficiency, pericardial effusion, and cardiac arrhythmia.

DIZZINESS AND VERTIGO

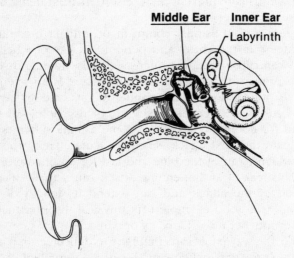

Figure 1. Cross-section of the ear.

The terms *dizziness* and *vertigo* cover a broad range of complaints. *Dizziness* is a broad term that can include light-headedness, faintness, wooziness, a "swimming" sensation in the head, a floating feeling, double vision, a feeling of "everything spinning in circles" or of whirling in space. *Vertigo* refers to the more specific sensations that either the body or its surroundings are turning or the head is swaying or revolving. The physical causes of these two symptoms are numerous, including problems of the middle and inner ear, dental problems, infections, head injuries, drug effects, and disorders of the cardiovascular, neurologic, and central nervous systems.

The ear is responsible for our sense of balance as well as our hearing. The inner ear includes a structure called the *labyrinth,* which monitors the brain. When injury or infection disrupts the action of the labyrinth, vertigo may occur.

PHYSICAL CAUSES OF DIZZINESS AND VERTIGO

Ménière's disease	Postural orthostatic
Labyrinthitis	hypotension
Nystagmus	Stroke
Benign positional vertigo	Cerebral thrombosis
Ear infections	Cerebral embolism
Dental problems	Cerebral hemorrhage
Head injury	Transient ischemic attack
Hypertension	

Ménière's disease is a common disorder of the labyrinth in adults, in which excess fluid builds up and increases the pressure within the inner ear, causing vertigo and occasionally a ringing or other noise in the ear, tinnitus. Labyrinthitis is an infection of this same region, often caused by a virus, sometimes associated with an upper-respiratory infection. This can produce severe vertigo, occasionally with some nausea and vomiting during the first episode. The individual may also experience a rapid flickering of the eyes, nystagmus. Calcium crystals floating within the labyrinth can cause benign positional vertigo. In this condition, a shifting of position, such as rolling over in bed, can produce vertigo and nystagmus moments later, lasting no more than thirty seconds. Several kinds of ear infections, such as otitis media and mastoiditis, can cause vertigo, but they also have other distinguishing symptoms, such as drainage of fluid, fever, or redness of the eardrum. Because the teeth and jaw are so closely aligned with the ear, dental problems such as an abscessed tooth, malocclusion, or temporomandibular joint (TMJ) abnormalities can also produce vertigo.

Any head injury can cause a cerebral concussion or a

labyrinthine concussion, which may result in vertigo or a sense of feeling dazed, unsteady, or faint.

A number of cardiovascular and neurovascular diseases may affect a person's sense of balance. Hypertension, or high blood pressure, is often a symptomless disease. However, a swimming or woozy sensation may be the initial symptom that brings a patient into a physician's office for evaluation.

If dizziness and light-headedness are experienced when you rise in the morning or change from a lying to an upright position, postural orthostatic hypotension may be the cause. This is a problem of low blood pressure, and results in poor circulation of blood through the body. Typically, when a person shifts positions, the blood vessels reflexively contract to maintain proper blood pressure. In hypotension, this mechanism fails to respond appropriately. Since the needed pressure is not maintained, the flow of blood to the brain is temporarily reduced, causing dizziness and even fainting. Diabetes, minor complications in pregnancy, or hardening of the arteries can cause postural hypotension. It can also be a side effect of antidepressant medication, major tranquilizers, and even medications prescribed for high blood pressure (hypertension).

The most serious vascular ailment, one that requires immediate medical attention, is *stroke*. A stroke occurs when the blood supply to the brain is significantly altered, causing damage to the brain itself. Three types of vascular problems produce stroke: cerebral thrombosis, cerebral embolism, and cerebral hemorrhage. In cerebral thrombosis, some portion of an artery that supplies blood to the brain has been reduced in size. A large deposit of fatty tissue in that portion allows blood to clot, causing a partial or complete blockage of the blood flow to the brain. A cerebral embolism occurs when a bit of blood clot or arteriosclerotic plaque from the heart or the wall of a large artery breaks off and travels to an artery within the brain, where it lodges and causes the stroke. In a cerebral hemorrhage, the artery leaks or bursts, causing blood to seep into the surrounding brain tissues.

A *transient ischemic attack* is usually caused by a small blood clot or piece of fatty tissue. While passing through the brain, it briefly becomes lodged in a blood vessel, reducing the blood flow through that area. These symptoms resemble those of stroke, but are temporary and do not cause serious harm, since the clot or embolus eventually is dislodged. Although emergency medical attention is not necessary, a transient ischemic attack does require medical evaluation and possible measures to prevent a recurrence.

Dizziness alone is insufficient cause to fear stroke. However, if you experience one or more of the following symptoms, you should consult your physician: numbness and/or tingling in any part of the body, blurred vision, confusion, difficulty speaking, loss of movement in the arms or legs. These symptoms can also indicate a panic attack rather than stroke. If you have experienced such a reaction several times and your doctor finds no sign of a physical disorder, you should consider the possibility that some psychological disturbance is precipitating the symptoms.

MULTIPLE SYMPTOMS

Many physical illnesses can produce nervousness in individuals who are not emotionally troubled. Certain other physical disorders—those discussed in this section—can cause a cluster of symptoms that resemble those of panic.

Hypertension is the predominant cardiovascular disorder that can produce multiple symptoms. It is caused by a narrowing of the arteries. As your heart pumps blood through your body it exerts a certain amount of pressure on the arterial walls. If these passageways become constricted for some reason, it requires greater force to maintain a steady flow of blood. The entire circulatory system is then under strain, and hypertension is the diagnosis. As mentioned earlier, this is often a symptomless disease, but you might notice such symptoms as palpitations, nervousness, dizziness, and fatigue, as well as a general sense of ill health.

PHYSICAL CAUSES OF MULTIPLE SYMPTOMS

Hypertension	Hypoxia
Mitral valve prolapse	Carcinoid syndrome
Menopause	Compression neuropathies
Premenstrual syndrome	Temporal lobe epilepsy
Hyperthyroidism	Caffeinism
Hypoglycemia	Amphetamines
Pheochromocytoma	Cocaine
Anemia	Phencyclidine (PCP)
Iron deficiency anemia	Hallucinogens
Folic acid anemia	Marijuana
B12 anemia	Alcohol withdrawal
Sickle-cell anemia	Pulmonary embolism
Heart attack	Withdrawal from antidepressants, narcotics, sedatives, barbiturates, benzodiazepines, or beta-blockers

Mitral valve prolapse is a common condition found in approximately 5–15 percent of the adult population. In this disturbance a valve leaflet within the heart balloons into the left upper chamber, the left atrium, of the heart during contraction. About half of all people with mitral valve prolapse complain of heart palpitation sometime in their lives. Other possible symptoms are rapid heartbeat, shortness of breath, dizziness, and an increased awareness of the heart's action. This is a rather minor cardiac problem, but people can erroneously pinpoint it as the sole cause of panic attacks. More often, though, it is the patient's fearful preoccupation with the action of his heart that produces panic. There is a more extensive discussion of mitral valve prolapse in chapter 6.

There is growing evidence that hormonal changes can dramatically affect a person's physical disposition and mood. Approximately 50 percent of women experiencing menopause report some major physical and/or emotional changes. Another 25 percent have uncomfortable, even distressing, symptoms that can include intense moments of palpitations, sweating, hot flashes, and anxiety. The term *premenstrual syndrome* refers to a complex of symptoms, including panic, occurring in the days just before menstruation. You will learn more about premenstrual syndrome in chapter 5.

Hyperthyroidism, overactivity of the thyroid gland, is another hormone-caused problem. The thyroid gland is located in the lower part of the neck and is controlled by a thyroid-stimulating hormone produced in the pituitary gland. In hyperthyroidism, the normal control mechanisms are disrupted and the thyroid continues to produce an excessive amount of its own hormone, thyroxine. This overproduction causes a general speeding up of all chemical reactions in the body. The person may feel shaky and anxious, with heart palpitations, breathlessness, and increased perspiration—as though he or she were experiencing a constant anxiety attack. Additional symptoms make this disorder easier to diagnose: increased appetite associated with weight loss instead of gain; thinning hair; chronic tension and a sense of needing to keep moving despite fatigue and physical exhaustion. Instead of feeling cold, as the anxious person might, the person suffering from hyperthyroidism will feel hot, and his skin will be warm to the touch. Your doctor may order a thyroid screening test for you if you have several of these symptoms. Physicians treat hyperthyroidism in one of three ways: through antithyroid medication, by surgically removing either a lump in the thyroid or the whole thyroid, or, more commonly, by the administration of a radioactive iodine fluid that controls the overactivity of the gland.

Hypoglycemia produces several unpleasant symptoms caused by a lower than normal level of glucose in the bloodstream. This state of low blood sugar generally produces a feeling of being uncomfortable, with cold, clammy skin and profuse sweating. Other symptoms can be dizziness, weakness, trembling, tingling in the lips and hands, palpitations, and fainting. The condition is most often found in diabetics who take insulin. Many nondiabetic individuals erroneously believe that hypoglycemia is the cause of their panic symptoms and therefore fail to explore other possible diagnoses. For further information on hypoglycemia and panic, see chapter 5.

The adrenal glands are located on top of each kidney. The adrenal medulla produces two hormones that play an important role in controlling your heart rate and blood pressure: epinephrine (adrenaline) and nonepinephrine (nonadrenaline). Very rarely a growth, or tumor develops within or near an adrenal gland and causes an increase in the production of these hormones. Tachycardia, sweating, anxiety, faintness, nausea and pallor—all resembling panic—can occur as a result of slight exercise, exposure to cold temperatures, or minor emotional upset. Typically the blood pressure becomes extremely high, and the patient may have the frightening feeling of being about to die. This extremely rare disorder, called pheochromocytoma, is cured by surgically removing the tumor.

Anemia is the abnormal decrease of either hemoglobin or red blood cells. Red blood cells carry oxygen from the lungs to all parts of the body. Within each of these blood cells is the protein hemoglobin, which combines with the oxygen while in the lungs and then releases it into the tissues as the blood circulates through the body. Characteristic symptoms of anemia are light-headedness, rapid heartbeat, difficulty breathing, and faintness. The anemic person may experience palpitations, because the heart is attempting to compensate for the lower levels of oxygen by pumping blood faster than normal. A diagnosis of iron deficiency anemia means that lower than normal levels of iron in the body are limiting the production of hemoglobin. Folic acid anemia and B12 anemia mean that the body has insufficient amounts of these two essential vitamins, which are required for the production of healthy red blood cells. *Sickle cell anemia* is an inherited disease found almost exclusively among people of African descent. In this condition, the red blood cells contain an abnormal hemoglobin, called hemoglobin S. It is associated with a deformed, sickle shape, cell, which impedes the smooth flow of blood into smaller vessels. Premature destruction of red blood cells, and anemia, results. A physician should diagnose and treat all forms of anemia.

Pulmonary embolism occurs when a blood clot detaches from the wall of a deep vein, moves through the bloodstream, and becomes lodged in the pulmonary artery close to or within the lungs. This reduces the volume of fresh blood returning to the left side of the heart and may produce sudden chest pain, rapid heart rate (tachycardia), rapid shallow breathing, and coughing up of bright red spit.

A heart attack often involves crushing chest pain as the predominant symptom, as mentioned earlier. Other symptoms can include dizziness, shortness of breath, sweating, chills, nausea, and fainting.

Hypoxia means diminished availability of oxygen to the body tissues. It is a symptom of several possible underlying problems, such as altitude sickness or a pulmonary disorder. Symptoms can include difficulty breathing (dyspnea), rapid pulse, fainting, and chest pain (angina pectoris).

A carcinoid tumor is a small yellow growth occurring in the small intestine, appendix, stomach, or colon. Carcinoid syndrome develops when a carcinoid tumor produces excess amounts of serotonin, a blood vessel constrictor. Exertion, intense emotion, or food or alcohol intake can trigger symptoms, which include one or more of the following: brief flushing of the neck and face, brief abdominal pain, diarrhea, racing heart (tachycardia), low blood pressure (hypotension), facial puffiness and difficulty breathing caused by bronchoconstriction. Carcinoid tumors are rare.

Compression neuropathies, such as carpal tunnel syndrome, are disorders caused by some form of compression to localized nerves. Symptoms may include a tingling or "pins and needles" feeling similar to that which occurs during hyperventilation.

The symptoms of a temporal lobe epilepsy (TLE) attack are highly variable, but in some cases sufferers experience them only as a sudden attack of immense fear or panic. In 60 percent of the cases, fear is the primary emotion. The patient may also have a feeling of unreality, as though he is far away from his surroundings (derealization), or may feel that his body is strange or dreamlike (depersonalization). Highly charged emotional responses such as these can lead to a misdiagnosis of the problem as a psychologically based one. A distinguishing feature of a TLE attack can be the victim's sensing an aura, a sudden experience that often takes the form of a strange aroma or taste at the moment of fear.

Caffeinism refers to the uncomfortable side effects that can occur with high intake of caffeine from coffee, tea, cola drinks, chocolate, and over-the-counter medication such as Excedrin and Anacin. Symptoms include anxiety, irritability, insomnia, headaches, stomach irritation, agitation, increased respiration, rapid heartbeat, and irregular heart rhythm. These side effects can occur with daily consumption between 250 and 500 mg. Between 20 percent and 30 percent of Americans consume more than 500 mg of caffeine a day; four to five cups of drip coffee contain over 500 mg. Some panic-prone persons are highly sensitive to caffeine, and symptoms can occur from less caffeine intake than the average person. If you experience any of these symptoms, you may wish to review your intake of all forms of caffeine. Use the following tables as a guide.

PRESENCE OF CAFFEINE

In Medications (Per Tablet/Capsule)

Vivarin	200 mg	Fiorinal	40 mg
Caffadrine	200 mg	Medigesic	40 mg
Cafergot	100 mg	Triad	40 mg
No Doz	100 mg	Vanquish	33 mg
Excedrin (Extra Strength)	65 mg	Midol	32 mg
Amaphen	40 mg	Anacin	32 mg
Esgic	40 mg	Beta-Phed	32 mg
Fiorecet	40 mg	Empirin	32 mg

In Beverages

COFFEES, TEAS, AND COCOA (PER 5–6 OZ. SERVING)		COLA BEVERAGES (PER 12 OZ. CAN)	
Drip coffee, automatic	137 mg	Barg's Root Beer	33 mg
Drip coffee, nonautomatic	124 mg	Coca-Cola, Coke II Cherry Coke, Diet Coke	45 mg
Percolated coffee	110 mg	Dr. Pepper	41 mg
Instant coffee	60 mg	Diet Dr. Pepper	40 mg
Decaffeinated coffee	3 mg	Mellow Yellow	51 mg
Brewed tea	40–65 mg	Mountain Dew	55 mg
		Diet Mountain Dew	54 mg
Instant tea	33 mg	Mr. Pibb	40 mg
Decaffeinated tea	1 mg	Tab	45 mg
Hot cocoa	5–13 mg	Pepsi Cola, Diet Pepsi	38 mg
		7-Up, Sprite, Fresca, Hire's Root Beer	0 mg

In Chocolate

Baker's baking chocolate (1 oz.)	25 mg	Milk chocolate candy (1 oz.)	6 mg
Sweet dark chocolate candy (1 oz.)	20 mg	Chocolate milk (8 oz.)	5 mg

Amphetamines, whether taken for treatment of depression, for weight control, or illicitly for recreation, can cause severe anxiety to the point of panic. This extreme reaction is also possible with illicit drugs such as cocaine, phencyclidine (PCP), and the hallucinogens, such as LSD, and mescaline. It is possible that these drugs stimulate brain receptors associated with anxiety, making panic attacks more likely. Marijuana causes increased heart rate that can lead to a severe anxiety reaction.

Alcohol withdrawal can produce nervousness, rapid heartbeat, confusion, high blood pressure, and panic as well as other symptoms. Too rapid withdrawal, especially after long-term use, from antidepressants, narcotics, sedatives, barbiturates, benzodiazepines (Valium, Librium, etc.), or beta blockers can cause symptoms such as anxiety, rapid heartbeat, high blood pressure, and panic.

SIDE EFFECTS OF MEDICATIONS

Sometimes a medication may cause unwanted side effects along with its needed effects. If these occur, you should check with your doctor. In addition to other possible side effects, each of the medications listed below may produce paniclike symptoms. All medications are listed by their generic names.

Aminophylline relieves shortness of breath and wheezing in acute bronchial asthma and is prescribed to reduce asthmalike symptoms in chronic bronchitis and emphysema. Side effects can include nervousness, rapid heartbeat, and dizziness.

Heterocyclic antidepressants are used to treat depression and, more recently, panic attacks (see chapter 19 regarding the use of tricyclic antidepressants within the treatment of panic). Possible side effects are dizziness and irregular or rapid heartbeat.

Antidyskinetics are used in the treatment of Parkinson's disease. Side effects may include dizziness, irregular heartbeat, and anxiety.

Atropine is a medication used to dilate the pupil of the eye. It can produce an unusually fast heartbeat. A number of drugs are atropinelike in their effects. These are usually called anticholinergic medications.

Inhaler forms of beta-Z adrenergic agents, such as *isoproterenol* and *metaproterenol* (Alupent) relieve acute bronchial asthma and bronchospasms associated with chronic bronchitis and emphysema.

Side effects can include general anxiety, dizziness, rapid strong heartbeat, and shaky hands.

Cycloserine is an antibiotic medication whose side effects may include anxiety, irritability, confusion, dizziness, and restlessness.

Digitalis is prescribed to improve the strength and efficiency of the heart, or to control the rate of the heartbeat. It can produce an unusually slow or uneven pulse.

Ephedrine is prescribed for lung problems. Side effects can be nervousness, restlessness, dizziness, difficulty breathing, palpitations, and rapid heartbeat.

Epinephrine is used in the treatment of the eyes, the lungs, and allergies. Side effects can include faintness, trembling, rapid heartbeat, palpitations, nervousness, and difficulty breathing.

Insulin helps control diabetes. Increasing the dose of insulin can occasionally trigger a hypoglycemic reaction, which includes sweating, cold clammy hands, dizziness, palpitations, and trembling.

Isoniazid, an anti-infection medication, may produce rapid heartbeat and light-headedness.

Monoamine oxidase (MAO) inhibitors are in the antidepressant family. Physicians prescribe them to reduce symptoms of depression, and also to treat panic attacks (see chapter 19). Possible side effects are dizziness or light-headedness, especially when getting up from a lying or sitting position, and rapid or pounding heartbeat.

Nitrates are used to improve the blood flow to the heart and to relieve angina attacks. Possible side effects are dizziness, light-headedness, and rapid heartbeat.

Prednisone is the most commonly used of the corticosteroids and is prescribed to relieve inflammation. Its side effects can include irregular heartbeat, nervousness, muscle weakness, and mood swings. Other corticosteroid medications may cause similar side effects.

Reserpine is used to treat high blood pressure and certain emotional conditions, as well as a few other problems. Side effects may include dizziness, faintness, anxiety, and palpitations. Some individuals have even developed phobic reactions while taking reserpine.

Synthetic thyroid hormones are used for treating hypothyroidism. Excessive levels of these hormones can cause rapid heartbeat, palpitations, shortness of breath, nervousness, unusual sweating, and anxiety.

3
Panic Within Psychological Disorders

When the symptoms of panic persist, most sufferers become increasingly alarmed. Even when they can identify what they believe to be the immediate cause of these intense moments of anxiety, they are left with a bewildering array of questions: "Why me? Why now? What does it mean? How serious is it? How do I stop it?"

Few panic symptoms persist because of a physical problem. Most difficulties, even if associated with a physical disorder, are sustained through a pattern of thinking that is reinforced by past life experiences—or the lack of them. For instance, cardiac patients have suffered a physical trauma associated with the heart. A recent study found that up to 14 percent of these patients can also be diagnosed with panic disorder. Their episodes of severe anxiety start after their heart trouble but are not caused by it. If the physical trauma were the cause, then more people who have heart problems would also suffer from panic attacks. Actually, the problem stems from the way each cardiac patient reacts to his problem. The more fearful he becomes about the prospect of another physical trauma to the heart, the greater his chances of suffering from extreme anxiety or panic.

Researchers have identified a number of different patterns that help us categorize types of panic. Not everyone is so troubled by symptoms that they suffer from one of these psychological disorders. Some people simply pass through a difficult time with symptoms of anxiety, then continue on their way. However, if the symptoms remain over time, they will usually fall within one of six different categories of psychological problems: panic disorder, agoraphobia, generalized anxiety disorder, phobias, obsessive-compulsive disorder, and post-traumatic stress disorder.

PANIC DISORDER

Panic disorder is the only psychological problem whose predominant feature is recurring panic (or anxiety) attacks. Although the first panic attack may take place in a distinct situation, later episodes are unpredictable as to time or place.

The physical symptoms are the same as those described in chapter 1. One or more of these can be present in a severe form during an actual panic attack or in a milder form at other times: dry mouth; sweating; acute tension in the stomach, back of neck, or shoulders; increased heart rate; dizziness or light-headedness; feeling faint; increased respiration; trembling hands, legs, or voice; weak, numb, or cold extremities; shortness of breath; body fatigue; difficulty swallowing, a lump in the throat; irritability; blurred vision; inability to concentrate; and confusion.

After a number of panic episodes, the individual can become afraid of being a helpless victim of panic. She may hesitate to be alone, to venture far from home, or to be in public places. Even when not experiencing an anxiety attack, the person with panic disorder often becomes increasingly nervous and apprehensive. She attempts to remain physically and psychologically tense in preparation for the next attack.

Although the first panic attack may seem to appear out of the blue, it typically comes during an extended period of stress. This stress is not caused by a few days of tension, but extends over several months. Life transitions, such as moving, job change, marriage, or the birth of a child often account for much of the psychological pressure.

For some individuals, learning to manage this stressful period or to reduce the pressures eliminates the panic episodes. For others, it is as though the stress of the life transition or problem situation uncovered a psychological vulnerability. If the panic-prone individual accepts increased responsibilities—for instance, through a job promotion or through the birth of a first child—she may begin to doubt her ability to meet the new demands, the expectation of others, and the increased energy required for these responsibilities. Instead of focusing on mastering the task, she becomes more concerned with the possibility of failure. This attention to the threat of failure continually undermines her confidence. Through a series of steps, described in part 2 of this books, she translates these fears into panic.

Certain people experience symptoms while asleep. These are either caused by panic disorder or are "night terrors." Most nocturnal panics take place during (nondreaming) REM sleep, which means they do not tend to come in response to dreams or nightmares. They occur from a half hour to three and a half hours after the person has fallen asleep and are usually not as severe as daytime panics. These are distinct from night terrors, known as *pavor-nocturnus* in children and *incubus* in adults. The similarities are that they both produce sudden awakening and autonomic arousal and tend not to be associated with nightmares. However, a person who experiences a night terror tends to have amnesia for it and returns to sleep without trouble. He also can become physically active during the terror—tossing, turning, kicking, sometimes screaming loudly, or running out of the bedroom in the midst of an episode. Nocturnal panic attacks, however, tend to cause insomnia. The person has a vivid memory of the panic. He does not become physically aggressive during the panic attack, but remains physically aroused after the occurrence and has difficulty going back to sleep.

AGORAPHOBIA

Each person diagnosed with agoraphobia (the literal meaning is "fear of the marketplace") has a unique combination of symptoms. But common to all agoraphobics is a marked fear or avoidance of being alone or of being in certain public places. It is a response strong enough to significantly limit the individual's normal activities.

For the person who experiences panic attacks, the distinction between agoraphobia and panic disorder is based on how many activities he avoids. In panic disorder, the person remains relatively active, although he may avoid a few uncomfortable situations. If the panic-prone person begins significantly to restrict his normal activities because of his fearful thoughts, agoraphobia is the more appropriate diagnosis.

For some, agoraphobia develops from panic disorder. Repeated panic attacks produce *anticipatory anxiety,* a state of physical and emotional tension in anticipation of the next attack. The person then begins to avoid any circumstances that seem associated with past panic attacks, becoming more and more limited in his range of activities.

The fearful thoughts that plague the agoraphobic often revolve around *loss of control.* The person may fear the development of uncomfortable physical symptoms familiar from past experiences, such as dizziness or rapid heartbeat. She may then worry that these symptoms could become even worse than they were in the past, such as fainting or heart attack, and/or that she will become trapped or confined in some physical location or social situation such as a restaurant or party. In the first two situations, the person senses that her body is out of control. In the third, she feels unable to readily control her surroundings. The agoraphobic may avoid one or many of these situations as a way to feel safe. The need to avoid is so strong that some agoraphobics will quit their jobs, stop driving or taking public transportation, or stop shopping or eating in restaurants; in the worst cases they never venture outside their home for years.

The following list shows the types of surroundings that can provoke these fears.

Listed below are the types of fearful thoughts associated with the dreaded situations. These are irrational, unproductive, and anxiety-producing thoughts that last anywhere from a few seconds to more than an hour. At the same time, these thoughts are the primary cause of agoraphobic behavior; they serve to perpetuate the agoraphobic's belief that "If I avoid these situations, I'll be safe."

FEAR OF SURROUNDINGS

Public Places or Enclosed Spaces

Streets
Stores
Restaurants
Theaters
Churches

Travel

On trains, buses, planes,
    subways, cars
Over bridges, through
    tunnels
Being far away from
    home
Traffic

Conflict Situations

Arguments, interpersonal
    conflicts, expression
    of anger

Confinement or Restriction of Movement

Barber's, hairdresser's, or
    dentist's chair
Lines in a store
Waiting for appointments
Prolonged conversations in
    person or on the phone
Crowds

Remaining at Home Alone

Open Spaces

Parks
Fields
Wide streets

FEARFUL THOUGHTS

Fainting or collapsing in public
Developing severe physical symptoms
Losing control
Becoming confused
Being unable to cope
Dying
Causing a scene
Having a heart attack or other physical illness
Being unable to get home or to another "safe" place
Being trapped or confined
Becoming mentally ill
Being unable to breathe

Some agoraphobics experience no symptoms of panic. Although fearful thoughts continue to control these individuals, they have restricted their lifestyle, through avoidance, to such a degree that they no longer become uncomfortable.

When agoraphobics retreat to protect themselves, they often have to sacrifice friendships, family responsibilities, and/or career. Their loss of relationships, affections, and accomplishments compounds the problem. It leads to low self-esteem, isolation, loneliness, and depression. In addition, the agoraphobic may become dependent on alcohol or drugs in an unsuccessful attempt to cope (see chapter 4 for further discussion of this complex disorder; see chapter 5 for the problem of alcoholism. Part 2 addresses the specific ways in which agoraphobics can take control of their fears and their anxiety attacks).

GENERALIZED ANXIETY DISORDER

With generalized anxiety disorder, panic is not the predominant feature. However, many of the panic symptoms are present to a lesser degree. Instead of brief moments of intense anxiety, the person feels symptoms throughout most of the day. Although the specific manifestations of anxiety vary for each person, this chronic state of tension can affect six major systems of the body.

1. In the cardiovascular system, anxiety increases blood pressure, which causes tachycardia (rapid heartbeat), constriction of the blood vessels in the arms and legs, and dilation of the vessels surrounding the skeletal muscles. These changes produce symptoms of palpitations (an uncomfortable awareness of the heart rate), headaches, and cold fingers.

2. In the gastrointestinal system, anxiety leads to reduced salivary secretions, spasms within the esophagus (the hollow muscular tube leading from the nose and mouth to the stomach), and alterations in the stomach, intestines, and anal sphincter. These systemic changes result in symptoms of dry mouth, difficulty swallowing, butterflies in the stomach, the gurgling sounds of gas in the intestines, and mucous colitis (an inflammation of the colon), causing spasms, diarrhea and/or constipation, and cramplike pains in the upper stomach.

3. In the respiratory system, anxiety leads to hyperventilation, or overbreathing, which lowers the level of carbon dioxide in the blood, with symptoms of "air hunger," deep sighs, and pins-and-needles sensations. (See chapter 11 for further information on hyperventilation.)

4. In the genitourinary systems, the anxious person can experience the need for frequent urination. Men may have difficulty maintaining an erection during intercourse; women may have difficulty becoming sexually aroused or achieving orgasm.

5. In the musculoskeletal system, the muscles become tense. Involuntary trembling of the body, tension headaches, and other aches and pains may develop.

6. Through changes in the central nervous system, the anxious person is generally more apprehensive, aroused, and vigilant, feeling "on edge," impatient, or irritable. He may complain of poor concentration, insomnia, and fatigue.

As you can see, there is often a fine line between the diagnosis of panic disorder or agoraphobia and that of generalized anxiety disorder. Three features distinguish them. First, the symptoms themselves: if an individual is chronically anxious (as he would be with generalized anxiety disorder) and also experiences episodes of panic, then panic disorder or agoraphobia will be the more likely diagnosis.

Second, different kinds of fearful thoughts are associated with the two problems. In most people with generalized anxiety disorder the worries are about the kinds of interactions they will have with others: "Will I fail in this work setting?" "Are they going to accept me?" "I'm afraid he's going to leave me." "What if they discover how little I know?" "I'll never perform up to their expectations." With panic disorder and agoraphobia, the imagined response of others is secondary to the fear of personal catastrophe or loss of control, and the person's internal statements and questions will reflect this apprehension: "What if I faint [become hysterical, have a heart attack, cause a scene], and people see me?" The panic-prone person focuses more on her ability to be in 100 percent control of all her physical and mental capacities. The anxious person focuses more on her inability to cope with the expectations and responses of those around her.

POSSIBLE PHYSICAL SYMPTOMS DURING ANXIETY

Cardiovascular System

Tachycardia (rapid heartbeat)
Palpitations (uncomfortable awareness of the heart rate)
Headaches
Cold fingers

Gastrointestinal System

Dry mouth
Difficulty swallowing
Butterflies in the stomach
Gurgling sounds of gas in the intestines
Colon spasms
Diarrhea and/or constipation
Cramplike pains in the upper stomach

Respiratory System

Hyperventilation symptoms (see chapter 11)

Genitourinary System

Need for frequent urination
Difficulty maintaining an erection

POSSIBLE PHYSICAL SYMPTOMS DURING ANXIETY *(cont.)*

Cardiovascular System

Difficulty becoming sexually aroused or achieving orgasm
  (women)

Musculoskeletal System

Muscles tense
Involuntary trembling of the body
Tension headaches
Other aches and pains

Central Nervous System

Apprehensive, aroused, and vigilant
Feeling "on edge," impatient or irritable
Poor concentration
Insomnia
Fatigue

The third difference has to do with the person's response to her fears. The anxious person thinks about withdrawing from situations that increase her anxiety, and may procrastinate on performance tasks. The person with panic disorder or agoraphobia, on the other hand, is quick to use avoidance as a way to diminish discomfort. In a matter of days he will begin to identify the situations that are associated with the symptoms and determine how she can steer clear of them, immediately viewing avoidance as the single best solution to the problem.

SOCIAL PHOBIA

A social phobia is an excessive, unreasonable fear that others in public will notice and negatively judge some particular activity. The person with a social phobia becomes anxious even at the thought of this activity, for fear that he will be humiliated or embarrassed. Avoidance is his primary defense, which he feels compelled to use.

The types of social phobias range from those that seem to be an exaggeration of common fears to those that seem bizarre to others. The most prevalent are the fears of speaking or performing in public. Most people understand and have experienced the normal anxiety associated with public speaking: trembling hands and legs, increased perspiration, "butterflies," worries about performing poorly. The social phobic not only becomes highly anxious if he is forced to approach such a situation but will do all in his power to avoid it.

Any situation in which others may observe the person's behavior can become a phobic preoccupation: urinating in a public bathroom; signing one's name while being watched; being watched while eating. One client became anxious in almost every public situation because she feared people would begin watching her eyes. This belief was so real and so overwhelming that she was in a constant state of anxiety when not in her own home.

Anxiety, potential for panic, and avoidance behavior link the social phobias with panic disorder and agoraphobia. The distinguishing feature is, again, what the person fears. The social phobic becomes extremely anxious about people's reaction to seemingly normal behavior such as eating lunch or walking on the beach. The agoraphobic has the predominant fear that his body will not perform normally.

The person with generalized anxiety disorder is sometimes in the midst of a change in his personal or career life that diminishes her self-confidence. Social phobics, on the other hand, may never have mastered some basic social skills. Some report being shy and isolated as children and adolescents, long before this problem began. Many, cases can be viewed an extreme manifestation of a long-standing sensitivity to the opinions of others.

If you suffer from the symptoms of social anxiety or shyness, many of the chapters of this book will be relevant to you. Begin by reading chapter 20. It will organize the book into a self-help model that will help you approach your specific problems.

Specific Phobias

When a person has a persistent, irrational fear of an object or situation and a strong urge to avoid that object or situation, he has a "simple phobia"—an inappropriately intense reaction triggered by a *single* stimulus. Most people have met someone with a significant fear of a particular object or situation, such as closed spaces (claustrophobia), heights (acrophobia), water (aquaphobia), snakes (ophidiphobia), or lightning (astraphobia). The most prevalent phobias are of specific animals and insects, of the natural elements such as storms or water, of heights, and of closed-in spaces.

The person with a specific phobia may react with mild anxiety or even with panic when confronted with the prospect of facing the fearful situation. However, his fear is not of his symptoms (as in panic disorder or agoraphobia) but of the situation itself, which he believes to be a dangerous one. Some may fear that they will lose their senses and do something foolish. The person with a height phobia, for instance, might fear that he will forget what he is doing and accidentally leap off the cliff on which he is standing. Others with phobias fear that something will go wrong with their circumstances. The individual with a flying phobia might vividly imagine the tail falling off the plane, or the pilot losing consciousness with no one to take over, or the oxygen running out in midflight. Such fears defy rational thinking. Most phobics know that they are being excessive and unreasonable in their thoughts, but this knowledge is of no use to them. The fearful thoughts come automatically in spite of rational thought and thus the phobic may believe the only recourse is to avoid the problematic area.

Specific phobias may develop rapidly, as after a particular traumatic event, or gradually over the years, as a result of childhood learning and the examples set by parents and others. Some phobics are people who have not gained enough knowledge and experience during their childhood to successfully face new, frightening life experiences—whether real or imaginary—as adults. Instead of gaining some perspective during fearful times, the phobic becomes a passive victim to his fear. The only action he takes is to back away.

Diagnosing the true fear is an essential part of the cure. For instance, the person with a flying phobia may be afraid of heights or, instead, might actually be afraid of being contained, being far away from home, having a panic attack, or a combination of these. (If you are troubled by the fear of flying, chapter 21 will help you sort through your fears and guide you in responding to them.)

When a person has several specific phobias, the relationship between them may not seem evident at first. One agoraphobic patient also developed an intense fear of knives and of children. While discussing the problem during a treatment session, she reported that one day several months earlier she had found her seven-year-old son threatening his sister with a kitchen knife. After admonishing her son, she found herself dwelling on the many dangers of knives. Within a day, she began to question her own ability to control a knife. She then developed a spontaneous mental image of herself hurting a child with a knife. In a brief few days she began avoiding knives as well as becoming anxious whenever she looked at young children. The internal belief that has driving her fear was "I don't have enough self-control [to handle knives, to be with children]."

This case illustrates another pattern present in some phobics. The phobia can develop from a current internal conflict and/or a real-life fear. With this client, the real-life fear was of her young son hurting someone with a knife as a result of poor self-control. This legitimate fear was coupled with her own internal conflict. She was considering having a third child, but her marriage was unstable. Her husband was consumed with his business, and she felt unsupported and unloved. As we talked I realized that she was not consciously aware of the degree of her conflict.

Notice, though, how her phobia was, in a sense, helping her solve a problem while at the same time causing her distress. By unconsciously developing these fearful thoughts about her personal inability to control her aggression, she could now say, "Obviously I'm not capable enough to have another child." This irrational fear resolves her internal conflict. It also prevents her from confronting the pain in her marriage. If she maintained her desire to have a third child, she would want her husband to offer her more emotional support. What if he refused? What if he decided their marriage was no longer "workable" for him and suggested that they get divorced? Her fear of abandonment probably played a major role in the development of her new phobia. With the increase in her self-doubt, she no longer had the ego strength to risk making demands on her husband. Instead, she became more dependent and less likely to speak up for her needs.

Thus, phobias, are often more complex than they at first seem. Their "irrational" nature may relate to the person's attempt to solve a real-life problem. After a time the irrational fear takes on a

life of its own, just like a habit, regardless of its initial unconscious purpose.

OBSESSIVE-COMPULSIVE DISORDER

Obsessive-compulsive disorder has two components, obsessions
and compulsions. Obsessions are repetitive, unproductive thoughts
that almost all of us have experienced from time to time. We can
be driving down the road, ten minutes from home, heading for a
week's vacation. Suddenly the thought enters our mind, "Did I
unplug the iron after I finished with that shirt?" Then we think, "I
must have . . . but I don't know, I was rushing around so at the last
minute. Did I reach down and pull the cord out of the socket? I
can't remember. Was the iron light still on as I walked out the
door? No, it was off. Was it? I can't leave it on all week; the house
will burn down. This is ridiculous!" Eventually we either turn
around and head home to check as the only way to feel relieved,
or we convince ourselves that we did indeed take care of the task.
This is an example of what can take place inside anyone's mind
when we are worrying about a particular problem. In the mind of a
person with obsessive-compulsive disorder, this pattern of thought
is exaggerated and persistent.

Compulsions are repetitive, unproductive behaviors that people
engage in ritualistically. As with obsessive thoughts, there are a few
compulsive behaviors in which the average person might engage.
As children, we played with superstitions, such as never stepping
on a sidewalk crack or turning away when a black cat crossed our
path. Some of these persist as we become adults: many of us still
never walk under a ladder.

Obsessive-compulsive disorder, however, is much more serious
than these unbreakable habits. The obsessive person is driven by
persistent negative thoughts that are involuntary, uncontrollable,
and consuming. Self-doubt, ambivalence, indecision, and impulses
fill him. These thoughts are a defense against making any mistake.
His internal belief often is "If I keep worrying, I will prevent anything tragic from happening." At the same time, the person knows
that these thoughts are irrational, and he tries to resist them. The
more he resists, the stronger they become.

The general directions of obsessive thoughts that are most common are violence (poisoning one's spouse or stabbing a child), committing an immoral act, doubting whether one has performed some action (turning off the kitchen stove), and contamination (catching germs by picking up objects or touching someone).

Compulsions are also motivated by a need to relieve anxiety through rules or required rituals. Common compulsions are hand washing, as often as ten times an hour throughout the day, ritualistic touching of specific objects, and checking behavior. One compulsive client felt compelled to check if she had left the stove on each time she left her house for an errand. She would lock the front door as she was leaving, then feel a strong urge to return to the kitchen and touch each burner control knob as she checked it. As soon as she was back outside she would again feel a strong compulsion to repeat the process. After twelve or so times, she usually felt free enough to leave the house. Sometimes, however, this fear forced her to cancel her plans. High anxiety and even panic can result whenever the person attempts to stop the ritual. The tension and anxiety build to such an intense degree that she surrenders once again to the thoughts or behaviors. Unlike an alcoholic, who feels compelled to drink but also enjoys the drinking experience, the obsessive-compulsive person achieves relief through the ritual, but no pleasure.

Obsessions can sometimes intrude into the life of the agoraphobic, as was the case of the woman who feared she would stab a child with a knife. Such obsessions can lead to a phobic avoidance of the objects. You might think of it as a two-stage defense system. The person uses obsessions as a way to control some problem: "As long as I keep worrying, I won't make a mistake." If the individual begins to lose faith that those worries are enough to stop the feared response, then she must find another "solution," and phobias provide the answer: "If my thinking won't keep me safe, then the sure way to prevent a mistake is to avoid the situation altogether." The person with obsessive-compulsive disorder will cope with such situations by either avoiding the situation or engaging in compulsive behavior.˙

We have written a self-help book specifically for anyone suffering from OCD, titled *Stop Obsessing! How to Overcome Obsessions and Compulsions,* by Dr. Edna Foa and Dr. Reid Wilson (New York: Bantam Books, 1991).

Post-Traumatic Stress Disorder

Post-traumatic stress disorder (PTSD) identifies a specific emotional distress that can follow a major psychologically traumatic event. This uncommon event would typically produce fear and anxiety in anyone who experienced it. Examples are rape or assault, a natural disaster, being in or seeing a serious accident, major surgery, and wartime combat duty. Symptoms may begin immediately or may not surface for six months, a year, or even longer.

Severe anxiety and panic are just two of several possible symptoms. The person will have recurring images of the traumatic event, often with the same degree of anxiety as during the event itself. Or he will suddenly feel as though the event is occurring in the present. Recurring nightmares of the trauma are dramatic and disturbing. Nightmares, anxiety, or depression can disturb sleep. The person may remain tense and anxious throughout the day and may startle easily.

As they become more physically involved with these experiences, traumatized individuals begin to withdraw from the world, show less emotion, and become uninterested in people and activities that were once important. They avoid any situations that might stimulate memories of the traumatic event. Guilt, depression, and sudden outbursts of aggressive behavior may also surface. Drug and alcohol abuse develop in some as they attempt to manage these responses.

The largest group to experience this problem is the combat veteran. In the United States, the largest percentage of PTSD cases are Vietnam vets. In fact, it was after studies of Vietnam veterans were added to studies of civilian post-trauma sufferers that the American Psychiatric Association in 1980, created the diagnostic category post-traumatic stress disorder (acute, chronic, and/or delayed).

The major task in overcoming this problem is to incorporate the traumatic event into a person's sense of the world and into his understanding of his personal life. It is possible that the nightmares and spontaneous reliving of the trauma are unconscious attempts to heal the psychic wounds.

The experience of Vietnam combat veterans illustrates how traumatic changes can be difficult for the mind to incorporate and how this "working through" process is essential. The Vietnam War was like no other in American history. The average age of the combat soldier was nineteen, not twenty-six, as in World War Two. The military flew soldiers into duty as individuals, not as teams. Once there, nothing seemed straightforward. Those already fighting did not readily accept arriving soldiers. The enemy was not easily identifiable or necessarily in uniform; women and children could kill you in the streets. Women and children civilians were therefore sometimes killed by U.S. soldiers. There was no "front line," and soldiers had to win the same territory over and over again. Leadership was young and inexperienced. The object was to kill as many people as possible and survive.

The coming-home process of the Vietnam soldier failed to account for the mind's need to assimilate this experience in a slow-paced manner. After twelve to thirteen months of combat duty, the military flew soldiers back to the States in a matter of hours—again, as isolated individuals rather than as part of a team. This is in stark contrast to the weeks or sometimes months that World War Two veterans spent on ships en route to the United States, while sharing time with other soldiers close to them. In forty-eight hours the Vietnam combat soldier could go from a unit assault in which he killed four North Vietnamese soldiers with an M-16 to sitting on the front steps of his parents' house in the United States. In Southeast Asia, American soldiers would dream of that day. But when it arrived they weren't prepared. For the first time in U.S. history, the American people turned against its war and the returning soldiers. Antiwar marches replaced ticker-tape parades. A soldier in uniform on the streets of our country might be spat on. The heroes were now the villains.

It is no wonder that some Vietnam veterans have continued to experience chronic post-traumatic stress disorder, since the primary cause of the disorder is an inability to assimilate the experience into current life. A combat veteran needs time and the support and understanding of other people to assimilate a trauma of this significance. The person with post-traumatic stress disorder must have an opportunity to talk about the traumatic experience and, eventually, to feel the emotions associated with it. As he works through these feelings, he can begin to connect the trauma with the rest of his life. Part of that connection will be an ability to let past events remain in the past instead of continuing to surface in the present. For the Vietnam veteran, the return to present life can still be eased by the responses of those around him. Back in 1985, one of my colleagues who worked with these men and women said that even twenty years after returning from Southeast Asia, these soldiers needed to hear three things from us that weren't said long ago: "Welcome home," "Thank you," and "Thank God you're alive."

4

Agoraphobia and the Panic-Prone Personality

The nature of agoraphobia is so complex that it must be viewed as different from all other phobias. It is not the moment of panic that distinguishes agoraphobia, nor is it simply that a broader group of fears is involved. The physiological reactions of a claustrophobic who is facing an open elevator can be as severe as those of an agoraphobic, and the claustrophobic may avoid just as many situations for fear of being trapped.

The primary difference between agoraphobia and all other phobias lies in the beliefs that sustain the fear within the individual. These beliefs are established by the past life experiences of each agoraphobic and are supported by current relationships and by memories of the past.

If you are agoraphobic, you must do more than learn to master the moment of panic. You will need to take every opportunity to learn more about yourself, your relationship with the significant people in your current life, and your childhood development. The issues in agoraphobia include not only how you feel about frightening situations, but what you think about yourself, how you compare yourself with others, how you treat others, and how you let them treat you.

Learning how to handle your thoughts and your physical sensations as you approach a feared situation is an essential skill, just as it is for people experiencing panic from any source. In addition, though, you must learn about your self-perception and any limitations you feel as a human being. You will need all the strength you can muster to conquer this problem. In this chapter I will show you how self-perception, current relationships, and past relationships or events can set the stage for panic and weaken your stand against fear. In chapter 3 you read that the major fear of the agoraphobic is loss of control. Keep that in mind as you read this chapter. I will be illustrating a number of ways that people "learn" to feel out of control, not only in the panic-provoking situation but in their entire lives. The loss of control during panic is only one reflection of the belief system within each agoraphobic's personality.

Recent studies have found that women constituted 59 percent of the pure panic disorder cases and 89 percent of panic disorder with agoraphobia. Since approximately 85 percent of agoraphobics are women, I will focus primarily on the difficulties of the female agoraphobic.

Researchers have not yet established why such a disproportionately high percentage of agoraphobics are women. In the years to come we will most likely find that there are a number of influencing factors. Here are several hypotheses that have been suggested but have not been validated by scientific method:

1. Traditionally, parents and our culture have focused little attention on preparing young women to manage independently after leaving their parents' home. Girls' fairy-tale fantasies that turn on a delicate female being protected by the dominant, caring male can be shattered by the actual pressures of marriage and parenthood. If young women believe that their skills are no match for the tasks they face, they can become vulnerable to anxiety, self-doubt, and overdependence.

2. Agoraphobia develops within a person who succumbs to the fear of panic by avoiding situations. The stereotypical image of the macho male may pressure men to tolerate anxious symptoms and face fearful situations. By continually confronting anxiety you desensitize yourself to those symptoms. In this way, some men learn coping mechanisms that prevent anxieties from building into panic. Possibly women are "allowed" to give in to fearful feelings.

3. In this same vein, those who work at home are at a disadvantage compared with those who must travel to work each day in order to maintain their jobs. Consider a married couple with a new infant, where the husband has a full-time job and the wife is the primary caretaker. If the husband begins to feel panicky as he gets up in the morning, he also feels a strong, competing pressure to

tolerate his symptoms and make it to work on time. He feels the responsibility to provide his family with that weekly paycheck; he cannot easily avoid facing work. If the wife begins to feel anxious about going grocery shopping this morning, her schedule often permits her to postpone the trip until tomorrow. If driving to the park with her child might be anxiety-provoking, they can play at home today. So the spouse with a flexible schedule runs the greater risk of using avoidance to control panic instead of using the more successful methods of direct confrontation. You might say, "She who hesitates is lost." Soon, the need to avoid can become predominant, and agoraphobia develops.

4. Biological differences may play a role in increasing a woman's susceptibility to panic. Changes in the endocrine system are considered the strongest influencing factors: a large number of agoraphobic women develop their first symptoms after the birth of a child, a time when there are great changes in hormonal levels. Other agoraphobic women report increased anxiety symptoms or increased frequency of panic during their premenstrual week, a time when estrogen and progesterone levels temporarily drop. Premenstrual syndrome is further discussed in chapter 5.

Although these biological factors may prove to be significant in agoraphobia, psychological influences may play an equally important role during postpartum or premenstrual times. Agoraphobia usually develops during a prolonged period of stress. Every mother knows of the surprisingly large number of adjustments that are faced physically, psychologically, interpersonally, and economically as a new baby enters her life. Stress stems from the degree of change in one's life, regardless of whether that change is viewed as positive or negative. The stress of new parenthood can take its toll. Regarding premenstrual influences, if a woman regularly experiences physical and emotional discomfort during a certain week each month, then she will inevitably begin to anticipate that week. If she hasn't found any successful way to manage her symptoms, she will most likely anticipate with anxiety. In other words, the actual discomfort caused by biological factors is intensified by fearful expectation. This soon leads to a conditioned response: the woman unconsciously begins to brace in preparation for discomfort. Such bracing increases tension levels and makes her more susceptible to panic.

Another biological factor is the difference between males' and females' levels of testosterone. This hormone, which is found in much higher levels in men, is linked with dominance behavior. Thus men may be somewhat less likely to experience fear and might confront fearful situations more aggressively than women.

5. It is possible that the disproportionate ratio of female to male agoraphobia reflects an underestimation of male agoraphobia. One argument for this hypothesis is the suggestion that men mask their panic symptoms through abuse of alcohol (see chapter 5). That macho male image may stop men from admitting problems or asking for appropriate help, whereas women more readily admit to psychological causes of problems and are more likely to seek out mental-health professionals. Abuse of alcohol is a convenient self-treatment that offers short-term relief. However, when alcoholic agoraphobic men do seek help, they are more likely to end up at Alcoholics Anonymous meetings or alcohol treatment centers than with a mental-health professional who can spot their agoraphobia. A.A. programs address the substance-abuse problems directly but offer help with agoraphobia issues only indirectly.

Since such a small percentage of men have been identified as agoraphobic, our understanding of their difficulties is less developed. As a group, men who are agoraphobic seem more extroverted, aggressive, and ambitious than some of the women discussed in this chapter. Their greatest difficulty is in expressing their emotions directly, especially in intimate relationships. For this reason, the first symptoms may develop soon after conflicts arise within a marriage. Learning self-confidence within an intimate relationship, and learning to accept some of the changing roles of women today, may be an important factor in helping some agoraphobic men.

THE POWER OF BELIEFS LEARNED IN THE PAST

Each of the psychological themes in this chapter will be illustrated through the reflections and insights of five women who have suffered from agoraphobia. Before you meet each of them, there are several things you should know. First, these women generously agreed to permit an audio recording of our interviews. All names and biographical information have been altered to protect the confidentiality of our relationship. Second, their childhood experiences are typical of those suffering form severe forms of this disorder. Their long-term struggle with agoraphobia—lasting from twelve to forty-nine years—is common for those who do not receive appropriate professional treatment. With our new treatment approaches designed specifically for agoraphobia, people no longer need to remain trapped by panic for so many years. However, the accounts of these women provide an understanding of the workings of agoraphobia, which could not be so clearly and briefly illustrated by less dramatic cases. Third, it is not within the scope of this book to outline the complex treatment of all aspects of agoraphobia. Instead, I will describe each of these women as they appear at the initial stage of treatment and will summarize the therapeutic tasks ahead of them as they learn to control panic attacks.

And, fourth, I am limiting the details about these women's lives to those that help support the themes of this chapter. Many issues come to bear on complex psychophysiological problems, and those issues can be different in each individual.

As each woman shares her story, reflect on whether your experiences or feelings are similar. Take this opportunity to learn about yourself. Each theme that is not a problem for you is a positive sign of strength. When you do relate to an issue, consider it an area in which you will need to find strength. Make use of this important guideline: *Every time you gain strength in your personal life you will be laying a solid foundation for mastering panic.*

Karen L. is a thirty-four-year-old mother of two who began experiencing anxiety at the age of seven. She can remember at that age running home from friends' houses because of overwhelming feelings of fear. Once back in her own room she felt momentary relief from those strange tensions but would cry alone on her bed. After several years of psychological treatment, she became free of symptoms. Then, during her senior year in high school, her father died. For the next twelve months she withdrew into depression and rarely ventured outside her bedroom. The following year her family moved to another city. Within a few months, Karen began to have panic attacks, first in restaurants, then at movies and on trips.

Now, thirteen years later, Karen continues to experience panic, especially when traveling anywhere alone. Her symptoms include rapid heartbeat, blurred vision, clenched jaws, weakness, numbness, shooting headache pains, chest pain, and physical imbalance. Although she can comfortably travel with a companion, she rarely makes commitments for activities with others for fear that she will have to cancel plans.

Undoubtedly there were many experiences in Karen's childhood that contributed to her susceptibility to panic. But more relevant to this chapter is how Karen's symptoms are supported by her current self-image. In the following pages you will hear how she feels inferior to her peers, how she constantly criticizes her own actions, how she seeks approval from others yet refuses to accept their compliments. She believes that she is socially inept, that she is not capable of carrying on a normal conversation with her women friends. And she is so afraid of her husband's anger that she placates him through concession after concession.

When we place Karen's symptoms within the context of her current life we can see how they reflect a basic self-distrust. She doesn't believe she has what it takes within her to handle the adult world. Therefore, whenever life places a challenge in front of her, she naturally becomes afraid. Although quite uncomfortable and distressing, her panic symptoms are only one part of her fear of being forced into adult responsibility.

As she recovers from agoraphobia, Karen will learn to face traveling alone. But she will also learn that she is a unique and important member of our world, deserving of respect from others and deserving of her own self-respect. She will find that if her marriage is a good one, her husband won't leave her just because she sticks up for her needs. And she will learn that she can survive losses, that she can tolerate mistakes, and that she doesn't need the approval of others in order to feel O.K. about herself.

Sheryll W. is a forty-five-year-old housewife who has experienced the symptoms of agoraphobia for twenty-two years. Her greatest difficulties come when she begins to plan for some event, large or small. As she contemplates going shopping, entering a crowded place, or driving to the beach, she begins to feel smothered, as if she can't breathe. She feels dizzy and nauseated, her heart rate increases, and her legs become weak. At the same time, her mind races through a series of fearful thoughts about the activity. If she decides to venture out, all she can think about is getting back home. After several hours of this anxious anticipation, Sheryll becomes physically and emotionally depleted and withdraws into her house for several days.

Sheryll became pregnant on her honeymoon, and the symptoms started when her oldest child, Susan, was born. After Susan's birth, Sheryll's husband worked seven days and nights a week while she remained home. Thus, her life was dramatically altered: from enjoying a carefree, single life, she became isolated at home alone every night. Then, three months later, the family was evicted when their rental house was sold. This was the straw that broke the camel's back. Sheryll became depressed and anxious. One day, while trying to locate an apartment, she started having chest pains and thought she was dying of a heart attack. Her mother rushed her to the hospital, where the doctor diagnosed the problem as anxiety and prescribed tranquilizers. From that time on her symptoms became progressively worse. She began having difficulty attending church. Before long she became fearful at the supermarket. Within a year she was housebound, too afraid even to step outside her front door. During the past seventeen years she has gone through phases of improvement followed by dramatic setbacks. Like many agoraphobics, Sheryll has been evaluated again and again by physicians. She spent several years in psychotherapy, tried a number of medications, and was in and out of the hospital for two years. In addition to her agoraphobia symptoms she has suffered several bouts of severe depression.

But agoraphobia is more than being afraid of powerful physical symptoms. It is also the way each person views herself and her role in this world. Sheryll describes herself as the "worrier" in her family. She is always preparing for the worst, always on guard. Her biggest daily fear is that her husband will abandon her, even though she has no information that supports this dread. In general, her life revolves around her anxious bracing for some loss. Her fear of losing control in the grocery store is symbolic of a deeper belief about her life: if I let go and enjoy myself, something bad will happen.

Sheryll talks about her childhood, about how she lived in fear, confusion, and secret emotional pain, always worried that her alcoholic father would seriously injure her mother during his frequent Saturday night beatings. She talks about how her mother dominated her life; about how when she was a teenager her mother took away her independence, made decisions for her, and attempted to control her thinking.

Such experiences in childhood leave a young woman unpre-
pared for the responsibilities of adulthood. As she overcomes agoraphobia, Sheryll will master many new skills. But in addition she
will develop a special sense of independence. As a child she had
little choice but to be afraid of her father's violence and to follow
the overprotective directives of her mother. Today, however, she
will learn a new self-trust that gives her a sense of freedom, choice
and independence.

Donna B. is a forty-seven-year-old married woman with three
children. She has been agoraphobic for twenty-one years. For many
of those years her agoraphobia symptoms were overshadowed by
prolonged episodes of severe depression. She has been hospital-
ized several times for treatment of her depression and her thoughts
of suicide. Her treatment, however, never involved extended psychotherapy. Instead, it was limited to medications, such as antidepressants, tranquilizers, and electroconvulsive therapy (ECT), a
neurological treatment for severe depression. Such extended use of
ECT is no longer practiced. When used with discretion, as it is
today, ECT can produce spectacular changes in some severe
depressions within three to four sessions. However, Donna was
given more than one hundred ECT treatments over a seven-year
period. Because of this she now suffers long-term memory loss.

Her first anxiety attack came three months after the birth of her
oldest child. Over the past ten years she has become completely
housebound for about two months each year. During her worst
episodes she is unable even to leave her bedroom without panicking.

Donna is most susceptible to panic during the two-week period
before and after her monthly menstruation. In her panic attacks she
becomes dizzy and has blurred vision, poor concentration, weak
leg muscles, clammy hands and cold feet, nausea, and tight jaw
muscles. She also experiences depersonalization, the feeling that
her mind and body are separated, as though she is in a dream. Her
thoughts turn to the fear of losing control, and she wants to run. "If
I stay here, I'll faint . . . I'll humiliate myself . . . I'll be overwhelmed
by these feelings." Even more frightening is the fearful question,
"Am I about to become housebound again?"

Donna speaks of childhood experiences that I believe are relevant to her struggle with agoraphobia. She was the youngest of five
children; the next youngest sibling was eight years old when she

was born. When she was seven her father died in a car accident. Her mother then became reclusive: she stopped socializing, never dated, and never remarried. Donna withdrew as well. For the next five years she went to school, came home, and helped prepare supper while her mother was at work, then spent the rest of the evening in her bedroom.

During her teenage years Donna allowed her mother to dominate her life. She never argued, never said no. In her eyes her mother had made great sacrifices, so if Donna ever thought about opposing her, her sense of guilt would stop her assertive actions. Her most important task was to please her mother, and the easiest way to do that was to give up her own decision-making power. Donna explains how this relationship generalized to others later in her life, how she learned to hide her own needs while trying to do what others wanted.

There are several reasons why Donna puts on this facade. One is her long-standing fear of abandonment. After her father died, Donna's only relationship for years was with her mother. Possibly her thinking was "As long as I'm good, she won't leave me." And how does someone figure out how to be "good"? By ignoring her own needs while focusing attention on what would make others happy. And that is what Donna does to this day.

The best way to ignore our needs is to ignore our feelings, for our emotions guide a great many of our decisions. As a young girl Donna paid a high price for her desire to keep her mother's love: she stopped paying attention to her own feelings. After years of practice, she is no longer able to distinguish her different feelings and manage them.

Donna's struggle with panic is closely related to her fear of abandonment, her depression, her need to please others, and her suppression of her own desires and feelings. She will not win over panic without also facing these lifelong issues. Over time she will learn that adults live interdependently. Each of us has the right, even the responsibility, to express our emotions directly and to strive for our personal goals in life without fearing the repercussions of isolation and abandonment. Close, caring friends and relatives want to know our feelings, even if different from their own. It is only through openly and honestly sharing our authentic feelings and needs that we establish ourselves as unique, special human beings. As Donna learns to trust this sharing process, she will not allow trapped emotions to express themselves through the vehicle of panic.

Ann C. is a thirty-nine-year-old married woman with one child. She began to experience panic attacks at twenty, just one month before her wedding day. After returning to work after the end of the honeymoon, she remained highly anxious throughout her day, with headaches and episodes of panic. With the encouragement of her family she finally began treatment with a psychiatrist, who also placed her on a tranquilizer. After several months of weekly sessions without improvement, Ann stopped all treatment.

When her son was born four years later, Ann began self-treating her panic by avoiding more and more situations. This solution helped reduce her anxious episodes but at the same time greatly diminished her freedom of travel. Today, twelve years later, Ann never drives outside of her town. Whenever she drives within town, she must first devise an "escape route" back to some "safe" location, such as a friend's house. She is able to travel alone, but usually enlists the companionship of her son, her husband, or her mother. Her greatest difficulties are staying at home alone at night, grocery shopping, and standing in lines.

But what about the rest of Ann's life? These difficulties relate to her attitude about herself, to her ability to handle conflict, her relationships with those close to her. Her rigid perfectionism keeps her from enjoying her achievements. She also has difficulty sorting out her emotional responses to events. Expressing anger or experiencing the anger of others is to be avoided at all costs. She fears that if she truly lets herself feel angry, she will become explosive, and she goes to great lengths to prevent anyone from becoming mad at her.

Ann's need to please others and her fear of rejection are partly responsible for her overdependence on her husband and her mother. She speaks of how they fight her battles for her, how they "have always bailed me out whenever I've had to do something that makes me anxious." Within this protective system that Ann has created, she can always run away from conflict. But every time she runs away she reinforces her belief that she is incapable of handling life as an independent adult.

In addition to taking control of anxiety attacks, Ann will learn how to take charge of her self-esteem and pride. Her belief in her own self-worth will be based on something other than perfectionism or the opinions of others. She will find, through experience,

that she can handle her own emotions and can manage her conflicts with others. Some of the changes will come easily, like learning to say thank-you when someone compliments her instead of
rejecting the compliment with some self-deprecating comment.
Other changes will take more time, since they are part of the
deeper fear of abandonment. As Ann recovers she will be less and
less troubled by her profound sense that to think, feel, and act for
herself will cause her to lose everyone and everything she values in
this world.

Dorothy P. is seventy-two years old. She has experienced agoraphobia for almost fifty years now, but hasn't had an anxiety attack
in over thirty years. Long ago she learned that if she avoided all
uncomfortable situations she could avoid panic, and that is just
what she has done. She never travels outside the city limits, never
drives a car, never stays home alone or goes out alone. She sits in
the aisle seat at the movie theater, walks out into the lobby several
times during the show, and always leaves before the end of the
movie. If she goes to a restaurant she sits next to the door and
watches the door throughout the meal. In other words, she never
challenges her fears; she stays away from all things that might produce a sense of being trapped.

A brief review of Dorothy's early life shows how one's past can
have a direct bearing on one's current susceptibility to the fear of
panic. Her father died during World War One, when she was a
young child. A few years later her mother remarried. Dorothy
explains how her mother rarely left the house—she was probably
agoraphobic—and her stepfather did all the shopping. Her stepfather continually ridiculed her and her sisters and controlled and
physically abused their mother. Her loving, caring mother eventually broke under the pressure. Dorothy developed the traits of a
perfectionist at an early age so as not to give her stepfather any jus-
tifiable reason to attack her verbally. When she was fourteen their
family doctor placed her on tranquilizers because of her anxiety
symptoms.

At seventeen she married in order to escape from her home life.
Her new husband was as strong as her stepfather. To Dorothy this
was an important trait, because while growing up she never
learned how to think independently about her own needs. It was
important to marry someone who would also take care of her.

But soon this relationship turned on her as well. After the birth of their second child, her husband's alcoholism flared. As he drank he became violent. When their new daughter was only three months old, he came home one night in a drunken rage. Dorothy ended up in the hospital with a fractured jaw and a concussion. With the help of the courts she pressed charges, became legally separated, and then divorced her husband.

But her problems didn't end. Her ex-husband began to appear at her house randomly during the day or night, sometimes breaking down a door or window to demand "visitation rights." Dorothy lived in constant, anxious fear of being violently surprised.

It was during this traumatic period in her life that Dorothy's panic symptoms began to surface. Returning home on the train after a day at the beach with her two children, she suddenly became overwhelmed with fear and the need to escape. Within a matter of two weeks she restricted her travels to within her hometown.

Dorothy explains how she married the second time not for love but for security, how she never wanted to "cause trouble" by making demands of her children or her second husband. She kept herself from expressing angry feelings by thinking, "They're going to lock me up." In her mind she believed she could never be in control of her anger; she'd be angry every day if she allowed it. In chapter 7 Dorothy says that she never attempts to drive a car for fear of completely losing control: "If there was a detour, or if traffic backed up, I'd have to either get out and run, or jam on the brakes, knock everyone down, knock the policeman down, go through red lights. . . ."

Dorothy's recovery from agoraphobia will depend on her willingness to face fears she has avoided for almost fifty years. Her central fear, however, is not driving a car or being alone at home. It is the fear of her own emotions. She has a number of legitimate emotions that she has held inside year after year. She keeps them in check by scaring herself with exaggerated images of losing control.

Dorothy will not resolve this problem by herself. She will do it with the help of new friends and a supportive professional who will help her express her authentic emotions a little at a time. As she does this she will learn how her emotions express her personal values and her self-esteem. She will begin to reassess her priorities with regard to personal relationships. Being protected by a strong individual will be less and less important as she learns to manage her own life. And the desire to be close to loving, active friends will slowly increase in value. While these changes are taking place, she will begin to face panic by gradually expanding her restricted limits.

Her very first task, however, will be to stop verbally degrading herself. Dorothy's stepfather was wrong; she is not stupid, incapable, or worthless. The sooner she changes these personal beliefs the sooner she can start taking control of panic.

"I've Always Felt Inferior."

When the agoraphobic is a person with low self-esteem, she places others above her in life. She usually "talks herself down" and is self-critical. She may not attempt to take on a new challenge because she doubts her ability or competence. When looking back over her past she sees only a series of failures.

What's more, a person with low self-esteem will tend to think that other people see her in a similar light. "Who could possibly like me?" is the question in the back of her mind. Since she doubts people could like her for just being who she is, she will try to "make" people like her through her generosity and self-sacrifice.

The major problem with this approach is that she attempts to get others to like her before she learns to like herself. If it really were true that other people needed to be persuaded to like her, the problem would not be so difficult. But truly she is her own worst critic; when someone says, "Good job!" she says in her mind, "No, it wasn't."

This is quite a painful process. So much time is spent seeking the approval of others, so much thinking, worrying, physical and emotional energy is spent in the wrong direction, that the woman is actually out of control. She allows other people to have control over her self-esteem. How *they* act determines how *she* feels.

> KAREN: We lose our self-confidence. That's what agoraphobia does to us. We just don't deserve it. We're not good enough. We overcompensate because we're just not worthy.
>
> I probably spend all my waking hours looking for approval, recognition, and attention. I think I've always felt inferior, thinking that everyone else can do better than me. I need

someone to build me up constantly, which is bad because no one's going to do that.

Acceptance. That's my biggest issue. I am so critical of myself. I'm never content with my performance. Even when I am complimented on something, I think, "That's just not my best." It's strange, but I think deep inside I hate myself—I really do.

Here, Donna discusses her current relationship with her mother. As she speaks I notice her eyes beginning to water and her face flushing with color.

DR. W.: There's that sadness again.

DONNA: No, it's resentment. Resentment that I've let myself be pushed around all my life. I've allowed it to happen. I never said no to my mother. Never. If I thought about it, I felt guilty. And the guilt was difficult to deal with. Even today, she will constantly try to lay guilt on me—that she's all alone, I should spend more time with her, that other mothers and daughters are so close. Well, I can't tolerate much of her.

DR. W.: This inability to say no to your mother—does that generalize into other relationships?

DONNA: Yes. I have always been a people pleaser. If you wanted to go to a restaurant, you'd decide the restaurant and I would say, "Fine." I could hate the place, but I would say, "Wonderful."

Karen speaks of needing acceptance and approval. Although this is a natural need for all of us, Karen allows her entire life to revolve around her fear of disapproval. At the same time she says, "I'm never content with my performance." Before she can believe that other people accept her, she must learn to accept herself.

She explains that she continues to give and give because she wants to make up for being "not good enough." Where did that standard come from? What are her criteria for "good enough"? For some reason, Karen has set standards for herself that she can't meet; because she doesn't meet the standards, she is not "worthy." Belief in one's self-worth is essential to conquering panic.

Donna presents another dimension of low self-esteem. She doesn't deserve to say yes to herself. She will say yes to everyone else in her life; she reserves "no" for her own needs.

Here are the components of one typical belief system of a person who won't say no to others:

1. I am not worth much as a human being.
2. Therefore, I'm lucky this person has stayed with me for so long.
3. Since I don't deserve all that this person has generously given to such an unworthy; person as myself,
4. I owe him or her a great deal.
5. Therefore, I would feel guilty if I refused this request.

This faulty line of reasoning is often supported by a second set of beliefs:

1. Besides, I must not forget that I am not worth much as a human being.
2. If this person left me because I didn't keep pleasing him or her, then most likely I would end up alone in the world.
3. Not only would I be isolated and lonely, but I would not be capable of managing my life.
4. Therefore, I must forget myself and think of others at all times.

"I Can't Stand Making a Mistake."

The strongly self-critical person often demands perfection, but only in herself.

DR. W.: Do you feel as if you have to be perfect at everything you do?

DONNA: Oh, yes. In the sense that either I do it up to my expectations or I don't do it at all. I have a real problem being a perfectionist.

I don't demand perfection of other people, only of myself.

I'll always say to someone else, "That's fine! You did the best you could do," but I can't seem to apply that to myself. And I can't stand making a mistake. Doing paperwork, even if nobody knows that I make the mistake, and even if I correct it on the next line. I get this really frustrated feeling—it's just unacceptable to me.

DR. W.: Is there any other time that it gets in your way?

DONNA: Yes, in my hesitation to try things. I don't venture to try certain things for fear of making a mistake or not being perfect. I'd rather not do them at all.

Notice the significance of Donna's last statements. She is not speaking of hesitating about going shopping or moving in a crowd. She is speaking of not attempting *any* new, creative tasks that might be pleasurable or rewarding, such as painting a picture or writing a poem. Some agoraphobics, if they take time to notice, can see that they don't just avoid phobic situations; they avoid any chance of making a mistake—because to make a mistake is one more way for them to feel out of control. If they can't guarantee that an undertaking will be done perfectly, they will not even begin the task.

ANN: I can't say, "Well, that's good enough." It might be a question of one little detail that nobody will notice. But anything that I do that reflects me, that I'll get praise for, I have to do perfectly. Somebody might see it and say, "Oh, isn't that beautiful! Oh, you're so talented. Isn't that nice!" But while they're telling me that, I don't believe them. I just kind of laugh it off. I say, "Oh, it's silly, you can do it. Anybody can do it." I always put it down. Or if I make something, and there's something about it bothers me, I'll always point it out. I'll say, "See, I didn't do so well right there."

Ann works compulsively at any task that might bring praise from others. After tremendous effort, she finally receives her deserved acknowledgment and praise. Even at the exact moment the person is speaking, Ann is discounting the compliment in her own mind. And as if that weren't enough, she then explains to her friend that the praise was undeserved, since there was a flaw in the workmanship.

Can you imagine a carpenter spending all weekend remodeling his kitchen, then on Sunday night taking a sledgehammer to his handiwork? Can you imagine a secretary spending all day typing a thirty-page report, then at five o'clock placing it in the shredder? Think of the carpenter or secretary repeating that same procedure every week, and now you are getting the picture of an agoraphobic's life. People like Donna and Ann make a career out of earning self-worth, then never accepting it. It is an exhausting cycle.

Strong self-esteem is important as you begin to control panic. When you start to believe in your own worth, then you can start to believe that these symptoms of panic are standing in the way of an important person—you. You will feel more energy to push through setbacks and tough times. You will devote more energy to yourself and less to having to please others.

Here are some questions to reflect on:

- Do I think I am a lovable person?
- What do I have to do to be loved?
- What are my good qualities in each of my roles (spouse, friend, parent, employee)?
- What are my weaknesses in these same roles?
- How do I describe myself? What kind of language do I use to describe my weaknesses? Do I call myself derogatory names (lazy, childish, stupid, chicken, worthless, etc.)?
- Am I "devastated" by others' criticisms?
- Do I tend to point out all my mistakes to myself and others?
- Do I accept compliments? Do I really believe people when they speak well of me or my accomplishments?
- Do I need to do everything perfectly? Can I accept my mistakes?
- If I can't do something perfectly, do I avoid it?
- Do I have trouble setting limits on how much I give to others?
- Do I have trouble setting limits on any projects I undertake?
- Do I hesitate to try new tasks for fear I will fail?
- Do I consider mistakes to mean the same things as "failure"?
- Am I constantly watching and monitoring myself? Do I evaluate my every move?
- Do I consider everything that I do to be of great signifi-

cance? Or, do I use good judgment to determine the difference between small and large tasks, significant and insignificant projects?

- How many times have I said yes to myself this week? This
  year?

No one has to earn the right to be loved; we are already lovable.
Your answers to the above questions will indicate how much you
withhold love from yourself and how hard you work at gaining the
love of those around you.

If your self-esteem could use some strengthening, you must first
learn how to love yourself, including all your weaknesses. Then,
look around to find people who are willing and able to love you
just the way you are. Once you truly love and appreciate yourself
every day, you will begin to notice what kinds of people will love
and appreciate you. You will also notice the many people who
have been appreciating you all along.

Here are a few guidelines to help you on your way:

- Praise yourself every time you accomplish something, no
  matter how small.
- When you make a mistake, give yourself a helpful suggestion for your next try, or find someone who can.
- Refrain from calling yourself names or putting yourself
  down for your mistakes. Life is hard enough. No one
  deserves to be humiliated, even silently by themselves.
- Consider the idea that you deserve to be loved, not solely
  for how much you give to others, but simply for being a
  unique human being.
- If you are failing to meet your goals, change them.
- If you are failing to live up to your standards, lower them.
- Never stop setting goals and standards for yourself, only
  bring them within reach. Success breeds success.
- Set a small enough goal, work to reach it, praise yourself for
  your accomplishment, then set yourself a new reachable
  goal.
- When someone compliments you, be a sponge; absorb the
  compliment, believe it, feel it.
- When someone criticizes you, don't swallow it whole. Chew
  on it to see if you can learn anything for next time. Spit out

any name-calling and hostility. Digest only what you believe is beneficial.

- Reevaluate your self-expectations. Make certain that your expectations are based on your own belief system, what you think is good and right today. Do not allow beliefs taught years ago to rule your life without questioning them. Take control of your expectations and you will have control of your self-esteem.

- Find ways to say yes to yourself every day of your life. If you are unwilling to say yes to yourself, why should anyone else?

"But if I Didn't Have Him ... "

Self-doubt can have a major impact on all parts of your life. In the context of your panic symptoms, self-doubt can produce a multitude of questions. At a party, for example: "Will I be able to stay the whole time? Will I embarrass myself? Will it get worse? Will anybody see me?" Those same types of doubting questions can be found elsewhere in an individual's life, and nowhere will self-doubt have a more dramatic effect than in the realm of personal relationships.

Consider, for example, a woman who has an underlying belief that she is inherently a weak person. If I honestly believe that I am incapable of caring for myself, than I have to find someone in my life who will protect me. I might hate being dependent, I might detest my subservience to another human being, but those feelings will never be stronger than my fear of going it alone. If I believe I will be helpless if left alone, my basic survival is at stake. All other considerations take on lesser importance. I must survive. Therefore I must keep people around me, at whatever cost.

This is a crucial issue in the understanding of panic. Our basic belief systems will always overpower any other thoughts or emotions. Many of these beliefs were adopted years ago and are outside our conscious awareness. This is what is so confusing for agoraphobics. They really would love not to have to depend on others; they want independence more than almost anything else in the world. But their belief systems tell them that they won't survive without a strong person next to them. Keeping this significant conflict in mind, see how it has caused so much pain in these women's lives.

DOROTHY: When I met my second husband, something should have gone off in my head, I should have known that he was not going to be a friend. We had no common interests, we had nothing to talk about. Something told me—I don't know what it was—that I was going to be sick and unable to work; I was going to need a roof over my head. I had had it up to here trying to make ends meet. I was really wanting security. I didn't love him, not at all.

Dorothy made a major life decision based on fear. In order to gain security, she surrendered love, happiness, and companionship.

KAREN: I think I don't want to grow up—that's what I really feel. I just don't want to admit it. I don't want to be thirty-four, with two children; I don't want my responsibilities. I know that I can get rid of agoraphobia tomorrow, but then where do I go? I'm not ready for the adult world. I don't know how to act. I mean, I don't know how to pull up in people's driveways and talk to them.

ELIZABETH (to Karen, in a group therapy session): One night when we came out of here, you were rushing to go to your husband, and I wanted to talk to you for a minute. Your husband was outside and you said, "If I keep him waiting for too long, he'll get mad. If he sees me crying, he'll get mad and say, 'You can't come here anymore.'" And I say, "The hell with him, the hell with him!" You can use us, the hell with him. Lean on us, that's what a support group is for.

KAREN: You're right, you're right. I know that. It's a nightmare the way it is now. But I don't know how much of a nightmare it would be if I didn't have him.

ELIZABETH (still angry): So therefore you would rather do everything his way?

KAREN: I get up in the morning and I say, "How low do you have to lay? I mean, how low does someone like me have to go? How long will I let him treat me this way?" But to turn around and say, "Knock it off, I want to be my own person"— I can't say that to my husband. I need him too badly.

Karen says that she doesn't want to grow up. That is probably based on her belief that she is not capable of handling her responsibilities. She worried so much about failing as a mother that she gave her entire attention to her children. She monitored her every move and left no time for her own pleasures. She now believes that the world has passed her by, that she no longer knows how to communicate with her peers.

Her belief that she is incapable is so strong that she allows herself to be completely dominated by her husband. She hates what she is doing to herself. And I am sure some of her friends have said, "If you hate it so much, why don't you change it?" But, as Karen says, she believes she "can't," that she is not capable of independence. Therefore, her actions continue to lower her self-esteem. She fears the loss of her husband's support because she believes she cannot survive without him.

> KAREN: When I need to get my daughter to the doctor for a checkup, or I need to shop for new clothes, I have to say to my husband, "Three weeks from Saturday, would you take me to the mall?" And I have to build him up. I think, "No, I'd better not antagonize him because he'll say, 'OK, we're not going.'" What a way to live! I have no control over my own life.

> ANN: My mother will still do my fighting for me, and I'm thirty-nine years old. My husband does a lot for me, too. He's the "take charge" kind of person. So I have these two people that have always bailed me out when I've had to do something that makes me anxious.
>
> Even now, if I go to a group meeting my husband will say, "What time are you going to be home?" And if I'm a little bit late, he gets upset. I always say I'm his oldest child, because he treats me like a child in a lot of ways. But I let him treat me like a child, I don't assert myself with him. It doesn't seem worth it. I'm just happy to go along like this.
>
> My husband and my mother are always around to help me with this, to help me with that. I don't want to lose them but, deep down inside, I know that it's wrong. Still, I fear what will happen if I start to get really independent.

As you may be starting to sense, if a person feels as though she is incapable of managing the demands of the world, she will search out someone who can manage them for her. Perhaps she is skilled at giving to others, being kind and sensitive, but feels unable to stand up for herself when necessary. Within the logic of that belief system, she believes that she would be smart to marry a man who is powerful, dominant, and controlling. Together they make a whole person, one who can be kind, compassionate, and giving, and also strong and forceful if need be.

Unfortunately, they are *two* people, not one. This has caused many a painful marriage. They may stay together because they satisfy certain basic needs (simply put, he remains dominant and receives nurturing while she feels protected). But other needs go unmet or get stifled, because each person behaves completely differently. He controls and dominates, she surrenders and submits. They don't have a common, shared relationship between two equals. It is very difficult for them to have fun together, to solve problems together, to plan the future together.

"If I Stop Worrying, Something Bad Will Happen."

Over time, our roles and self-perceptions begin to solidify within our relationships. In the above example, Ann sees herself as always the child, both with her mother and with her husband. Sheryll sees herself as the worrier.

> SHERYLL: Nothing ever bothers my husband. And my kids take after him. Nothing ever gets on his nerves. Everything's very easy for them.
>
> DR. W: So what role does that leave you?
>
> SHERYLL: I do all the worrying. Somebody's got to worry in my family! [Laughs.]
>
> DR. W: Or what would happen?
>
> SHERYLL: I've never thought of the consequences. Nothing would get done. All my husband cares about is his tennis.
>
> DR. W.: "I have to keep worrying about the kids, because if I don't . . . "? Fill in the blank, Sheryll.

SHERYLL: Well, I'm afraid something will happen if I stop worrying about this, that, and the other thing. If I relax and take it easy, if I stop worrying, something bad will happen. Does that make sense?

I'm always prepared. I've been married twenty-three years. And still, every night when my husband walks through the door, I wait for him to say, "Sheryll, I've found somebody else." This is how I live.

DR. W.: "I'm always on guard . . . "

SHERYLL: I'm always on guard, you'd better believe it.

Sheryll first states that she must worry or nothing would get done in her home. But with just a little prodding, she reveals a deeper, more significant concern. Sheryll expresses a basic fear of something bad happening to her, especially the fear of being abandoned. It is not a minor fear; she thinks about it every day. But it is an irrational fear, one based on an internal belief system rather than any real evidence. She tells me that her husband has given her no reason to doubt his commitment to the marriage.

But she does give us a very important piece of information, something that I doubt she understood at the time she said it. It is as though she has a magical strategy to prevent anything bad from happening. Her belief is "As long as I keep worrying, as long as I remain tense and on guard, nothing bad will happen. If I relax and take it easy, if I stop worrying . . . "

This is exactly the same feeling that a person has about panic attacks. She remains tense in anticipation of a negative experience (at a store, in a car, or in a crowd). She remains on guard, expecting the worst. For Sheryll and other panic-prone people, that fear epitomizes the way they think about their life in general.

Looking back over Sheryll's therapy we were able to see this thought pattern more clearly. The interview you just read took place during our tenth session. Prior to that I had taught Sheryll a relaxation process (which you will find in chapter 12). She was petrified at the thought of listening to the exercise on an audiotape. "I *can't* relax," she said. I instructed her to do some household chore, like her ironing, while playing the tape on low volume in the background, just as a way to get used to the sound. She was so afraid of the concept of relaxation that she would not take the risk. At that point, "relaxation" meant "loss of control."

After this tenth session, I learned that her unconscious fear was long-standing and of a much stronger nature. She feared great harm or loss if she let go of her tension and worry. Her tension was her protection. Unfortunately, this belief was causing her great discomfort in her current life. But in her mind, her worry and tension seemed to be working, because she had averted any trouble. Since she always remained tense, she assumed her method of self-protection was successful. You may remember the old joke of the man who constantly paces around the outside of his house to keep away the tigers. "There aren't any tigers loose around here," exclaims his neighbor. "See how well it works," responds the man. The agoraphobic's use of physical as well as psychological tension to guard against mistakes or harm takes this same strategy. Even to experiment with relaxing holds too many risks.

"I Am Deathly Afraid of That Anger. "

There are few people who could say that they enjoy conflicts. Most people feel somewhat uncomfortable before, during, or after an argument. For many agoraphobics, though, conflicts are to be avoided like the plague.

> ANN: Last winter I was hemmed in in a parking space downtown. Someone parked illegally behind me, and I became livid. It was very cold and I had one child with me. Just driving into town with my children was a big step, because I was really feeling housebound at the time. Well, I came out and said, "How am I going to get out of this space? Look at that jerk parked there."
>
> It started welling up in me—the anger. I thought that I should stay and give him a piece of my mind, that I should call the cops because he'd parked illegally. Then all I could think about was getting out of there, getting the heck out of there and getting home. I didn't want to confront this; I didn't want this person to come out because I would have had to get mad and I wasn't sure what that would do to me.

DR. W.: So you'd start to have those feelings about getting mad, and you even had the image of getting angry at the person. At the same time you'd be thinking, "Let me get away from it."

ANN: Yes, but not all the time, because I can get mad, too. But that happened to be a particularly sensitive week, when I was feeling a lot of panic; I was highly sensitized.

Women such as Ann will expend much energy to avoid a confrontation. They may also attach themselves to a husband who will fight their battles for them. Ann expresses not only a fear of conflict but also a fear of her own anger. From my observations, such comments by agoraphobics reflect two types of fears. First is the fear of conflict and the repercussions it might bring, such as a separation or loss of relationship. Second is the fear of one's own intense emotions. Ann did not want to confront the driver of that car, "because I would have had to get mad and I wasn't sure what that would do to me."

Earlier you heard Donna talk about being a "people pleaser": she never expresses her own desires if she believes that they conflict with yours. Notice how that same pattern continues with regard to her feelings.

DONNA: I've had an awfully hard time with anger. I have trouble sorting out my emotions. Sometimes I think my feelings get tangled into a big ball. I don't know if I'm mad, or what.

I really don't get mad at all. And if I do, I keep it all in. I mean, I don't direct it at anything. I suppose I'm directing it at myself and just running away from it.

My husband never knows what I'm feeling. I never share negative feelings. I'm one of those people who talks positively and feels negatively. And I always play that game. I tell people what they want to hear or what I judge they want to hear. If I feel angry, they never hear about it—I never show it. I don't even think I give nonverbal cues for anger. A person would have to be very in tune to me to see a nonverbal. I just suppress a lot of stuff. And I think the reason isn't so much that I don't want to show I am angry as that I never really feel just anger, I feel rage. And I am deathly afraid of losing control of that anger, of hurting somebody. Consequently, it is unusual for me to even raise my voice in the house. When I yell at the kids, they move, because I so seldom do it.

DR. W.: So your anger has to evolve to a bigger level before you even begin to notice it yourself.

DONNA: Yes, I have to feel it to an extreme. And then I sometimes don't know exactly what I'm feeling. When I feel anger and rage it's usually mixed with self-pity. When I feel fear, it's more terror than fear.

DOROTHY: I was too lenient with the kids, and I'm still too lenient with my husband. If he says something, I think to myself, "Why cause trouble? Why have an argument? I'll just let it go." But once in a blue moon, I hit the roof.

DR. W.: And what would happen if you did that more often?

DOROTHY: Well, I'd be doing it every day of the week. Why bother getting upset over something that's not going to change? My fear is that they're going to lock me up.

Donna and Dorothy speak of holding in their emotions. Whenever we hold on to something tightly, we feel tension. Try physically holding your fist in a tight squeeze for one minute, and you'll be experiencing the amount of psychic energy we must use to hold in our secret emotions. It is exhausting physically and emotionally.

In order to incorporate our emotions into our lives in a beneficial way, it is important to do these three things:

1. *Notice* what emotion you are feeling.
2. *Respect* that emotion as a legitimate expression of who you are and what you value as a human being.
3. *Take care* of that emotion in some manner. Simply acknowledging the presence of a feeling inside you and permitting it to exist can sometimes be enough. If the emotion is in response to another person, you may need to express it directly to the person who stimulated your reaction. In still other situations it may be more beneficial for you to express your emotion to another, more objective and supportive listener instead of the person to whom you are reacting.

Your values and your emotions are the two essential ingredients that distinguish you as a unique individual. When you cut other people off from knowing your values and emotions, or if you only present the values and emotions you think they want to see, then you do yourself and them a disservice. You don't give people a chance to treat your true self with respect. You do the same thing when you cut yourself off from knowing your feelings. You don't respect your rights and your values as a human being.

In addition, when you refuse to pay attention to your milder emotions, they tend to grow stronger in order to be heard. Everyone knows what it's like to be in a noisy environment calling out someone's name. "John?" (in a normal tone). No answer. "John?" (a little louder). Not even a turn of the head. "JOHN?!" you yell with force, finally grabbing his attention. John will probably jump, startled.

Your emotions work the same way. As you ignore them, they grow and grow. Once they are so big that you can't ignore them, they scare you instead. This is how Donna's fear turns into "terror."

Dorothy is afraid that if she expresses her anger,

1. It will never end. She will be angry forever.
2. It will fail to change anything.
3. She will go crazy and be locked up.

Here are my answers to those fears:

1. *I'm afraid that if I let myself feel this emotion, I will be unable to stop feeling it.* Anything that is fully experienced will disappear. As soon as you begin to express an emotion, you begin to change it. Of course, if you remain within a situation which stimulates new anger inside you every day (such as your boss treating you with disrespect), you will have a new sensation of anger each day. If you never face your old anger, that new one just gets piled on top.

2. *What good will it do? It won't make the other person change.* Expressing anger rarely changes the person you are angry at; it changes you! Don't think of anger as a weapon, something you use to fix the other person. Those of us who are parents know how poorly it works on our kids. For starters, expressing anger can keep it from balling up inside you. Left unattended, it can do much dam-

age. It can turn into self-hatred and self-pity. It can contribute to such physical problems as headaches, muscle tension, ulcers, colitis, and high blood pressure. And it can grow into anxiety, emotional tension, or depression. Second, noticing your angry feelings over some incident helps you learn about your personal values, what is important to you, how you need to be treated by those around you, and how you need to respect yourself. These lessons are invaluable.

3. *If I really feel my emotions, I'll totally lose control.* Expressing an authentic, honest feeling has never driven anyone "crazy."

"And He Never Came Back."

Thus far I have presented several traits that are sometimes present in the panic-prone personality: low self-esteem, self-criticism and self-doubt, worrying, the need to do every task perfectly, the need to please others, and the fear of anger or conflicts. These characteristics do not develop after symptoms of panic begin in the agoraphobic's life; they are part of the individual's makeup, part of her personality.

Most of our behavior patterns are shaped between birth and our teenage years, so our personal histories can tell us a great deal about our current lives. The primary decisions we make about our future, most of the beliefs we hold, and the ways we view ourselves and our world come from what we learned long ago. And we act on that learning with little, if any, conscious thought.

When we are first born into this world, we are completely helpless and vulnerable. We are dependent on our parents for our every need, our very survival. The process of development from birth to late adolescence is a progressive maturing—physically, emotionally, intellectually, and socially. Critical to that maturing is learning independence—thinking for ourselves, trusting our instincts, setting personal goals, having confidence in our own abilities, and being capable of independent living.

In normal development, by the time a child is two years old she has begun to strike out on her own by opposing parents (through a broad range of "terrible twos" maneuvers) and by learning to feed herself. By age six, she has learned that it is O.K. to disagree, to speak up, and to ask questions.

By the time the normally developed child is eleven years old, her interactions with her peer group have evolved to a sophisticated level. She is skilled at arguing, competing, achieving, and negotiating. By sixteen, the teenager is in the process of adopting a comfortable sexual identity and self-image. She has learned to be assertive and to initiate activities while taking adult responsibility for many of her actions. By young adulthood, the woman has acquired a sense of self-worth. She can take risks and take time for her own activities, even if they conflict with the activities of others.

As you can see, achieving a sense of independence is a gradual, step-by-step developmental process, equal in intensity and importance to our physical growth during those same eighteen years. If we miss the achievement of certain developmental tasks when we are young, our ability to experience independence as adults will be restricted. None of us had perfect parents, nor can any of us *be* perfect as parents. It is not beneficial to blame anyone for what happened in the past. Every parent does the best that he or she can. Very few parents purposely hurt their children.

All of us have the ability to overcome any developmental limitations. We have the power now, as adults, to identify the strengths we are missing and to train ourselves in independent thinking, feeling, and living. Childhood experiences are not excuses for our adult difficulties.

I look to the past with my clients for one primary reason: to identify what new learning is needed. For the client, however, this looking back helps her to understand certain of her current beliefs in light of past experiences. And it guides her in seeing what changes need to take place today in how she thinks, feels, and acts. Studying the past does not in itself change anything. Only positive action today changes how we think, feel, or act, and only thinking, feeling, or doing something new today produces change.

Some of my agoraphobic clients are women who had quite traumatic experiences in their pasts. I share their particular stories with you because they can best illustrate how some unconscious learning takes place. I do not intend to imply that all agoraphobics have had unhappy childhoods, because I don't believe this to be true. I do want to suggest that some of the agoraphobic's beliefs may be irrational, acquired unconsciously. Many of the lessons we receive during our lifetimes are quite subtle. But nonetheless they shape our belief systems, and what we believe strongly determines how we act.

DONNA: My father died when I was seven. And I don't really remember the next five years of my life. I spent a lot of time in my bedroom during those five years. I would go to school, come home, help out around the house, and then I would go upstairs and listen to the radio.

I was one of five kids, but when I was born, my brothers and sisters were much older than me. They were already in junior high school. So it was really just my mother and I. She never socialized or dated any other men and never remarried. She worked very hard, was very loving and giving.

DOROTHY: My father joined the service during the war. And he never came back—he was killed. I can remember the day we heard of his death.

I think maybe that's when it started. From that point on my mother gave up her life for us.

Both of these women experienced a significant loss during childhood. Both Donna and Dorothy have a traumatic scene etched in their minds, one in which their fathers disappeared and never returned. At seven years old, Donna was given no explanation of death or of how to manage her feelings in response to death. She became depressed and remained that way for many years, withdrawing form the world and feeling a "void." She now has no memories of those years, but we can presume that she had great difficulty understanding or expressing her emotions, in part because of this early childhood experience.

While we are children, our parents serve as our models of how to act in life. Dorothy's mother withdrew from the world after Dorothy's father died. She watched her mother become isolated, stop taking care of herself, and rarely leave the home. Donna's mother made the same decision. Both girls watched their mothers surrender their personal lives while continuing to give to their children.

Four issues are significant to our understanding of childhood learnings. First, the experience of a loss of a significant person in the child's life is highly traumatic. If a person disappears from a child's life, she becomes confused as to why the person left. Death, separation, and divorce can cause a child to wonder, "Did I cause that?" The child may become fearful of her actions, not being sure which of her behaviors was "wrong." According to a child's logic, if you can be abandoned once, you can be abandoned again. That is a terribly frightening thought. A child might make a variety of decisions to protect herself from another loss or separation. One is to resolve not to get close to anyone else, to prevent further hurt. Another is to be very good, no to make waves, because if you are bad, people might leave you.

These are examples of unconscious decisions that can be made by a child and can remain in place into adulthood. Such behaviors are based on a belief system and logical framework which is not part of our conscious thought. They have been "implanted" into the brain without our awareness. But this store of beliefs influences many decisions in adulthood. It can lead the agoraphobic to resolve, "I'd better keep pleasing the people around me, or I'll be left alone."

Second, when one parent leaves or dies, the child can develop a strong attachment to the remaining parent. That attachment can become a powerful unconscious force which plays havoc with the person's life in the future. As adults we have responsibilities that require us to think, feel, and act independently. Adults with unresolved attachments can suffer great internal conflict. Many of my agoraphobic clients speak of their resentment of parents who are too close to them emotionally, or who attempt to run their lives. At the same time, they feel incapable of setting limits on the relationship and are unable to bring about a separation as adults. They make statements such as "I'm angry about how my mother treats me, and yet she is my closest friend. I don't know what I would do without her." This same kind of relationship can be found with an agoraphobic's spouse instead of the parent.

The third issue is that experiencing a loss produces a great many emotions. For a child, it can be the first time she has felt so many feelings so intensely: sadness, fear, surprise shock, even anger. She will probably feel confused and overwhelmed by these new sensations. Unless special care is taken, it is possible she will never sort out those feelings. I believe that Donna, for example, remained swallowed up by that confusion for years. Agoraphobics like Donna, beginning treatment some thirty years later, may still be unable to manage any extreme emotions.

The fourth issue is the concept of "modeling." When we are young, our parents or guardians constitute out entire world. They probably model 90 percent of all our learned behaviors. As we grow up with them, we learn, by observing their actions, how to share our feelings of love and affection, how to solve our problems, how to communicate with others, how to respect ourselves, how to face the world. Most of these lessons are absorbed unconsciously. Automatically, we begin, to imitate the actions of those close to us. Both Donna and Dorothy watched their mothers become socially isolated and withdrawn. What they did *not* see was a woman who had self-pride and self-esteem, who looked on life as a challenge. At the same time, though, both received a great deal of love and affection from their mothers. This, I am sure, was a positive, nourishing experience, which they remember and appreciate to this day. No one's childhood is all bad or all good.

> DONNA: My mother went out to work after my father died, though she had never worked before in her life. I felt I was a burden, so I never made waves. I never gave her any aggravation. I always did what I could do around the house to help out. I was very grateful that we were able to keep the house that I grew up in, that we didn't have to move, change our environment.

> DR. W.: What makes you think she thought you were a burden?

> DONNA: The fact that she had to go out to work in order to maintain that house, that she had never worked, and so forth.

> DR. W.: So this was something that you decided on your own, as opposed to any cues that she was giving you?

> DONNA: I think so. I don't really remember any particular cues.

Here Donna describes her belief (that she was a burden) and her decision (not to make waves) based on that belief. Notice that her belief was not based on anything that her mother did or said. She also felt grateful that nothing else was taken form her after her father died. She was careful to be good, so that her mother wouldn't leave her also. Now as an adult, Donna has incorporated these early childhood decisions into all of her relationships. She hides her needs if they might conflict with others' and works hard to please those around her. Even with her closest friends, she smiles on the outside when she is actually feeling sad or hurt. It is as though the same childhood fears continue to plague her: "If I express my needs, I'll be too much of a burden and others will abandon me."

"I Lived in Fear That Something Would Happen."

Dr. W.: Tell more about what it was like in your home.

SHERYLL: Oh, Saturday nights I'd wake up and my father would be beating my mother up, and ... oh, I don't know ... [Voice trails off. She looks down at the floor.]

DR. W.: You don't want to talk about it.

SHERYLL: It was tension. What else can I tell you? It just stunk. I used to be mad because other families seemed so intact, and I had to put up with this. There was always this fear. I guess I lived in fear that my father would do something to my mother. Don't get me wrong, it was weekends that he was really frightening. Other that that, he'd put up with a lot of garbage from her. She was an aggressive woman in her own way.

I didn't feel secure in the house. I always felt that something bad would happen, that one Saturday night, something was going to happen. The situation was at its worst during my teens. Maybe going to school and being a cheerleader and being in clubs was my way of blocking all this out. I don't know.

Long before Sheryll ever developed agoraphobia, she lived in fear. She had no control over her environment. She had reason to be afraid that "something bad was going to happen," since her father physically abused her mother. But it was not something that she could prevent as a young girl. Her only option was to avoid the situation, to be outside of the home as much as possible.

Again, notice how this is similar to the response an agoraphobic has toward fearful situations: to worry about something bad happening over which one has no control, and to avoid the situation as much as possible. This early life experience provided Sheryll's first lesson in such behavior.

> SHERYLL: I was very confused as a child. Sometimes I wished that my father would leave or my mother would pull herself together. It was very difficult. But on the outside, I always acted as if everything was fine. People on the outside would never know there was anything going on in the house.

Sheryll made a generous, unselfish decision to protect her family's secret. She hid her feelings from all her friends so that they wouldn't discover the problems within her household. But she did this to her own personal detriment. She pretended to be a happy-go-lucky, active child on the outside, while on the inside she was sad, confused, tense, and scared. Since no one knew of her emotional pain, no one could respond to it in a caring manner.

Sheryll decided at a young age to withhold her emotions. This decision and all its repercussions served as the foundation of many personal difficulties later in life.

> KAREN: I have suffered from anxiety since the age of eight. I can remember actually having to run home because of overwhelming feelings that I had, but couldn't logically understand at the age and mentality of five. And from that point on, I was labeled an emotionally disturbed child. I was also asthmatic. I coped with it as best I could. I just accepted it, and if I didn't feel well while over at a friend's house (this is at the age of eight), I'd just go home. I always knew what I had to do. And then when I got home I'd feel relief. But I'd go in my room and cry; I'd have deep depression.
>
> In grammar school and in junior high school, I always had a lot going for me. Then, when I was a teenager, I went to an analyst at some type of clinic because my mother thought I was depressed.

> DR. W.: Why?

> KAREN: As I look back on it I can remember that I spent a lot of time in my room—one whole year, in fact. And I had no goals, no achievements, no ambition.

DR. W.: When was that?

KAREN: Right at the time that my father died. I was a senior in high school. During that year after my father died I'd shut myself in my room. I just wanted time out, wanted my own time. And I caused my own depression, I'm sure. In fact, when I was depressed, I had no anxiety, I just secluded myself from everybody.

I remember that my first anxiety attack came when we were moving. I left the place where I had grown up. My mother had remarried, and we were moving to another state. And I had to leave my boyfriend. All this was happening at once. Important things—my house, my security . . .

DR. W.: How old were you then?

KAREN: Eighteen. And shortly after that I started having my spells. In restaurants, movies, theaters, on ski trips.

In this brief exchange, Karen describes three patterns that are common in some agoraphobics.

1. She had a long-standing tendency toward anxiety.
2. She also suffered bouts of depression. In fact, her year of being housebound was more likely a depressive reaction to her father's death than it was a sign of agoraphobia.
3. Her panic attacks began during the time when her mother remarried and she had to move away form many important people and things in her life. This fits the pattern we have seen so far: agoraphobia tends to manifest itself during a stressful period in the person's life.

A new and significant psychological issue is evidenced by Karen's history. Many women who suffer from agoraphobia have difficulty coping with separation, not just in childhood but throughout their lives. As adults, developing an independence from their parents or choosing to separate from an unhealthy marriage can produce feelings of overwhelming anxiety. Even though they may intellectually believe that a change is needed in the relationship, psychologically the task is untenable. As a psychologist I can frequently identify experiences that agoraphobic clients have had during their childhood and adolescence that reflect this difficulty in coping with separation.

Karen's extreme reactions to her father's death and to the family's cross-country move are examples. This single issue can place a powerful roadblock in the way of recovery.

"So I Allowed Her to Dominate Me."

DONNA: When I got married, I had absolutely nothing to do with the wedding. I didn't pick out the gown, I didn't pick out my maid of honor. My mother wanted a particular girl and that was it. I was always trying to please her, because I felt that she had sacrificed for me. And so I allowed her to dominate.

SHERYLL: My mother had always been a very domineering woman. She wants to control the world. She's got to be in control at all times. When I was a teenager I was never allowed to do anything; she used to do everything for me. I never had any independence. She tells me that this is because she was the youngest of nine and had to do everything in her family. Well, she shouldn't take it out on me!

From those brief excerpts we observe that neither Donna nor Sheryll developed independent thinking and behavior during their teens. Regardless of the reason, they left their developmental years lacking an essential skill. Each of them has suffered greatly from that deficit.

In order to conquer panic, each of them must learn now what they should have learned then. If they fail to develop independence of thought, feeling, and action, they will remain trapped by their symptoms, because those symptoms are generated by fear, hesitation to act, and self-doubt.

DOROTHY: My stepfather, no matter what we did, always bossed us. We never could do anything on our own. If we did one thing we were "stupid," if we did another we were "wrong." My mother was phobic, I guess, because he took charge of everything. He did the food shopping, my mother stayed home. He bossed my mother, he bossed me. He meant well, I'm sure he did, because we had a very good life, materially. But as I got older, I used to hear her crying a lot in bed.

My stepfather had to be right. She did try to fight him; as a child I remember them arguing about different things. But if they didn't go his way, he'd hit her. My mother was once lovely and strong. She ended up having a nervous breakdown. She's a nothing now, she just takes pills.

My mother would allow him to boss us. She'd say, "Just do it. Make him happy." In other words, we never had our own minds. We couldn't say, "I'm doing this because I want to do it."

After a while, I think it was ingrained in me. I was a perfectionist even as a child. I wanted everything just so. And I worried about everything. They called me "anxious." I was more of an emotional type. At fourteen the doctor put me on a tranquilizer.

I married my husband at seventeen to get away from the place. He was as strong as my stepfather, he also had control. So it's as if I never got the chance to find my own way.

These passages from Dorothy's session contain a wealth of information about her limitations today. First, Dorothy learned from her mother's modeling. It appears that her mother, too, was agoraphobic. Her world was no larger than the walls of her house. Remember that simply *observing* the significant people and events around us in childhood provides us with a great many of our beliefs. Dorothy also watched her mother attempt to stand up to her stepfather—and fail. Standing up for what she thought was right produced not only physical pain but humiliation as well. Independent thinking or acting became associated with discomfort, over and over again. In that setting it was natural, even smart, for Dorothy to become passive and dependent.

Dorothy made two other decisions in attempting to cope at home. She became a perfectionist, and she worried about everything. Could her belief have been "Maybe if I do things perfectly, he'll stop criticizing me?" Did she become anxious because she never knew what bad thing would happen next? "Will he get angry about this?" "How will he react if I do this?" No matter what she did, her stepfather would never let her have control. In that setting, attempting to avoid his criticism may have been her best move.

The problem is that Dorothy's coping strategies as a child (to be passive, dependent, worried, and perfectionistic) became unconscious patterns that she continues to use today, even though the situation that made these strategies necessary is no longer present. In order to change, she will have to experience a new trust in the benefits of activity, independence, and an acceptance of mistakes.

The lessons we learn don't necessarily come from major, traumatic experiences; they can come from subtle influences, as illustrated by these comments from Helen, another agoraphobic client: "I was an only child, and I always wanted to please my father I think. If I was doing anything wrong, he never hit or scolded me, or yelled. But he'd give me a look—that was all it took. My mother was a very passive person. She'd hold the peace at all costs, and I think I always wanted that, too—peace at all costs." Regardless of what actually took place in the home, it is what the child learned and decided to believe in response to what took place that determines her current behavior. We are not run by our past, we are run by our learned beliefs. Helen watched her mother "hold the peace at all costs" by being a quiet, undemanding wife who would never argue. She also experienced a loving family and observed a happy marriage between her father and mother. One belief Helen adopted was that "keeping the peace" would produce a happy marriage, and she decided to follow that rule in her adult life.

COPING IN THE PRESENT

Although panic can rise seemingly from nowhere in a person's life, in other people the causes are more obvious. The phobic has learned to become fearful on the basis of past traumas or from modeling others. The post-myocardial infarction patient fears a second heart attack. However, the experience of panic in an agoraphobic is the physical manifestation of a complex constellation within the personality.

Certainly a great many people in the world suffer through traumatic events, perhaps the death of a parent or physical brutality. Even more people have experienced stressful periods during their lives that have produced brief episodes of anxiety and panic. All of us go through times of self-doubt and self-criticism, of wanting to please others and of avoiding conflicts.

So what "makes" an agoraphobic? Just as with most other psychological problems, we are not certain, and probably never will be. The understanding of personality cannot be an absolute science. However, the patterns illustrated in this chapter reflect some of the common experiences of the present and the past that shape and support the panic-prone personality of the agoraphobic.

There is no going back to fix the past. There is no way to get today the things you failed to receive when you were younger. What is done is done. But, fortunately, knowing the causes of agoraphobia is a different issue than knowing how to cure it. Panic is maintained by our current beliefs and attitudes, our current emotions, and our current behaviors. These three parts of us *are* changeable, regardless of our past.

One difference between an agoraphobic with panic and other panic-prone persons is that the agoraphobic may feel more "stuck" and have a sense that "I'll never change." So many variables come into play during the treatment of this disorder. You might say that with the agoraphobic, the moment of panic is much like the tip of an iceberg. For this reason it is the general agreement of experts in this field that agoraphobics require the assistance of a specially trained mental-health professional to master panic.

Part 2 of this book takes into account the many issues facing the agoraphobic with panic. Most important, it reflects my firm conviction that by attending to current beliefs, emotions, and actions one can overcome any obstacles in one's way.

5

Four Complicating Problems

There are four specific problems that can complicate the diagnosis and treatment of panic. The symptoms of panic closely resemble those of premenstrual syndrome and those of hypoglycemia. This can cause some difficulties in diagnosis. An incorrect diagnosis can delay appropriate treatment for some sufferers. Depression and alcoholism greatly disrupt the treatment process by lowering motivation and by contributing additional serious problems to an already complex picture. In most cases, the depression or alcoholism must be treated before significant progress is made toward controlling panic,

PREMENSTRUAL SYNDROME

Premenstrual syndrome (PMS) is the occurrence of a wide variety of physical and psychological symptoms in women during the days of weeks prior to menstruation. Studies have found that 30 to 95 percent of all healthy females may experience a premenstrual increase in depression, irritability, and anxiety in addition to physical discomfort. Central to diagnosis of this disorder are both the type of symptoms present and the time they occur.

A woman suffering from PMS experiences moderate to severe emotional and/or physical symptoms; they may begin up to fourteen days before menstruation, but usually start five to seven days prior. The discomfort comes in almost every monthly cycle and only during the premenstrual phase. The symptoms disappear during the week after menstruation begins.

The menstrual cycle is one of the most complex of the body's

functions. Despite fifty years of research, we do not fully understand its process. There is no known cause of PMS that has been
substantiated by large-scale research findings. No one treatment has
achieved solid support, either. We can now say, however, that this
is a physical, not psychological, disorder.

Since the possible kinds of symptoms are so numerous and can
vary dramatically among women, I will present here only the psychological and behavioral symptoms that frequently occur during
the premenstrual phase. If your symptoms are so severe that they
seriously disrupt your life and if you have four or more of these
sets of symptoms, discuss it with your physician:

- Irritability, hostility, anger, "short fuse"
- Tenseness, restlessness, jitters, upset, nervousness, inability
  to relax
- Decreased efficiency, fatigue
- Depression, crying, spontaneous mood swings
- Poor coordination, clumsiness, proneness to accidents
- Distractibility, confusion, forgetfulness, difficulty with con-
  centration
- Change in eating habits, usually cravings and overeating
- Increase or decrease in sexual desire

Although most women with PMS suffer both physical and psychological symptoms, the psychological can be the more devastating.

PMS is one of several problems described in this book that often
go undiagnosed; since so many of its symptoms are psychological,
the women, their families, and health professionals can dismiss it as
"all in the head." Failure to receive a proper and early diagnosis
can greatly complicate the problem.

We know that stress has a direct effect on the menstrual cycle. It
can cause a delayed period or a missed period. When troubles and
tensions increase in a PMS sufferer's life, they also take their toll by
increasing her symptoms, such as irritability and depression.

Panic can be one symptom of PMS, and the stresses of life as
well as the stress of having undiagnosed symptoms only serve to
increase the possibility of panic. In fact, professionals who fail to
consider this syndrome may misdiagnose the problem as panic disorder. The best way to distinguish the two is for the sufferer to

keep a daily chart of symptoms for two or more months. By matching the discomfort with the menstrual cycle, a clear pattern should emerge if you have PMS.

Treatment for PMS must be individualized, since medical science is still exploring the exact causes. Several approaches are considered to have potential benefit. The broadest recommendation is an attention to food, vitamins, exercise, and emotions. Foods to avoid are highly processed foods, those containing chemicals, and those high in sugar, salt, or fat. Controlling eating binges and weight gain can also lower risk. Foods that may be beneficial in reducing symptoms are those high in protein and whole grains, the legume family, seeds and nuts, vegetables, fruits, and foods containing unsaturated vegetable oils. Vitamin A and the B-complex vitamins, especially B, may be needed. Increased physical exercise promotes an increase in metabolism. And finally, counseling to help in coping with stress is important.

Other treatments are still in the exploratory stage, with either mixed findings or too little research completed to adequately support their wide use. These include progesterone suppositories (if a hormone imbalance is found) and medications such as diuretics (to reduce water in the body), oral contraceptives, and biomocriptine or danazol (for breast symptoms).

You may find that, even though your symptoms are not identifiable as PMS, they become stronger prior to menstruation. A number of my clients have remarked that they are more likely to panic during this time. Their comments support my belief that hormonal changes can influence susceptibility to anxiety attacks. Specifically, the female hormone progesterone has been found to increase the sensitivity of certain chemical receptors in the body. Progesterone is secreted during the premenstrual phase of a woman's cycle. It is possible then that these alarm systems become too sensitive, causing the brain to respond to misinterpreted signals. This may account in part for the far greater frequency of panic in women than men, as well as the increase in anxiety and irritability during the premenstrual phase.

The symptom of panic in a PMS sufferer can begin to take on a life of its own, causing many complications. In part 2 of this book you will learn to "desensitize" this alarm system so that your symptoms remain under your control. You will learn how to manage panic and eventually eliminate it from your life as you find the best treatment for your other PMS symptoms. While some anxiety may persist, no one needs to feel swallowed up by the fear of unexpected, uncontrollable panic attacks.

HYPOGLYCEMIA

As mentioned in chapter 2, hypoglycemia (meaning "low blood sugar") is the experience of uncomfortable physical symptoms during times when there is a lower than normal level of glucose in the blood stream. This condition is quite rare and is found predominantly in people with diabetes mellitus. Other causes of "functional" or "reactive" hypoglycemia include high fevers, liver disease, pregnancy, stomach surgery, some kinds of cancers, a reaction to certain foods or drugs, and anorexia nervosa.

In diabetes mellitus, the pancreas produces insufficient amounts of insulin, a hormone used to break down and store sugar in the body. One result is a higher than normal amount of glucose in the bloodstream. The disease is managed by means of daily insulin injections and/or a controlled diet. If the diabetic takes too much insulin, does not keep to the prescribed diet, or is engaged in extended strenuous physical activity on a particular day, she may experience a drop in the blood glucose level, leading to symptoms of hypoglycemia.

Severe symptoms of hypoglycemia are indistinguishable from those of a panic attack: trembling, light-headedness, perspiration, anxiety, irritability, tachycardia, unsteadiness, and weakness. The similarity in symptoms is not coincidental. To combat low blood sugar, the medulla of the adrenal glands secretes the hormone epinephrine, which helps release extra sugar from the liver and dump it rapidly into the bloodstream. In addition, epinephrine stimulates the sympathetic branch of the autonomic nervous system. During times of emergency, fear, anger, or threat, epinephrine prepares the body by increasing the heart rate, raising blood pressure, increasing the rate of respiration, tensing muscles, and causing a number of other rapid changes. (This process is fully described in chapter 8.) During a panic attack, the individual believes he is threatened in some way. That belief is enough to signal the brain to cause epinephrine to be secreted.

Since hypoglycemia and panic attacks are so closely related, misdiagnosis is a serious problem. In the past hypoglycemia has been diagnosed by physicians through a five-hour glucose tolerance test preceded by three days of a high-carbohydrate diet. Even such a rigorous evaluation is insufficient, since 25–48 percent of normal individuals will experience random periods of low serum glucose levels. An accurate diagnosis requires that the patient experience *symptoms* during those times of low blood sugar and a *relief of symptoms* as the blood sugar rises.

Important information can be obtained by evaluating the patterns of your panic episodes. Ask yourself the following questions:

1. Do you wake up with panic attacks? Blood sugar levels are lowest in the morning, since the body has experienced its longest period of time without a meal. If symptoms occur every morning, not just every few mornings, hypoglycemia might be a factor.

2. Are there regular patterns to your panic attacks? Blood glucose levels are lowest just before lunch, just before dinner, and two to three hours after lunch and dinner. If your panics consistently coincide with one or more of these periods, low blood sugar may be contributing to the problem.

3. Does sugar in some form completely remove the symptoms? If you are prone to panic during these times, experiment with consuming sugar in some form (a sweet roll, fruit juice, candy, or pure sugar) when you begin to panic. If your symptoms consistently diminish within ten to thirty minutes, you should check with your doctor to consider a diagnosis of hypoglycemia.

A number of popular books have proclaimed hypoglycemia to be the undiagnosed culprit behind a vast number of physical and psychological problems. In fact, the exact opposite may be true. Poor diagnostic procedures by professionals and self-diagnosis by lay people account for the inordinately large number of false cases of hypoglycemia. For instance, in a recent study of 135 patients who claimed to have or were suspected of having hypoglycemia, only 4 could be confirmed with the diagnosis. Eighty percent of the other patients manifested some kind of psychiatric condition, especially depression and somatization (continual focus on multiple physical complaints).

The misdiagnosing of hypoglycemia is a dangerous affair, since a false confirmation of this illness prevents the true diagnosis from being identified and treated. Serious physical problems such as hypertension and hyperthyroidism (described in chapter 2) may be present, as may treatable psychological problems.

The diagnoses that may be missed are depression, panic disorder, and agoraphobia. There are several reasons for this. First, of course, is the fact that paniclike symptoms can be present in hypoglycemia. There is also a relationship with the times in which panic might occur. If a person has panic attacks routinely while standing in line at the grocery store or waiting for a meal in a restaurant, is it panic disorder or hypoglycemia? If the person hasn't eaten in a few hours, she may feel the same jitteriness and other symptoms that any of us might get when our bodies react to a low blood sugar level.

The panic-prone person will not only notice her symptoms while in the store or restaurant, but will react fearfully to them. Unlike the situation with hypoglycemia, consuming some form of sugar to diminish the physical symptoms will not relieve her worry; leaving the scene will.

Many people with panic disorder cling to the belief that they have hypoglycemia instead. This provides them with a number of benefits that all fall under the category of avoidance. Psychological problems continue to carry a stigma for many in our culture. By deciding that they have a physical disorder panic-prone people avoid facing the psychological and stress-related problems in their lives. Hypoglycemia provides relief by placing a clear label on some perplexing and ambiguous symptoms. Treatment of panic disorder also requires dedicated effort on the individual's part. Hypoglycemia offers an easier solution, since the sufferers simply pay special attention to their diets. Some putative hypoglycemia patients not only limit what they eat but begin to restrict their social functioning. This may be a clue that the individual is keeping a firm hold on the label of hypoglycemia as a way to avoid facing more fearful possibilities.

As mentioned earlier, to make the diagnosis of reactive hypoglycemia, the physician must determine that the patient's symptoms are present when the blood sugar levels are at their lowest and are relieved when the blood sugar level rises. Merely performing a glucose tolerance test on patients who experience spontaneous panic attacks is insufficient, since a large minority of normal subjects can show random low glucose levels.

Even when a positive diagnosis of hypoglycemia is made, the panic-prone hypoglycemic person may still have to work at managing her emotional reaction to times of low blood sugar. Here are a few suggestions. Carry sugar in some form with you at all times. When you notice the early signs of an attack, calmly eat some sugar until you begin to feel normal again. Explain to friends how to help you if you become disoriented. Instruct them to give you fruit juice or other sweets until you are able to help yourself. A general maintenance diet for hypoglycemia and any necessary precautions will be explained to you by your physician. Part 2 of this book presents information that will help you control the physiological reactions of your body during a hypoglycemia attack and remain emotionally calm so that your symptoms can be kept to a minimum.

DEPRESSION

It is not surprising that some people who experience anxiety attacks become depressed. When we begin to feel our world closing in on us, when we are unable to face situations that previously caused us no anxiety, when we experience physical symptoms that seem to have no clear cause, self-doubt, discouragement, and sadness are understandable side effects.

Many people who experience panic also complain of symptoms related to depression: a low energy level, feelings of hopelessness, low self-esteem, crying spells. irritability, difficulty concentrating, lack of interest in normal activities, a decrease in sexual desire, difficulty with sleep, and fluctuations in weight.

The relationship between panic disorder and depression has been well established through numerous controlled studies. At the same time, this research indicates that panic disorder, agoraphobia, and depression are distinct problems that happen to coexist within the same individual. A large majority of patients with panic disorder or agoraphobia have had episodes of serious depression. One study found that half the panic disorder and agoraphobia patients entering treatment with a history of depression had experienced at least one major depressive period prior to developing panic disorder or separate from periods of panic. In other words, depression doesn't develop simply in reaction to prolonged struggles with panic but can predate the panic attacks. And your depression can lift, even though a problem with panic continues.

For the person suffering from panic, the most important issue regarding depression is the way it complicates and slows the recovery process. Consider for a moment the thoughts of an anxious person who experiences panic attacks. She looks to a specific future event and worries, "Can I handle it?" She considers the possibility of failure and says, "It's possible I'll fail." She desires to take some action but says, "I'm too afraid." The panic-prone person wishes actively to engage her world, but is doubtful she can manage specific tasks. As panic lingers in a person's life, her outlook and self-evaluation may take on depressive qualities. The person who is primarily anxious will look to the future with uncertainty. She is not sure how difficult future tasks will be; doesn't know whether or not she will perform up to par or if she will be able to control the situation. She doubtfully questions the future.

If she begins to adopt a more depressed attitude, this uncertainty is transformed into fatalistic expectations. She looks to a specific future event and says, "I won't be able to handle it." She considers the possibility of failure and says, "I'll fail." In the internal struggle between wishing to take action and feeling too afraid, the balance shifts. Instead of doubting the future she becomes more certain of what will happen: "I will not succeed." An even more self-destructive attitude may arise: "I really don't care that much."

These negative predictions and lack of drive are supported by a pervasive sense of personal worthlessness, as though she is missing the essential traits to be a complete, competent human being. Instead of thinking, "I'm not prepared for *that job*," or I doubt I can enter *that building*," he begins to think, "I'm inadequate. I don't have what it takes. I don't fit in." As he looks to his past, he finds justification for this feeling. "Things are no different than they've ever been. Nothing has ever made that much difference. My limitations are unchangeable."

Helping someone face panic when he or she has adopted a depressed attitude is a difficult task, for obvious reasons: If I believe that I am basically inadequate, that nothing ever really changes in my life, that tomorrow will be about the same as yesterday, then why should I bother considering alternatives to my present state of affairs? There seems to be no point.

If you are feeling this kind of depression, you must confront and shift your entrenched attitude in order to face the challenges presented by panic. Through some means, you must move your attitude from a position of certainty ("Nothing is going to change things") to one of uncertainty. Even an anxious attitude ("I don't know whether or not I can manage this") is an improvement. In fact, this is the position I want and expect my clients to take as they begin facing panic. It is not necessary to embrace some false sense of confidence and assurance,, because uncertainty is a major component of adult life. By saying "I'm not sure," you are opening your mind up to the possibility of change ("Maybe I won't handle this particular challenge, and maybe I will").

There are two ways to begin changing this depressive attitude. The first is to directly wrestle with your negative beliefs: to listen to how you state those beliefs in your mind, to learn how those statements influence your actions, and then to explore other attitudes that might support your goals.

The second way is to begin to change your activities even before you change your attitude. Try some specific, small activities, without needing to believe they will help you. Change your patterns of behavior during the day, alter your routine, do some things that you imagine someone else must consider "good for you." There is no requirement that you engage in these new activities with the belief that they will help you. At first, just do them. Don't predict how you are "supposed" to feel during or after them—that will usually be a setup to prove, once again, that "nothing will change." Simply change your patterns as a way of giving yourself experiences that might challenge your beliefs in a small way.

Let me illustrate the purpose of this process by describing its use with another kind of problem. In my practice as a clinical psychologist I specialize in the treatment of anxiety disorders and also in the management of chronic pain syndrome. Years ago I worked as a therapist at the Boston Pain Center, a medical in-patient unit for chronic-pain patients. The facility is designed to help those who have tried every known medical treatment and yet remain in significant physical discomfort because of a physical injury or illness.

The chronic-pain patient and the person suffering from panic disorder share the predominance of depression Consider the patient who enters the treatment unit with chronic low-back pain. He describes himself as "vegetating in front of the boob-tube all day for the past five years." He perceives himself as useless, since he hasn't been able to work in five years and his wife supports the family. He can't even mow the lawn or take out the garbage because of his back pain, much less figure out how to return to productive, paid employment. And "all of the doctors have given up hope" on him, so how could the future be anything else but just like the past, or worse?

The in-patient program takes him out of the normal routine of his home and provides a broad range of activities that are designed to challenge this attitude. He lives for four to six weeks among twenty other patients with similar pain problems. He is required to rise first thing in the morning, make his own bed, eat in a group dining room, and attend four support/therapy group meetings a week, plus medical sessions, community meetings, and special outings. To manage his physical pain he attends individual and group physical therapy session, receives massages and ice massages, hot packs, ice packs, and whirlpools. He is taught biofeedback and relaxation techniques. His pain medications are slowly diminished and eventually discontinued, as he learns alternative ways to successfully manage his pain.

This is the typical design of a therapeutic community, where the medical staff and patients work together to find the best treatment for each individual. We don't expect every approach to work for every patient. Instead, we provide as many options as possible in order to discover which combination will be most effective.

But one of the first things that must change is the patent's attitude, since a depressive outlook can prevent any learning. How does that attitude shift? Most frequently it changes because the patient begins to have experiences that don't fit into his negative expectations.

For instance, a low-back-pain patient may complain of an inability to stand or sit for more than twenty or thirty minutes at a time, after which he must lie down to relieve his discomfort. By altering his pattern of activities, the therapeutic community offers him a chance to have new experiences that can change his belief. On day 5 of the program he discovers that he just sat through an hour-and-a-half group therapy session without having to stand or lie down. Then he remembers that this is the third time in two days that he has sat for over an hour. It is this kind of awareness that can lead him to say, "Maybe I can do something to help myself. Maybe things can change."

This is usually the turning point for patients on the Pain Unit. Once they decide that change is possible, they tend to look at any new treatment with a ray of hope. They stop being so certain of failure and begin thinking of their options. Trying each new technique now involves curiosity. "How might I benefit from learning biofeedback?" "I wonder what results I'll get it I do these physical therapy exercises every day for a couple of months?"

If you are suffering from depression, this is the kind of curiosity you must strive for. In part 2 of this book I suggest a number of new techniques and activities for you to practice. This part also directly addresses your depressive attitude, giving you alternative ways of thinking about yourself and your future. As you proceed, keep in mind the need to confront your negative view. For a while you may have to try the suggestions in spite of your mind's saying, "What's the use?" Above all, you must take action. No matter how low you feel, some part of you believes that you can help yourself. Even if it is a small ember of hope deep within you, let that supportive self give you the gift of curiosity.

ALCOHOLISM

Alcohol can have a dramatic effect on the body. It is primarily a central nervous system depressant, similar to major and minor tranquilizers, barbiturates, narcotics, and nonbarbiturate sleeping pills. It is just as addicting as these drugs in that there is a specific physical and psychological withdrawal process after prolonged use.

As a central nervous system depressant, alcohol slows down and numbs the higher and lower brain and spinal cord center. The first centers affected are the inhibitory ones, so alcohol's first effect is usually the removal of tensions and inhibitions. This is the primary reason why people with anxiety, fears, or panic might turn to drinking. With alcohol, they typically experience warmth, relaxation, and a general feeling of well-being.

As larger amounts of alcohol are consumed, however, the entire nervous system becomes depressed, leading to impairment in judgment, motor coordination, speech, vision and balance. And of course, since the judgment is distorted, the person who has been drinking in excess is unable to judge the negative changes in his behavior.

Heavy drinking can lead to a hypoglycemic reaction, usually occurring twelve to sixteen hours after a drinking bout. As the liver metabolizes alcohol, it stops manufacturing glycogen (the precursor to glucose). Blood sugar levels are then maintained by using previously stored glycogen. Once that supply is used up, blood sugar levels drop, producing a hypoglycemic reaction. As mentioned in the earlier discussion of hypoglycemia, this reaction can be indistinguishable from panic. Some panic-prone persons are more susceptible than others to low blood sugar levels. For instance, drinking may diminish their anxiety level during an evening out. Twelve or so hours later, as the next morning begins, they experience panic symptoms that seem to come from nowhere. This of course reinforces their sense of being out of control and may encourage than to take another drink to "calm the nerves."

Several studies have explored alcoholism and phobias, bringing interesting patterns to light. It has been estimated that 5–10 percent of all phobic people are dependent on some chemical such as alcohol. Studies of alcoholics indicate a high correlation between the degree of the person's dependence and the presence of phobia.

One study of 102 alcoholics admitted into an alcohol treatment unit in England found that one third of them also suffered from agoraphobia or a social phobia. Another one third had phobic symptoms to a less disabling degree. A second study by the same investigators found that in a group of 44 alcoholics who were phobics, the majority had developed their phobic symptoms prior to their alcohol dependency.

It appears, then, that some panic-prone persons drink to relieve their anxiety and their crutch may end up causing them more serious problems. Often the drinking pattern becomes autonomous: the person still has the same fears and still avoids uncomfortable situations but is now also consumed by alcohol.

I predict that in the years to come, research will continue to confirm this significant relationship: for certain alcoholics, anxieties regarding their abilities to handle themselves in specific situations draw them to drink. For the short term they perceive the drinking to be helping them by diminishing their sense of fear. Yet, as time passes, the alcohol takes on a stronger, independent role in their lives. They increase their alcohol consumption, which actually increases their original problem, their emotional instability, and their isolation from family members and friends.

Because of the serious problems caused by alcoholism, the patient's phobic symptoms tend to go unnoticed, even within a professional treatment program. Since the symptoms of detoxification are similar to those of anxiety, both the patient and the alcoholism treatment staff may not consider any phobic or panic disorder as an additional diagnosis. When the anxious fears return, though, that patient may once again reach for the only relief he or she knows. The more skilled the staff can become in identifying anxiety-related drinking problems, and the more the patients can wrestle directly with these issues, the less that revolving door in the detoxification unit will spin.

Dependency on alcohol reinforces the panic-prone person's negative belief system. The person sees alcohol as a form of self-medication, but simultaneously his dependency reinforces the belief he is not in control. He feels safe only after he has had a few drinks. Any difficult situation becomes a cue to reach for a drink. In time, self-assurance, confidence, and pride are replaced by this numbing process.

As you might imagine, depression in the panic-prone person is another problem that is reinforced by alcohol. The scenario may unfold in dozens of ways. Here is a hypothetical example: One day, to my great surprise I have an anxiety attack just before making a presentation at a business meeting. Over the next several weeks I worry about losing control like that again. I'm feeling tense in general these days because of expanded job responsibilities and competition for some others in the company. Before my next presentation I down a shot of whiskey, "just to take the edge off." It actually works: I'm calmer just before my talk and during it. But I continue to remain on edge during the week.

Before a dinner party the next week I again become panicky. Out comes the whiskey, in order to turn the evening into a pleasant time. I am discovering that I can manage the tensions with this little helper, even though I notice an unusual increase in my anxiety level the next morning.

Time passes. It is four months later—four months of swings of tension followed by relief. Four months of doubt about my ability to handle the pressures of work. Four months of distortions in my normal thinking about my job, my life, my capabilities. My anxiety begins to change. Now, instead of thinking, "Oh, no, how will I handle these responsibilities," I begin to think, "I don't really care that much." The persistent drinking to ease the anxiety takes its toll as my anxious feelings become wrapped in a blanket of depressive indifference. "The job's not that important" might be my conscious thought. But underneath this is a growing sense that I am no longer the man I thought I was; I don't have what it takes to control my life, I am stuck and might as well surrender. Nothing will fix the problem, so I can only learn to cope with it.

Through the powerful combination of alcohol and depression, the symptoms of panic have led to a serious and complex syndrome involving denial, self-defeating behaviors, avoidance, loss of self-esteem, and physical deterioration.

If alcohol has become your crutch you must remain alert to its seductiveness. Facing your fears without it may seem tough, but your successes without this drug will provide your only avenue to long-lasting change. If you suspect that you may be dependent on alcohol, or if people close to you agree that you have a problem, seek out professional help or the help of Alcoholics Anonymous. A panic-prone person with alcohol dependency should treat his alcoholism first, then begin managing his fear responses.

6

Panic in the Context of Heart and Lung Disorders

It is easy to take the human body for granted. Its complex functioning is so phenomenal that we can scarcely imagine the process, much less appreciate it. With nourishment and upkeep, the body runs without any major complaints for decades. All systems work together for one single objective: to maintain equilibrium throughout the body and between the body and its environment.

The cardiovascular and respiratory systems work together as the primary forces behind this process. Through its smooth rhythmic action, the respiratory system ensures that adequate levels of oxygen are available instantly for any circumstance and maintains the delicate acid base balance in the blood. The cardiovascular system makes certain that every cell in the body is fed nutrients and oxygen and is cleansed of its waste products. The heart circulates five quarts of blood through the body every minute, which also helps it maintain a constant, comfortable temperature.

Because these two major systems are so vital to our moment-by-moment life, the body and mind will react faster than the speed of light if these systems are threatened. This automatic alarm, evolved over hundreds of thousands of years, directs all our human capabilities with two instructions: "Find any way to breathe, and keep the heart beating."

A dramatic moment eleven years ago still reminds me of this powerful alarm system. I am standing on the porch of my parents' farm in the mountains of North Carolina. My father is holding our twelve-month-old daughter as we talk casually about one thing or another. I glance at Joanna at the same moment her eyes bulge and she stops breathing. I lunge forward and slap her on the back while three other options to free her passageway instantly appear in my mind. Within five seconds from start to finish, the piece of ice that has lodged in her throat has melted and cleared through the esophagus.

As an infant, Joanna hardly knew anything had happened. I, on the other hand, experienced the remarkable speed and skill of my unconscious life-saving instinct. And my body and mind were left with the after-effects of this psychophysiological response. As soon as I saw that Joanna was breathing again I also noticed that my head was pounding from all the blood that had rushed there. And I mean *rushed:* my circulatory system pushed an abundant supply of blood to the vessels of my brain within my first two heartbeats.

This, of course, was only a minor crisis, because no harm was done. But the body doesn't wait around for some panel of experts to vote on the degree of the crisis. If the brain signals "crisis," the body responds. This instinct saves our lives.

The person with a chronic heart or lung problem faces many new challenges. One of these is how to adjust the signals from the brain so that the minor symptoms of the problem are not interpreted as life-threatening. If the patient with heart disease reacts fearfully to every pressure in his chest, he places unnecessary strain on his healing heart. If a patient with emphysema becomes anxious about every new activity, he directly aggravates his safe, comfortable breathing pattern. And yet, the brain has been trained for hundreds of centuries to shift the body into crisis gear when the heart and lungs seem to be threatened. Therefore, learning to cope with these chronic conditions can be quite challenging.

In disorders of the heart and lungs, panic arises when the body and mind respond to a relatively minor symptom with the weapons typically reserved to combat a life-threatening situation. This chapter discusses five of these conditions: mitral valve prolapse, recovery from myocardial infarction, emphysema, bronchitis, and asthma.

MITRAL VALVE PROLAPSE

The mitral valve is a structure within the heart that controls the opening between the left atrium and the left ventricle. In mitral valve prolapse (MVP), this valve leaflet balloons slightly into the left atrium during contractions. (Figure 2 shows the location of the mitral valve and the change in its appearance after ballooning.)

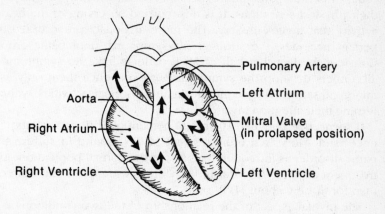

FIGURE 2. *Location of mitral valve and change in appearance after ballooning.*

This minor cardiac abnormality is found in approximately 5 to 15 percent of all adults and is especially prevalent among young women. Most people who have this problem are never aware of it, since 50 percent of those with MVP experience no symptoms. On average, even if MVP is identified, no medical treatment is needed.

In the 50 percent who do notice symptoms, the predominant symptom noticed is palpitations, the conscious awareness of some unpleasant sensation of the heart. They may be aware of premature contractions of the heart chambers, called extrasystoles, or of a rapid heartbeat, tachycardia. Other possible symptoms are shortness of breath or difficulty breathing (dyspnea), dizziness, chest pain, fatigue, fainting, and panic attacks.

Given these symptoms, what is the relationship between panic disorder and mitral valve prolapse? Demographically, they appear to be related. Both are found with the same frequency: in 5 to 15 percent of the population. Both are found more often among women, with symptoms beginning in early adulthood. Research findings indicate that some people with MVP may have inherited it, and so for some individuals there may be a genetic link associating these two problems. The question of genetic linkage remains unanswered.

Growing evidence indicates that MVP does not cause panic disorder. Instead, panic-prone persons become overly attentive to their physical sensations. It is this worried observing of the heart's activity that invites anxiety. The more anxiously preoccupied the person becomes, the stronger his symptoms, until panic erupts. Consider the fact that half of MVP patients have no symptoms at all. Others develop the symptoms but experience them only as a minor nuisance. They continue in their normal activities without turning their attention inward.

It seems that between 10 and 20 percent of MVP patients experience panic. Research indicates that MVP is found in sufferers of panic disorder as infrequently as it is in the normal population. And treatment of panic disorder in individuals with MVP is no different than for those without MVP.

The pivotal aspect of the relationship of the two conditions is in how the person responds to his awareness of symptoms. In order to panic, the person must not only notice some new sensation of the heart but must also become fearful of what that sensation means. The autonomic nervous system will then respond to the person's fearful thoughts, not to the heart palpitation itself. This process, fully described in chapters 7 and 8, produces more dramatic symptoms, such as a racing heart, dizziness, shortness of breath, and even a panic attack.

Since mitral valve prolapse can produce palpitations at random, it contributes to the panic-prone person's belief that he must remain "on guard" at all times to defend against mysterious "out-of-the-blue" attacks of panic. One advantage of receiving a clear physical diagnosis of MVP is that is can reassure the panic-prone person that these symptoms are not a sign of danger. By diminishing worry and anxiety you automatically diminish the potential for symptoms.

Diagnosis of mitral valve prolapse is made by a cardiologist through echocardiography (recording the position and motion of the valve by echoes of ultrasonic waves transmitted through the chest wall) and through listening to the sounds of the heart during contraction. Evaluation by a physician is recommended if a person experiences a sudden occurrence of physical symptoms, such as true vertigo (room spinning), fainting, or chest pains or palpitations.

If you are diagnosed with MVP, material in part 2 of this book will help you learn to manage your symptoms. It is important to understand a few points. First, changes in the rhythm of the heart are a frequent occurrence in most people, and are rarely harmful. By learning to accept, tolerate, even ignore them, you will diminish your anxiety. Second, don't let those symptoms frighten you into avoiding activities. By avoiding, you feed a negative pattern that unnecessarily restricts your life. Third, you can actually reduce your symptoms to a few annoying but not distressing sensations by learning to accept the normal process of mitral valve prolapse and by preventing panic.

RECOVERY FROM MYOCARDIAL INFARCTION

A heart attack is certainly cause for reflection. It is a traumatic blow to the ego which jerks us out of our mundane patterns and calls our attention to the fragility of life. The return to physical health is slow and steady for those with uncomplicated problems, but the psychological recovery almost always includes a struggle with two stresses: depression and anxiety. The depressed patient wrestles with thoughts and feelings of resignation: "My life is no longer worth fighting for." The anxious patient continually poses the fearful question, "When will I die?"

Time and the skilled maneuvering of the mind heal these psychological blows for most recovering myocardial infarction patents (post-MI patients). Many people will deny the significance of the problem just two or three days after a heart attack and become increasingly animated and cheerful with the staff of the coronary-care unit. Although the customary hospital stay is two weeks, they talk of their readiness to go home and get back to work immediately.

To concerned family members, such talk seems inappropriate, as though the patient is not facing up to the seriousness of the situation. Actually, this denial seems to be the mind's clever way of giving the body some rest during the early stages of recovery. To allow the person to experience the full blunt reality overstresses the cardiovascular system and slows the healing process. Eventually, though, this denial must gradually give way to acceptance of the true picture, or the patient will not take necessary precautions and follow medical advice and guidelines. As he faces reality his primary question will be "How cautious should I be?" After a heart attack this becomes a complicated question, since its answer affects hundreds of small daily decisions for years to come. It is no wonder that many of these patients continue to restrict their lifestyle and feel uncertain about activities for months and even years beyond the acute phase of the illness. "Will I die at the same age as my father? Should I ever risk having sex again? Will I die in my sleep tonight? I shouldn't be getting excited like this. Is that a pain in my chest as I inhale?"

A post-MI patient can make three basic life-choices:

1. *The healthy stance: Knowing my limits and my options, I work within them in order to expand them.* There is an old expression that runs, "Freedom is what you do with what's given to you." In order to experience freedom, this post-MI patient who has made this choice works with his physician and other medical professionals to understand his current physical state and capacity. He then learns what activities are possible given this stage in his healing process. He acts on his desire to live his life to the fullest within those limits, while simultaneously adopting a medical plan that can help expand those limits. This is the only life choice that will successfully control panic.

2. *The panic-prone stance: I must remain constantly on guard, since the slightest provocation could cause my death.* Panic arises because the post-MI patient is unclear about her limits or her options. She notices a symptom or potential symptom and has no specific plan for monitoring or controlling it. This lack of preparation turns her body against her. Without the proper signal of reassurance from the brain, the body reacts by shifting into crisis gear, which causes an increase in symptoms. This life choice encourages chronic anxiety and panic attacks, which seriously strain the heart.

3. *The depressive stance: There is no point in continuing to try, since my course is now charted.* This patient surrenders her power to heal herself. Because of her willingness to become dependent on others, helpless, and restricted in her activities, this type of patient has been labeled a "cardiac invalid." Often, she withdraws from friends and retires from work. This life-choice dissolves the

person's spirit to live. By becoming physically passive she worsens her medical status by weakening the cardiovascular and respiratory systems, since regular exercise helps maintain all organs and systems of the body.

The panic-prone stance can lead to the depressive stance; "If I continue to face situations that I believe might stress my heart and do not develop a plan to manage those situation, eventually I must alter my course. My only solution, then, is to avoid those situations." Soon avoidance is the first choice. Since preventing another heart attack is more important that some brief pleasure, the person also stops participating in the activities she enjoys. She becomes less anxious, but has lost her pleasures too. Depression steps in to fill the void.

If you are recovering from a heart attack, your physician will help you understand your physical limits and will design a rehabilitation course so you can return to your highest level of functioning. She will also help you understand and respond appropriately to any unusual symptoms you might experience.

Part 2 of this book offers you information and a number of skills for you to use within the context of your medical treatment: how to think clearly in case of any medical emergency, how your attitude toward your health affects your reaction to symptoms, and how to calm yourself if you become anxious of panic. We know from research and numerous clinical reports that simply mastering a few basic calming skills is one of the key ingredients to recovery from any of the cardiovascular illnesses, including hypertension and coronary artery disease. Most important, you will learn how to return safely to the physical and social activities that give your life meaning and pleasure. Before reading part 2 discuss with your doctor the appropriate response to various symptoms.

CHRONIC OBSTRUCTIVE PULMONARY DISEASE

"I'll never breathe again." That is the statement that screamed out in my mind. And for that instant, I believed it with all my heart, soul, and mind. There was not the tiniest sliver of belief that I would live. You don't live without air. I could not inhale, and I had no air in my lungs at that moment. I was dying. Good-bye.

That moment occurred during the second half of a soccer match this past summer. As a defensive fullback, I stepped in front of the offensive forward just as he followed through on a forceful kick toward the goal. The ball slammed into my chest at point-blank range. The power behind the blow knocked all the air from my lungs, leaving me, literally, breathless. The game continued as I stood there, frozen, leaning halfway forward, incapable of inhaling and incapable of speaking. This marked the moment of panic for me: I believed, on the basis of my physical experience, that I did not have the control to save my own life.

My panic lasted about twenty seconds. Within thirty seconds, action had stopped in the match, two teammates had helped me to lie down on the ground, and I had had my first taste of ever-so-precious-but-lost-forever air.

I can look back now and laugh a bit at my extreme reaction to such a benign occurrence. On the other hand, this was the second time in three months that I had lost my breath on the playing field. And during both moments I thought, "I'll never breathe again." The panic associated with heart or lung problems is special. You don't experience it as a passing moment, you experience it as your *last* moment.

Panic plays its most damaging role in patients suffering from chronic obstructive pulmonary diseases. The illnesses themselves interfere with the natural breathing process and diminish vitality and endurance. For some the symptoms become more severe over the years. If the illness progresses, the patient becomes less and less able to work or to enjoy social and recreational activities, since any kind of exertion or emotional shift could trigger a breathing problem. Thus, the patient with a chronic lung problem learns to brace himself for any sign of discomfort and often chooses to avoid activities in order to feel safe. This is the fearful stance, which is most vulnerable to panic.

The essential feature in many respiratory disorders is a narrowing of the bronchial tubes. In chronic bronchitis, the mucous membrane that lines the main air passages, or bronchi, of the lungs becomes inflamed. This leads to breathlessness, coughing that brings up phlegm, and an increased risk of infection. In chronic asthma, the muscles of the bronchial walls contract, causing a partial obstruction of the bronchi and the bronchioles, the smaller air passages in the lungs. The patient experiences attacks of wheezing and difficulty breathing, triggered by allergy-provoking substances, physical activity, or psychological stress. With chronic emphysema, the air sacs, or alveoli, at the ends of the bronchioles are damaged. Since these are the site of oxygen and carbon dioxide exchange, the lungs become less and less efficient at their job. The primary symptom is difficulty breathing, which worsens over the years. Figure 3 identifies the parts of the respiratory system affected by these diseases.

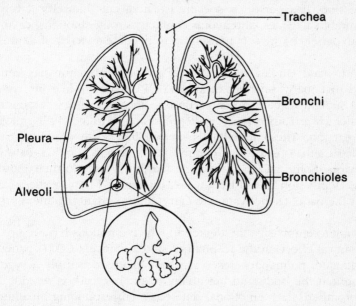

FIGURE 3. *Parts of respiratory system affected by chronic obstructive pulmonary disease.*

Since breathing is one of the two most prominent life-supporting processes (along with the pumping of your heart), patients with chronic obstructive pulmonary disease (COPD) are likely to develop anxiety, panic, and depression because of their inability to control this vital function. Their most-feared problem is having difficulty breathing. When an episode of difficult breathing begins, they may respond with panic, believing that they will die from suffocation as they gasp for breath. This brief period of panic becomes etched in their minds. The aftereffects of this trauma are maintained by vivid recollections of the attack, by nightmares of being unable to inhale, and by thoughts that the next attack could come anytime, anywhere. The results of one study illustrate the outcome of such recurring experiences: the researchers found that 96 percent of the subjects with COPD developed "disabling" anxiety.

As they withdraw from their world to protect themselves from anything that might cause breathlessness, the patients' general level of anxiety may diminish. But they then become susceptible to depression. If a person is socially isolated, cuts himself off from pleasurable activities, and avoids conflicts, strong emotions, or any new experiences, he sets himself up to become a victim of depression.

Dr. Donald Dudley of the University of Washington has aptly stated that many severely disabled COPD patients live in "emotional straightjackets." It is no wonder, since any shift in emotion, whether toward anxiety, joy, or depression, can trigger a physiological reaction. These individuals' impending sense of doom can translate into obsessions, compulsions, phobia, and ritualistic behaviors. Some will even become fearful of visits to their physicians. Depression fueled by low self-esteem and hopelessness can lower the patient's motivation to carry out important treatment programs.

I want to emphasize the degree to which emotions have a direct mechanical effect on the respiratory system. Since a COPD patient has limited pulmonary reserves, her ability to supply oxygen throughout the body and her ability to remove carbon dioxide is compromised. Each emotional state has a corresponding breathing pattern. For most people these changes are easily accommodated. However, the patient with a severe COPD problem becomes incapable of managing even minimal changes in respiration.

For example, as we become angry, afraid, or anxious, these more active emotional responses require an increase in metabolism. This need cues the respiratory system to increase breathing, to increase the oxygen supply, and remove excess carbon dioxide. The COPD patient may be physically incapable of accomplishing this increase in breathing. Instead of taking in more air, she begins to have difficulty taking in enough air. The oxygen level in her body drops as the amount of carbon dioxide increases. As the difficulty persists, of course she becomes anxious or panics, causing more symptoms, in a vicious circle of symptoms producing anxiety producing symptoms.

A similar process can take place if the patient experiences episodes of sadness, depression, or apathy. These emotional states lower the rate of respiration, which leads to low levers of oxygen and high levels of carbon dioxide in the body.

Even if the COPD patient is able to inhale sufficiently, she may still become anxious in her awareness of the increased demand placed on her lungs by an emotional state. In normal circumstances the breathing pattern matches the demands placed on the body. When I am involved in a vigorous physical activity, the increased oxygen my lungs supply is utilized efficiently during metabolism. During anxious moments, however, the body often cannot use the oxygen as rapidly as it is put into the bloodstream. At the same time, the lungs remove more carbon dioxide from the body than is useful. This is hyperventilation, which causes a number of uncomfortable symptoms in addition to those caused by the illness. A complete overview of breathing processes and hyperventilation is presented in chapter 11.

If you suffer from a serious chronic obstructive pulmonary disease, managing your daily living presents a great challenge. Often your predicament seems hopeless. But you can bring a beneficial attitude and set of skills to this challenge. I believe that those suffering the discomforts of COPD can begin to feel safe and more involved in their life and community by considering the suggestions and practicing the skills described in this book. Here are several guidelines which may help you along the way as you read part 2:

- Your central goal should be to find as many ways as possible to keep physically active and maintain your interest in life without harming yourself. Setting realistic goals and working progressively and safely toward them will improve your spirits, strengthen your respiratory system, and decrease any unrealistic fears you may have.
- When you socialize, find ways to make yourself comfortable. Some people become easily fatigued and must end an evening earlier than expected. Those with chronic bronchitis may have to tolerate a severe coughing spell and dispose of sputum discreetly. In order to remain active you will need to find ways to handle these situations without withdrawing in embarrassment.
- If you are taking medications, discuss with your physician

whether any of them might cause increased nervousness or irritability. For instance, certain drugs help open up the bronchi by activating the sympathetic nervous system, which may make you feel a little more jumpy. Knowing this can help you prepare for any mild side effects.

Three classes of medications used for COPD patients are most likely to cause unpleasant side effects. The oral medications used for bronchospasm, aminophylline and the beta-Z adrenergic agents, can cause general anxiety and a rapid heartbeat. Those who use an inhaler of the beta-Z adrenergic agents such as isoproterenol and metaproterenol can experience general anxiety and shaky hands. The corticosteroids, such as Prednisone, may briefly elevate the patient's mood, then cause a swing into depressed feelings.

- The problems of your life will not disappear just because you avoid them. Your best approach is to learn ways of facing and coping with any stressful changes. If you don't respond to the curves that life throws you, then you will eventually surrender control of your life.
- If you suffer from a severe lung disease, you may find it necessary to avoid any situation that causes anxiety or can lead to any rapid change in your emotional state. It is sometimes a tricky balancing act to remain an interested participant in your world and at the same time not become too caught up in the dramas of life.
- When nervousness, worry, and depression do come, learn how to diminish them by applying skills such as those described in part 2. The less worried you are, the fewer severe breathing episodes you will have, and the less you will need to use emergency care.

Most important, learn the best ways to think, feel, and act during an acute episode of difficult breathing. You can learn specific techniques that minimize symptoms and support your return to comfortable breathing. The breathing problems that confront COPD patients are quite unique. Our bodies and minds do not instinctively respond to these attacks in a supportive way. In fact, it appears that some of our instinctive reactions exacerbate symptoms. It is necessary, therefore, to study your individual patterns and adjust them, in order to diminish your anxiety and increase your sense of well-being. You must develop the ability to notice your symptoms without reacting emotionally to them. By learning a set of response skills, by creating a plan for when and how to use them, and then by repeatedly practicing them, you will begin to take control of the symptoms of your illness. Anyone would react with anxiety to the thought of not being able to breathe. Your task is to reduce your anxiety once you notice it, then take steps to improve your breathing pattern.

Part II

TAKING CONTROL OF ANXIETY ATTACKS

7

The Anatomy of Panic

The battleground of panic is not isolated to the few seconds or few minutes of an anxiety attack. The more panic attacks you experience without gaining mastery over them, the more they seem to invade other territories. Imagine for a moment that panic is an enemy that has chosen to wrest control of your life away from you. The cleverest of invaders will overcome their victims by undermining their foundations, withholding their nourishment, destroying their confidence. And that's just what panic will do, given the chance.

The first panic attack can be a surprise, to be dismissed as a fluke. Two panic attacks might be viewed as coincidence; you rationalize that too much stress caused the problem. You tell yourself to slow down, take it easy, don't get uptight. However, if the episodes continue, panic makes its first inroads into your life. You begin to question yourself, to doubt your strength, to wonder whether you are coping. This is panic's most powerful weapon. This is what begins to loosen the bricks in your foundation. By creating self-doubt, panic gains its first stronghold in your life. After a while, the panic attack itself plays a role in the ongoing battle. With all the cleverness of a magician, panic appears in your life; and with all the swiftness and power of a judo master, panic takes your mental energy and turns it against you. Before you know it, you've reversed the tables on yourself. Just as with any of the martial arts, the more you fight pain, the more you seem to lose.

Am I overstating the case? I don't think so. People who call my office for a first appointment usually have been experiencing panic attacks for anywhere from six months to dozens of years.

Here are some of the many ways panic, over a period of time, can use your thoughts, feeling, and beliefs as weapons against you.

- Some reminder causes you to hesitate before venturing back into the arena of that last attack.
- The need to avoid becoming "trapped" is given high priority each time you consider certain activities.
- You anxiously wonder when the next attack will come. "Will it be here, now?" Simply asking the question seems to bring on symptoms.
- You nervously think about the last panic attack, and then you doubt your control over your body.
- You worry that some unknown physical illness or an emotional breakdown is causing your attacks.
- If you have a diagnosed physical illness, you fear any undue stress or aggravation.
- You begin to avoid certain people or places as your principal defense against attack.
- You become more socially isolated and secretive, perhaps feeling trapped by appointments, roles, expectations.
- You brood, you worry, you criticize yourself and become discouraged.
- You may stop trusting yourself and turn to alcohol, drugs, or doctors to carry you through your days.

You can see that portraying the anatomy of panic requires a broader brush than you might at first imagine. Every individual is unique, and the ways panic affects each of us are different. There are no absolutes, this in not a black and-white picture of straight lines and curves. There are many gray areas and a number of frightening shadows. For each person the intensity, duration, and depth of the specific problem areas differ. To help yourself you must first paint an accurate picture of your unique situation. Only then can you decide how you must change that picture to regain control. I describe many serious problems encountered by my clients, but in no way do I mean to suggest that you will face these same difficulties. Please read these passages with a curious mind, asking yourself whether that particular aspect relates to your experience. For example, the inability to understand why you are experiencing an anxiety attack can dramatically increase your anxiety. I address this problem and ways to handle it in a number of sections of this book. On the other hand, readers who suffer from chronic bronchitis, emphysema, or asthma *know* why they panic; they become afraid that they won't be able to get enough air. These readers will not need to focus on this issue.

The first change you achieve will probably be a greater understanding of how panic affects you as an individual. But knowledge alone will never be enough. You must then evaluate your way of thinking about yourself and the world you have created around you, your beliefs about yourself and your roles, your emotions, especially the feelings you are afraid of, and your actions, the things you do and don't do. Panic invades all four arenas, so you must gain control of each territory to regain control of your life. The keys to long-lasting change are challenging your attitude about your present-day life, exploring the roots of your many beliefs, learning from your emotional responses, and experimenting with new actions.

One of your strongest resources for overcoming panic is knowledge, since panic uses doubt, uncertainty, and fear of the unknown as its powerful allies. At this point you should know whether your problem with panic is serious enough to merit a diagnostic evaluation by a physician or a mental-health professional. If a physical or psychological disorder is diagnosed, learn as much as you can about it: What is its cause? What are the other problems associated with it? What professional help will you need? How can you help yourself? A broad understanding of your situation will serve as the foundation of your success.

This book is designed to address all the issues central to panic attacks. Let's begin by separating panic into its component parts. How does it disrupt your confidence? How does it make you a victim of its surprise attacks?

The central element of panic, of course, is its symptoms, which I described in chapter 1. Needless to say, if this book is going to help you, it must advise you on how to manage those symptoms. In chapter 8 you will learn about the physiology of panic, and in later chapters you will gain the tools necessary to become master of your body again. Now, however, I want you to think about the ways brief episodes of anxiety can play havoc by disrupting your thoughts.

WINNING THROUGH INTIMIDATION

The only way panic gains control over you is through psychological intimidation. The actual panic attacks last only an infinitesimal amount of time; even if you had one panic episode every day and that episode lasted five minutes, you would be experiencing panic only one third of a percent of your life—and yet some people can become completely dominated by the repercussions of those moments of panic.

Consider the concept "losing control." What does that mean to you? For most people it means losing security, safety, protection. If we have a sense that we are out of control, we immediately, almost instinctively, begin searching for some small way to regain our equilibrium, whether we have lost control of that burst water pipe, or slippery roads have caused a momentary loss of steering, or our young child has disappeared from sight in a shopping mall.

And after you have lost control once, what do you do? You probably start checking *all* the pipes in the basement to make sure there aren't any more potential breaks. A few hours later you might go back down those stairs "just to check and see if everything's O.K." After momentarily losing control on the highway you may grip the steering wheel a little tighter, even chastise yourself for being overconfident and driving with one hand. Once you find your missing child in the mall you probably keep a constant vigil over her whereabouts. *When the mind fears loss of control, it begins to think more intensely about how to keep control in the future.*

Panic attacks—especially spontaneous attacks—stimulate the sense of being out of control. All of a sudden, you are not in charge of your body; heart, lungs, throat, head, legs—all seem to have minds of their own. That is very frightening. Just the thought of it can make you anxious.

And that is how it begins, how panic starts to invade your life. You fear that those uncomfortable physical symptoms might return yet again. And how bad will they get? Worse than before? You don't know. It is not knowing that proves to be a devastating weapon: "Since I didn't manage the last attack, how can I possibly handle this one?"

THE SURPRISE ATTACK

To add to your confusion, the attacks are not always consistent. You might get hit with symptoms at a restaurant one evening, have a problem only once over the next three times you go out for dinner, then on your fifth time out begin to feel the same trapped sensation again. It is like spinning the chamber of the pistol in Russian roulette. Mentally, and even physically, you begin to brace yourself in anticipation. You become constantly on guard. For some, these fears translate into a desperate need not to feel trapped, because being trapped implies surrendering control. "Staying in control" is the primary objective.

Katherine M. is a twenty-nine-year-old single woman who works as an editor for a computer software company. She had been experiencing anxiety attacks for about nine months when I first saw her.

Her first moment of panic occurred completely unexpectedly as she was walking to work from the subway station. But as is often the case, this morning was preceded by several months of stress: her boyfriend had broken off their relationship, her boss had been transferred, a close friend had been diagnosed with a terminal illness, and Katherine was seriously considering moving form her hometown of Philadelphia to California.

During the past nine months since the first panic attack, her fears and her self-imposed limits have gradually restricted Katherine's world.

Here is how she described some of her concerns when I first interviewed her: "I work downtown, but I won't walk around outside when I'm there. I'm afraid I'm going to pass out. If I went out to lunch I would be afraid I wouldn't make it back. I also have trouble driving. I get afraid I'll be trapped if I get into the outside lane or if I'm not near an exit. Restaurants bother me. Again it's that trapped feeling: once the order is taken, I can't leave."

Katherine and millions like her suffer from panic disorder. They experience unexpected anxiety attacks and seek a safe asylum from that sense of being trapped. Before venturing out of their place of security they mentally evaluate each new environment. If they can imagine any chance of being trapped, they avoid the situation. When such avoidance behavior dominates their lives, the diagnosis of agoraphobia is considered.

The fears are not only of being trapped but of any experience that might produce a sense of being out of control. In chapter 4 you were introduced to Ann C., a thirty-two-year old woman who has experienced agoraphobia for twelve years. Listen to her concern in this brief anecdote.

> ANN: When I had surgery for a biopsy, they were going to put me to sleep. The scariest part of the ordeal to me was being put to sleep. I asked the doctor to give me a local anesthetic instead of a general. He said, "You know, you're so brave. Many people say, 'Knock me out, knock me out.'" I said to myself, "Little does he know that my fear *is* of being knocked out, of just *letting go*."

Why does Ann fear general anesthesia? Because she believes that the way to remain in control of her life is always to be on guard, to monitor her every action, always to watch for potential threats. This belief is actually causing her physical and physiological harm. The mind and body cannot tolerate the pressure of constantly bracing for an emergency. It is no wonder that she also reports feeling tense, anxious, and physically and emotionally exhausted.

Panic plays on the imagination. It gains its greatest power through the thoughts and images that you create in your mind. A person who fears elevators doesn't get anxious only while standing in front of an elevator. When he thinks of calling his physician for an appointment, he remembers that the doctor's office is on the fifteenth floor. He reminds himself immediately of his fear. And now, weeks before the appointment, he feels afraid. While sitting in his living room he imagines himself standing in front of the elevator. Then he begins to feel a little light-headed, and he changes his mind about calling his doctor. Most likely he will rationalize his decision, attributing it to more than just fear ("I don't *need* an appointment, yet. I'll just wait a while").

Dorothy P. is another agoraphobic whom I described in chapter 4. In the following comments, notice how she anticipates losing control. She imagines the worst possible scenario, and this mental image scares her from driving.

> DOROTHY: I don't want to lose my license, so I just don't drive. If I had a panic situation driving somewhere—if there was a

detour or if traffic backed up—I'd either have to get out and run, or jam on the brakes, knock everybody down, knock the policeman down, go through red lights. . . . I would have to escape. I can't seem to say, "Well now, calm down. You know you can. It's only going to be a short time." I can't rationalize it, I don't think at all.

Dorothy is right: she *doesn't* think rationally about her driving skills. The fact is that she has never had an auto accident and has never responded with such hysteria while driving. But she imagined the *possibility,* and that image is enough to keep her out of the driver's seat.

CONTROLLING THE MIND

Panic controls more in its victims than just those brief moments of physical anxiety. It connects physical sensations directly with your thoughts, so that simply by entertaining an idea, you stimulate a physical reaction.

For example, the *thought* of biting into a lemon can cause the lips to purse. The *thought* of a violent crime can make the muscles tense with anger. The *thought* of sinking into a nice long, deep, warm, soothing, quiet, peacefully restful bath . . . can begin to relax those same tense muscles.

With panic, the body responds to the mind in a similar fashion. I asked Katherine what happens after she has ordered in a restaurant and then thinks of being trapped. "I get terribly anxious and panicky. I'll sit there and eat, so no one will notice. But I become very uncomfortable physically, even dizzy. It's the same when I stand in line at the bank. Once I get to the teller's window and hand my business through, I get very nervous. Because I think, 'I can't leave until she gives me my receipt. I'm stuck!' I start thinking that I'm going to pass out." Katherine remains under control while she is in line only because she tells herself, "I can just get out of the line and leave." But once she has begun her transaction, she imagines that she cannot leave without "causing a scene."

Another client, Michelle R., a regional manager of a national corporation, had been experiencing panic episodes for six years. Her first spontaneous panic was while driving her car: she became dizzy and light-headed and felt as if she was going to faint. After her second attack four months later, she visited her family physician, who diagnosed the problem as "nerves." During the months prior to the onset of her symptoms, Michelle had become involved in an extramarital relationship. Within one month, she and her husband separated. Even with the episodes of panic and her physician's diagnosis, Michelle remained calm and unemotional regarding the process and saw no relationship between her symptoms and her marital conflict. During those next six years she managed her panic disorder without any professional help. She divorced her husband and two years later married the man with whom she had become involved.

By the time of her first appointment with me, she had stopped driving. She never took a walk, or stayed home alone, or shopped alone. In her business she continually found excuses to avoid out-of-town meetings. In addition, I suspected that she was subtly sabotaging her chances for further promotion.

In one of our sessions Michelle described how she had gained some insight into the ways panic plays havoc with the mind. During her previous appointment I had asked her to listen for the silent statements she makes just prior to a panic episode. She entered this session with a satisfied smile on her face and said: "Now I know what you mean. I produced my own anxiety attack! I was sitting at a staff meeting this morning and I did it to myself without knowing it. I thought, 'What happens if you feel overwhelmed, or you get that panicky feeling?' And I started feeling it! I could sense my heart racing. I became intensely nervous."

Michelle had always described her panic attacks as coming out of nowhere. In fact, that was one of the worst parts of her experience: she never had a clue as to when or why they would appear. Once she learned that particular ways of thinking can influence physical symptoms, she started paying attention to some of her thoughts. In this way she was able to discover one typical line of patter: she would simply mentally raise the possibility of experiencing symptoms; then the symptoms seemed to begin. In the past she had not been aware of these thoughts going on in her mind, so the only thing she noticed was her physical reaction. As soon as she discovered that she could produce negative symptoms by the way she was thinking, her improvement was rapid. She realized that if thoughts could bring on panic, controlling thoughts could also get rid of panic.

FORECASTING THE FUTURE

Sheryll W., whom you met in chapter 4, became agoraphobic after the birth of her oldest child twenty-two years ago. She began to feel uncomfortable in church and in grocery stores. Then the anxiety attacks started. "When I panic, my heart rate increases, I hyperventilate, feel dizzy, my legs get weak, especially if I'm experiencing a lot of stress. If I even *think* about going to the beach or another crowded place, I get that smothering feeling and I can't catch my breath. That brings on all the other feelings." Her comments illustrate the same process that Katherine and Michelle speak of. As soon as they begin to think negatively about the future, they fall into the panic trap.

It is as though panic has implemented a small voice in your mind. Let's say that you have had some anxious feelings about driving long distances on the highway. Today you decide to drive to your sister's house, fifteen miles away. As the time to leave approaches, that little voice begins. "Now, can you get there without having an anxiety attack? Really and truly get all the way there?" That's all it needs to say, because that question alone plants a seed of doubt in your mind. "Are you a hundred percent certain you can get there? And what if you start to panic . . . then what?" These kinds of questions imply that you *can't* get there without being anxious, and that you can't handle the anxiety.

How does panic reach the body through the mind?

First, you contemplate venturing into a type of situation that has caused problems in the past ("I think I'll go grocery shopping today").

Second, you remind yourself that this situation has the *potential* to stimulate your physical symptoms ("Oh, no, last week when I went with the kids I got so dizzy I thought I'd pass out").

Third, you doubt your ability to handle those symptoms ("Who knows what would happen if I went alone? I'd be so humiliated if I had to run out of there. I'm already feeling queasy just thinking about it").

Your fears may be completely irrational. A part of you may even say, "I know I'll be fine. I've never fainted. Even if I do faint, I'll survive." But despite that voice of logic, the fearful doubts remain. You gradually become plagued by the *concept* of losing control, and that plaguing fear seems to defy logic.

You can now see what a powerful ally panic has if it can instill in your mind a fear of losing control. Add to that fear the uncertainty about when the symptoms will strike and how long the attack will last, and you can see why so many sufferers from panic become physically and emotionally exhausted. They must be on twenty-four-hour sentry duty.

THE PLANNED RETREAT

Only one defensive move sees to bring relief from panic: avoidance. "If I can just keep from having to give that speech [take an airplane, confront my boss, use an elevator], then I'll be fine." And so you retreat back to some safe ground. Remaining safe becomes the highest priority.

For certain fears, avoidance can be an acceptable solution. City dwellers needn't be comfortable confronting snakes. Nor does everyone have to be comfortable crossing suspension bridges. But for too many people, avoidance has a significant impact on the quality of their lives. I have worked with clients who have given up driving, who have stopped entering stores or taking buses, who have refused promotions or quit work altogether, who haven't been in a restaurant or to a party in years. I have had to visit some agoraphobics in their homes because they refused to venture outside.

In reaction to an actual physical illness some people will dramatically alter their lives. For instance, I worked with a twenty-four-year-old woman who had suffered from asthma since she was twelve. As you probably know, the symptoms of an asthma attack include wheezing, tightness in the chest, and difficulty breathing. Even though she had not had an asthma attack in over a year, Cynthia was profoundly fearful of having a spontaneous attack. She rarely traveled beyond her hometown. When she did drive outside the city limits, she would mark on her map the location of each hospital along her route. She would not venture a route unless she thought she could reach a hospital emergency room for oxygen within five minutes' time. In addition, she remained afraid of ever becoming "too excited," which might trigger a bout of asthma.

Dorothy P. had not traveled outside a two-mile radius of her house in over forty years, nor had she ever been alone during that time.

> I don't actually go someplace and panic, because I just tell myself I can't go. I never leave Chapel Hill. Anytime I travel in Chapel Hill I have someone with me. If I go into a restaurant I have to watch the door, even sit near the door. I very seldom go to the movies, and when I do go I take the aisle seat. I have to walk out to the lobby from time to time, and I always leave before the end of the show. I hate to say this, but I haven't had any anxiety symptoms in years, because I never push myself. I stay away from all things that might produce this trapped feeling.

Few people go to such extreme measures to protect themselves, but many people begin to hesitate in their everyday life. They start to delude themselves about what they want and need out of life. Actually, they begin talking in terms of what they *don't* want or need: "I don't really want to get all dressed up tonight. Why don't we skip that party?" "Who needs the added pressure of that promotion?" "I'd love to meet with you next week, but I don't want to make commitments so far in advance. I never know what might come up."

Some cardiac patients, frightened of overexertion or overexcitement, can become socially isolated and physically inactive. Their fear of triggering a heart attack becomes masked behind indifference and depression. "I'm too old to start taking walks around the block" really means "What if that walk is all that it takes to produce another attack? I don't want to die." Such fear is understandable, but when it begins to take primary control over most of your daily activities, you are being run by panic.

Sam S. was a sixty-three-year-old plumber referred to me by his family physician. He had developed the common signs of agoraphobia: he was afraid to ride the subway, take a bus, or drive. He remained home most of the time. And he had developed a peculiar fear of his plumber's tools, which prevented him from returning to work.

After our first interview I had a strong sense that I understood the cause of his problems. After four sessions, my hunch was confirmed. With my encouragement and a few simple suggestions, Sam was able again to take the subway and drive his own car. But his tool phobia was immovable. He said his fears were so great that he couldn't even consider the idea of touching the tools without starting to feel tense and anxious. In fact, he said, his fears were so great that he didn't wish to continue treatment. I never saw him again, but I learned from his physician that six months later he still remained out of work.

What did I believe was behind Sam's phobia? Three months before he first saw me, Sam had had his second heart attack. This brush with death triggered his fears of travel and activity. But most important, he feared causing his own death by bringing on a third heart attack. Sam had unconsciously found a way to prolong his life. By developing a phobia toward his tools, he would not have to pick them up again. He would no longer have to crawl under a person's house, lift a twenty-two-pound plumber's wrench, strain to tighten down a joint, place his weakened heart under that kind of stress.

At his age and after two heart attacks, perhaps Sam should have considered retiring his tools. But panic took that decision away from him. He did not feel consciously that he had any choice in the matter. Even explaining my sense of the problem to him had no effect. Panic won, and last I heard, Sam was applying for 100 percent disability because of his phobia.

This case illustrated how panic can even disrupt the healing process after a physical illness. Regardless of what produces the initial worries or anxieties—whether the cause is emotional or physical—panic can take on an identity of its own and continue to play havoc with a person's life.

WHY ME?

If you suffer from unexpected panic attacks that defy all methods of self-control, you want desperately to know *why*. Typically you discover one or both of the following: there is something physically wrong with you, or there is something psychologically wrong with you.

If you remain convinced that the problem is physical despite objective findings to the contrary, you will begin a long and frustrating pilgrimage from doctor to doctor. You might take that same route if you consider the problem to be psychological in nature. Or you may feel so humiliated by the possibility of being labeled "mentally disturbed" that you hide behind the cloak of secrecy. Some of my clients have never told a single person about their years of silent anxiety. Adding to the pain of social isolation is the destructive force of self-doubt and criticism. You begin to blame yourself for your "weakness": "Why am I so afraid? Why don't I just *do it?*" Panic attacks that defy simple cures can lead a person into a self-destructive downward spiral. Since you feel that you cannot control your life, you gravitate toward any person or thing that might prove that control for you. Through your physician, you may try tranquilizers, sedatives, muscle relaxants, or antidepressants. Or you may begin to self-medicate, using alcohol to "take the edge off." Some adults unconsciously choose to remain very close to their parents, even though consciously they feel ambivalent about that decision. Others gravitate toward strong and dominant friends, or unconsciously choose a spouse who is powerful and controlling as a means of feeling safe. These choices are the result of a belief system that follows the line "Since I know that I am inadequate, I must find someone who will stay close to me and watch over me."

Panic begins to erode your self-confidence by convincing you that you are no longer in control of your life. After a few months, you may face a new set of problems: a loss of drive, diminished motivation, a sense of hopelessness, helplessness, worthlessness. Not only are you feeling out of control of your body, but the people around you seem to be taking control of your life decisions. Thus, depression can complicate an already difficult life.

In other words, panic gains further inroads in your life by its ability to elude cure. It becomes the great unsolvable mystery. You surrender to the problem while watching desperately for something or someone powerful enough to conquer it.

The following paragraphs are excerpts from therapy sessions with four of my clients whom you met in chapter 4. I have taken these passages out of context, so of course a great deal of information is missing. Nonetheless, read between the lines to imagine how such experiences of helplessness can erode the self-confidence and hope of these women.

ANN: After my honeymoon I returned to work and felt utter tension all the time, with very bad headaches and several anxiety attacks. I finally visited the psychiatrist. He put me on Valium [a mild tranquilizer]. I would go to see him each week, but I never got anywhere because he never did any talking. In the end I said, "What's wrong with me? Just what is wrong?" And he said, "Well, you suffer from classic, classic tension." That was his answer.

DONNA: The doctor put me in the hospital for four weeks. During the first week I had all kinds of physical tests, and then I went over to the psychiatric unit for observation for three weeks. That cost us nearly five thousand dollars. And when they were through, they said to me, "We don't know what's wrong with you." The psychiatrist said, "You're as sane as I am," and the medical doctor said, "We can't find anything physically wrong with you." I've tried Valium, Stelazine, Tofranil, and Elavil. They had absolutely no effect. So the doctors said to me, "We're taking you off of all medication and we're discontinuing your psychiatric treatment because there's nothing we can do for you."

KAREN: When I had my second child, I finally was diagnosed as having "cabin fever." I tried to understand it and tried to rationalize it, saying, "Well, you've got two little babies under the age of two, and you have cabin fever. It's the middle of February, and it's a terrible time for people." But deep inside I knew it was something more than that.

SHERYLL: The symptoms began after Susan was born, my oldest. I had postpartum depression, but I also kept experiencing anxiety attacks. One afternoon I was on the phone trying to find an apartment. I started to have chest pains and other symptoms. I called my mother, and they rushed me to the doctor's. They thought I was having a heart attack. That's how it all started. I found that when I went to church I would have a problem. Before long, it was supermarkets. And then I think it all mushroomed. I went to doctor after doctor, and they all said it was my nerves.

As you can see, the mystery that surrounds panic also feeds the panic. To label anxiety attacks as "nerves" and to offer only medications rarely succeeds. In fact, when those medications fail to eliminate panic attacks, the sufferers will often become more distressed. Some people are very secretive. Here is how Katherine described her feelings:

> I think I was just ashamed. I thought I was having a nervous break-down. I mean, I couldn't just go up to my friends and say, "Hi. I'm having a nervous breakdown." I guess I didn't know how to talk to anyone about it. I thought they would laugh at me. Besides, I don't like to bother people with my problems. People have their own problems, they don't need mine. Or they won't take me seriously. They'll say, "Don't worry about it."

So instead of giving her friends a chance to support her and express their care, Katherine became more withdrawn and turned to alcohol for control.

> I didn't know what was happening to me. And I was also drinking a lot. I would get home at night and drink to calm myself down. There were some weeks when I'd go home and drink half a pint of whiskey at night. I didn't understand what was happening to me, and it seemed to be the only thing that would calm me down. But the alcohol didn't work, because the next day I would feel terrible and the symptoms seemed to be worse.

What accounts for such dramatic physiological changes that defy simple cures? How does panic remain so powerful, yet so mysterious? Part of the answer, discussed in chapter 8, lies in our inability to trust our bodies' unconscious control. And another part of the answer, examined in chapter 9, lies in the way we think during times of crises.

8
Who's in Control?

To me, there is little that brings such peace and serenity as a walk along the beach during the quiet of the early morning. It's as though it's just me and the universe having our private time together, undisturbed. The problems of home seem so far away as I let my mind just drift in its own easy thoughts. The sun slides up over the Atlantic; it looks so big and orange. Everything seems wondrous: the sand crabs swimming deeper, leaving only a small hole for the next wave to wash over; the school of dolphins in the near distance diving one way, then the next, through the surface of their playground; the seagulls seeming to hang carelessly in the sky. The ocean shore changes my perspective and slows my busy thoughts. Life seems simpler. The natural world surrounding me invites me to join in its rhythm.

There appears to be a balance in this universe of ours, which is maintained by constant change. The tides of the sea are either in the process of rising or in the process of falling. Nothing is still. Everything in nature is in constant flux, but it is not random change. Just as the pendulum swings, the rhythms of this world seem to produce a balance between two poles. Every molecule in the universe expands and contracts.

Our years on earth are balanced between the heat of summer and the cold of winter. Our days move from the brightness of noon to the darkness of midnight. The rhythm of living things brings movement between rest and activity. For many of us, every twenty-four hours bring sixteen hours of activity and eight of rest. We work five days and rest two days. Each year we balance months of work with weeks of play.

This rhythm is equally profound in the human body. Consider

the heart. It expresses a singular pattern as it beats within the chest: contract, relax, contract, relax, contract, relax. Blood doesn't flow through the body; it pulses. Push, relax, push, relax. Each blood vessel expands and contracts as needed, rhythmically.

When you receive a blood pressure reading, you are given two numbers. The higher number, the systolic pressure, indicates the greatest force exerted by the heart and the highest degree of resistance put forth by the walls of your arteries as blood is pumped. The second, lower, number, the diastolic pressure, identifies the lowest pressure in the arteries, at the time when the heart is most relaxed. Your pulse rate expresses how often this activity-and-rest cycle of your heart takes place each minute. Physicians are concerned only when this basic life rhythm is not in balance. A good strong heartbeat and pulse of blood through the body are signs of health to a physician, not a cause for worry.

Consider your breathing. The lungs fill with air as you inhale. When the lungs expand, they stretch the diaphragm, which is a sheetlike muscle above the abdomen. When the diaphragm is stretched, its natural tendency is to relax again. As it moves back to its relaxed position, air is gently pushed out of the lungs. They contract, and you exhale.

Expanding and contracting. Activity and rest. This is the principle polarity that maintains the equilibrium within all the systems of the natural world, whether we speak of the oceans, the seasons, our daily activities, or the organs of the body. This force which sustains life is self-generating. It need not be supervised. It is a force extending back to the beginning of time.

DISTRUSTING THE UNCONSCIOUS

When I speak of the life-sustaining rhythm in the human body, I refer to it as being managed by the unconscious. My working definition of the word *unconscious* is "*any part of the mind that we are not conscious of.*"

I needn't consciously remind myself to take my next breath, or to have my next heartbeat. All the important functions of my body and mind are controlled unconsciously. I can certainly control the rhythm of my breathing consciously, but if I tried not to breathe, I wouldn't succeed. Even if I did a great job of holding my breath, I would eventually be forced to exhale or to faint so that my unconscious could regain control.

When I sleep at night my conscious mind relinquishes complete control of my body to my unconscious. If I were injured and feeling severe pain I would probably faint (or "lose consciousness") while my unconscious regulated my essential bodily functions.

So, what am I leading up to? You are glad I like the ocean, you already know how long you work each day, and, yes, your heart beats regularly without constant reminders. What's the point?

The point is this: Panic erodes your basic trust in your body. Panic wins control over you by convincing you to doubt your body's natural *unconscious* monitoring system. Panic says, "Keep watching, keep listening, keep monitoring." These are the destructive messages of panic.

If you are constantly on guard over your body's sensations, you will need to start thinking about your body in a new way. How do you allow yourself to fall asleep at night? Sure, you are exhausted from the day and you need your sleep. But when you fall asleep, you are no longer going to be able to consciously monitor your vital functions. You can't listen to your heartbeat, you can't make certain that you'll get the next breath of fresh air. What lets you relinquish that conscious control? What is it that you are implicitly trusting?

If you have found an answer, it is probably along the lines of "trusting that something would make sure my heart kept pumping." Again, for simplicity's sake, let's label that something the unconscious mind. What if, at the time of a panic attack, you could convince yourself to rely on that same unconscious to help you manage your body's sensations? I can guarantee that when you learn this skill you will be back in the driver's seat. You will no longer be letting panic control, nor will you be forcing your conscious mind to do all the work. Instead, you will take full advantage of the remarkable control possible through a "team" effort. Your conscious thoughts will do half the work; your natural unconscious processes will do the rest.

As you may know, the "unconscious" has been viewed in the past as some dark and deep part of the psyche, full of painful traumas and repressed emotions from childhood. Psychoanalysis was seen as a decade-long process of dredging up these hidden memories by means of the patient's dreams and free associations. Its goal

was to gain conscious insight and control over negative unconscious impulses.

This I believe, is the wrong approach for coping with panic. The
unconscious is 99 percent brilliant in its ability to constantly direct
the body toward health. Perhaps 1 percent of the time the unconscious is functioning inappropriately. For winning over panic
attacks, the unconscious *needs no fixing* and *needs no supervision*
by your conscious mind. It's perfectly fine. It simply needs to be
permitted to do its work without intrusion. It is the conscious
mind's intrusion that is the problem—that little voice that says,
"What if these sensations get worse? Something bad will happen.
Watch out!"

THE EMERGENCY RESPONSE

A couple of summers ago, when I was living in Massachusetts, I
drove to the Outer Banks of North Carolina for a week's vacation at
the ocean. This was the scenario as I was heading south.

I am looking forward to being with my brother and his wife during that week on the beach, so part of my mind is drifting to images
of playful times as I drive down Interstate 95. Another part of me is
aware of how crowded the highway has become now that we are
close to Philadelphia. I move to the outside lane to keep up speed.
Driver's ed. classes teach us to keep a comfortable distance of one
car length for each 10 miles per hour. But today in this lane no one
is thinking of such things. The task is to keep close to the car ahead
of you so that no one else can squeeze in from the slower lane.
You jockey for position and keep a heavy foot on the gas pedal. I'm
cruising at just under 65 miles an hour, and no one's breaking in.

Suddenly I see a small car three cars in front of me sharply
swerve into the right lane and back again. In an instant the second
car ahead of me swerves in a like manner. My immediate thought
is "We're as good as dead. Here comes the crash." My eyes flash to
the rear mirror and back again. Just like a giant ripple in the stream
of cars, the Chrysler ahead of me also veers out, almost hitting the
truck to its right. And now I'm on top of it: a large eight-foot-long
metal bumper, lying diagonally in front of my car, ready to slam
into the left front tire. Before another thought registers in my mind,
I veer out and back into my lane, circumventing death.

The thought of our demise seems to slow the pace of all of us in the fast lane. I let out a deep sigh. My heart seems to be pumping out of my chest, my armpits are soaked, and I have a throbbing headache. I place my hand over my heart—partly to verify the pounding, partly to contain it.

Of course, I was not having a panic attack. My body and mind had just given a peak performance. Together, they had totally transformed their functions. The time between the instant that small BMW swerved and I passed by that bumper was probably less that eight seconds. In those moments, the pupils of my eyes dilated to improve their vision, absorbed in detail every movement of the cars in front of me, flashed to the rearview mirror to assess the distance and speed of the cars behind. Meanwhile, peripheral vision registered the vehicles to my right, and all this data was fed instantaneously to my brain. My hearing automatically became acutely sensitive to any relevant sounds. The blood flow to my hands and feet decreased and the excess blood was redirected to my deeper skeletal muscles. Blood also pooled in my torso to provide an abundance of nourishment to any vital organ in need during the emergency. My heart increased its pace to whatever degree was necessary to get blood near my vital organs. My blood pressure thus increased. My breathing accelerated to provide for the increased oxygen needs of my rapidly circulating blood. That newly oxidized blood rushed to the brain, where the increased supply of oxygen stimulated my thought processes and significantly improved my reaction time. The muscles in my arms, hands, legs, and feet tensed in readiness for instructions from the brain, and responded with precision. My liver released increased amounts of glucose (sugar) into the bloodstream to power my muscles and feed my brain and heart.

It is truly phenomenal, this body of ours. Nothing that humankind has ever created can come close to its performance. My conscious thought processes were not responsible for saving my life. Instead, they had one task: to prevent fear from interfering with the task. My life was in the hands of my autonomic nervous system, which signals the release of adrenaline and coordinates all efforts of the brain and the body with literally split-second timing.

Here are the major changes that take place in the body during such an Emergency Response:

The blood sugar level increases.
The pupils dilate.
The sweat glands perspire.
The heart rate increases.
The muscles tense.
The amount of blood in the hands and feet is reduced.
The blood pools in the head and trunk.

These are normal, healthy, life-saving changes in the body's physiology, produced by communication from the brain to the autonomic nervous system, the endocrine system, and the motor nerves of the skeletal muscles. When the brain receives word that a crisis is at hand, it flips the "emergency" switch. All systems react simultaneously and instantly.

TRICKING THE BRAIN

In all likelihood, you have recognized some of these changes as symptoms of panic attacks. Your panic attacks are not identical to the body's natural, healthy Emergency Response. However, since this is a self-help book and not a medical textbook, I will take some liberties with the technical details. View it this way: panic attacks are produced when panic deceives the brain into thinking there is imminent danger. There you are, standing in the aisle of the grocery store not bothering a soul. Flip. On goes the Emergency switch. "Red alert! All systems prepare for battle!" shouts the commanding voice of the brain, through the nervous system to the skeletal system, the muscles, the circulatory and respiratory systems, the endocrine system, and most of the organs of the body.

Since this is an unconscious response produced at an illogical time, you are consciously surprised and frightened. The reason you have more symptoms that those I just listed is that panic now induces anxiety. Anxiety exaggerates the normal, healthy Emergency Response, and anxiety also feeds on itself. I said that during an Emergency Response the best thing for the conscious mind to do is to prevent fear or doubt from interfering with the task at hand. Panic, however, instructs you to focus on your body (*wrong!*) and worry about what will happen next (*wrong!*). Those two instructions are responsible for extreme symptoms of anxiety that you experience during a panic attack. They can cause these changes:

The heart may seem to skip a beat or beat irregularly.
The stomach may feel as though it is tied in knots.
The hands, arms, or legs may shake.
You may have difficulty catching your breath.
You may feel pains or tightness in your chest.
The jaw, neck, or shoulders may feel tight and stiff.
The mouth may become dry.
You may have difficulty swallowing.
The hands and feet may feel cold, sweaty, or numb.
You may develop a headache.

Although several other changes are also possible (see chapter 1), I list these here because they are all clearly exaggerations of the normal, healthy Emergency Response. For instance, during a crisis the autonomic nervous system produces what is called a "sympathetic stimulation" throughout the body, causing the sphincter muscles of the stomach to contract while blood flow to the digestive system is decreased. Anxiety will then increase the chance of heartburn, nausea, and pain in the upper abdomen and chest.

In addition to exaggerating the normal physical changes of the body, making you focus your attention on your body, and inviting you to worry about the future, panic produces a fourth problem: it prolongs the symptoms.

After a normal, healthy Emergency Response, the brain signals the end to the sympathetic stimulation of the nervous system. The body begins its swing back to "normal mode." Panic and anxiety, on the other hand, tend to let symptoms linger. The headache throbs for the rest of the day, or the stomach churns through the night, disrupting your needed rest. The body feels depleted, exhausted; the mind seems to hang in a fog.

To summarize:

1. The human body and its organs, like those of all living organisms, maintain a balance between activity and rest, between expansion and contraction. A shifting from one of these poles to the other creates a healthy, natural rhythm.

2. The body is specially designed to handle extreme activity. It

responds to an emergency automatically, through instinct. It is well equipped to perform at an instant's notice.
3. Panic disrupts the natural balance of the body by sending false emergency signals to the brain and by telling you to doubt your body's natural abilities.

To conquer panic attacks as they occur, you must know and believe the following:

1. You can trust your body and your unconscious to perform their essential roles during crises.
2. The body also has another response that is exactly opposite to and as powerful as the Emergency Response, the Calming Response (see chapter 10).
3. When panic flips the emergency switch on, you can consciously flip it off.
4. With practice, you can consciously stop panic even before it takes control.

9

Why the Body Reacts

If the brain is such a brilliant machine with an incredible capacity for intelligence, why doesn't it block out panic? Since it is the brain that signals all the physical symptoms of panic, the brain, as executive, must take responsibility for failing to block panic.

For the answer to that question we must delve deeper into the workings of the mind and the brain. Most of the time I use the words *brain* and *mind* as synonyms, but occasionally they must be distinguished. I define the brain as the primary center for regulating and coordinating the body's activities. It also generates thought, memory, reason, emotion, and judgment. The brain is an actual physical object. The mind, on the other hand, is a concept, representing the ability to integrate the functions of the brain: perceiving our surroundings, experiencing our emotions, and processing information intelligently. In a sense, the brain is the workhorse of the mind. This is why I speak so much about altering your thoughts and beliefs. They are the keys to your brain's activity.

In a nutshell, here is what the brain does:

- It receives a stimulus.
- It interprets the meaning of that stimulus.
- It selects a response.
- It enlists the body to cooperate as needed.

For example, if you accidentally touch a hot radiator, the stimulus travels up the nerve endings of finger through the spinal cord to the brain (1), the brain interprets the stimulus to mean "I'm touching something hot. This is burning and uncomfortable" (2), the brain selects to remove the finger from the radiator (3), and it sends a communication through the nerves to the muscles in the arm, hand, and finger (4). Your hand instantly jerks away.

You might label it an "instinctual" response to jerk your hand off a hot object. It is also a learned response. The early experiences of your life, dating back to infancy, have trained your brain to interpret a hot radiator in that manner.

The brain interprets sensations on the basis of two criteria: memory- and sensory-based images. Significant events of your life are recorded in your memory with varying degrees of intensity. I have a distinct memory of poking a stick in a small fire when I was four years old. That memory is reinforced through a sensory-based image: the smell of the burning lumber, the sight of those flames, the touch of my hand on that stick. Interestingly, I don't have an image of that stick breaking, causing me to fall into coals. My next memory is sitting on the counter of my neighbor's kitchen. I can see several adults around me, feel the ointment covering the minor burns on my knees, and recall the grown-ups offering me a soft drink.

The memory of events like these lives on, reinforced by sensory-based images. The actual event is not the only thing recorded in the memory. In addition, our internal reactions are etched in our unconscious mind. A few minutes before I fell into that fire, my mother had instructed my six-year-old brother and me to "stay away from that fire." So in addition to the immediate pain I experienced from the burns, I suspect that in my memory I also hold the sense of guilt I must have felt for disobeying.

WELL-WORN PATHS

Our beliefs and values develop largely out of our life experiences and the memories of them. As adults, all of us probably notice that certain of our patterns and habits stem from our childhood experiences. Such things as our religious beliefs, our social skills, our use or abuse of alcohol, our choice of partners, are based in part on our childhood memories and in part on past adult experiences.

This past learning is of tremendous benefit to us today. So many decisions are simple for us because we already have the "circuits" in place. We don't need to put much conscious effort into remembering our phone number or writing a letter or tying a ribbon on a package. But as children, learning each of these skills was a challenge. Can you remember? As we mastered each skill, we literally created new neurological circuits in our brain, circuits that we have now used for years. They become like well-worn paths. Every time we learn new skills, we create new circuits.

But as I discussed in chapter 8, with every positive there seems to be a negative. Here is the rub: strong beliefs can *block* the natural protective mechanisms of the brain and mind. Left to its own, the unconscious mind will seek health. But social learning and certain traumatic experiences tend to override the unconscious mind.

After the panic response has become established, the mind stops working creatively in your favor. Instead it seems to be set on "automatic pilot" and stops seeking out solutions. The mind focuses on the problem instead of on its solution. When you walk into a situation that is similar in time or place to one in which you previously had a panic attack, the image of that last time rises up in your mind. This image alone can produce the same muscle tension and the mind can interpret it to mean "trouble." Instead of paying attention to all of its many problem-solving options, the mind focuses on its negative images: its messages to tense your muscles and produce all of your disturbing body sensations.

A panic attack may completely surprise you—consciously. But unconsciously a step-by-step process has taken place prior to your panic symptoms:

Step 1: When you enter a situation that is associated with panic, the brain registers this stimulus.

Step 2: It interprets the meaning of this stimulus as "harmful" or "dangerous."

Step 3: On the basis of your memory of past experiences, your brain doubts your ability to cope effectively.

Step 4: It therefore selects "emergency" as its default response, compounded by "anxiety" (since it doubts that you will cope well).

Step 5: The brain enlists the body in the Emergency Response and the Anxiety Response. After enough of those experiences, you develop a conditioned response, meaning the brain takes less and less time to evaluate each new situation. Instead, it more and more automatically selects the Emergency and Anxiety responses. You have created a "well-worn path." This explains why people who have their first panic attack in a car may gradually develop a fear of any form of transportation. The brain stops screening the stimulus. If a person has a panic attack in a restaurant, bank, or other closed space, eventually the mind might say, "All such situations are dangerous."

IMAGES AND INTERPRETATIONS

Images can produce brain responses just as well as the actual experiences do, and this creates further limitations. If you have experienced panic during public speaking in the past, simply the *image* of seeing yourself giving a talk next week can produce uncomfortable feelings right now. In your fantasy of the future you imagine having a rough time of it. You don't call up a view of yourself standing in front of the group, well organized and prepared, feeling confident, speaking distinctly, being well received by your audience. Instead, you envision yourself in front of the group, then you ask yourself, "What if I begin to panic?" That suggestion triggers an image of you panicking during your speech. And right now, one week before the event, you begin to have those physical sensations that you expect to have during the event. This is how powerful the tools of the mind are.

Here is a key point. Much of your ability to control is based on this principle: People, places, events are panic-provoking only *after* we apply meaning to them. A store is just a store, a speech is just a speech, a drive is just a drive, until the brain interprets them as "dangerous" or "threatening." To conquer panic, then, you must intervene at the *point of interpretation*.

TAKING AWAY CHOICE

There are two reasons why the brain selects the Emergency Response at inappropriate times. The first is that it is prevented from gathering relevant information. Many of our observations and beliefs about life were established during our youth, well before our adult intellect was mature. Other beliefs were formed after fearful moments or traumatic events. When these beliefs are fixed in place, they prevent the brain from evaluating new situations with an "open mind," so to speak. Once a belief is established, it closes off the mind from constantly reevaluating the facts associated with the belief. When the beliefs are useful ("Hot objects can burn you"), we benefit. But when an erroneous faulty belief is in place ("All forms of transportation are dangerous to me"), our lives become restricted and uncreative.

If you suffer from panic attacks, it means that a faulty belief prevents your brain from receiving a critical message. Remember the four steps of all brain activity. At Step 1 the brain receives a stimulus (e.g., entering a restaurant or thinking of giving a speech) and at Step 2 it interprets the stimulus. It is at Step 2 that the brain is missing a message. The faulty belief "This is an emergency!" prevents an accurate interpretation of the situation, namely, "There is *no physical danger.*" (Of course this is not so straightforward for the post-myocardial patient or the patient with chronic pulmonary disease. She must be able to assess whether she requires medical attention and at the same time keep herself from becoming too panicky.) The brain doesn't bother to look around this new scene, gathering information to make an assessment. Instead, it receives an immediate message that forces the Emergency Response.

The second reason the brain selects the Emergency Response is by default: it doesn't know of another, more appropriate response. From an evolutionary standpoint, the human intellect is a relatively recent development, when compared to the Emergency Response, which is also found in all lower animals. Perhaps our intellectual and psychological defenses have not evolved enough adequately to handle certain social threats, so our physical defenses respond first. The fact remains that the Emergency Response produces a handful of significant changes in the body that are strictly designed to help in a physical crises, yet actually handicap us in dealing with social or intellectual challenges. Most of us know the difficulty in trying to pass a final exam in mathematics while the hands sweat, the mouth dries, and the muscles tense.

My position, however, is that we have the intellectual and psychological capability to defend against social threats well enough not to need the intrusion of the Emergency Response. This book tells you how to identify these capacities, how to master them, and how to use them against panic. Your first task is to work on changing your interpretation of events. Over a period of time you must slowly reinforce this message: you are *not* confronting a physical emergency. To begin, you must start to believe it, to remind yourself of it: "This is not an emergency." (Heart and lung disease patients should replace this statement throughout the book with, "I can stay calm and think.") Sooner or later it will be one of the messages you tell yourself at the moment you sense panic creeping in. Eventually it becomes one of the automatic, unconscious interpretations of the brain.

It is perfectly fine for you to become highly alert and to experience an increase in your heart rate and respiration during a panic-provoking situation. These types of responses are positive and mean that you will have the capacity to think more sharply and clearly. As you face these fearful times and places, clear, sharp thinking will be your ally. Your goal should not be to eliminate all these sensations. A certain amount of anxiety and worry can be beneficial. In research comparing the test scores of students who enter exams either completely relaxed, somewhat anxious or very anxious, the students who were somewhat anxious performed the best. When we anticipate an event with excitement or anxiety, the adrenal glands secrete hormones that stimulate our creative intelligence, which we will need when facing such events. This same process takes place when you face panic. The goal is to keep your alertness while you change your interpretation. That alertness gives you a conscious choice, so that you don't have to respond with your old automatic fears.

You will now learn a series of strategies that allow you to remain alert and sharp to all that is taking place around you and with you, while at the same time consciously flipping off that emergency switch. With practice, you will be able to consciously stop panic before it begins.

10

The Calming Response

For all its apparent complexity, our body operates with great simplicity. The autonomic nervous system controls all involuntary bodily functions; within it, the sympathetic nervous system produces the Emergency Response. As is the case in most living organisms, if the human nervous system can produce a response at one extreme, it is capable of producing a response at the opposite extreme. This is a basic tenet of physics: every action has an opposite and equal reaction.

And so it is. The sympathetic response, or Emergency Response, is balanced by the parasympathetic response, what I call the Calming Response. When a crisis has passed, the brain doesn't just stop sending those emergency communications. An entirely different set of nerves sends *new* signals to all the affected parts of the body. Those signals tell the heart and lungs to slow down, and instruct the muscles to stop contracting. The blood pressure decreases, oxygen consumption is reduced, and blood sugar levels return to normal. These restful changes take place not accidentally, not haphazardly, but by instruction.

When I ask my clients what one change they would like to see more than anything else, changes, their response is "To feel *calmer* during those panicky times, so that I can *think more clearly*." The fact is, you already have the capacity to turn off the emergency switch—you just don't know it. You fear you are losing control, but your body has a built-in control which is yours for the asking: you can consciously activate the parasympathetic nervous system response. The central purpose of the Calming Response is to halt and reverse the Emergency Response. Its circuits cause every internal system to return to its normal state. Thus your parasympathetic system, with controlling fibers in all the essential parts of your body, can cancel out the Emergency Response.

Dr. Herbert Benson was the first to label this calming process the Relaxation Response, and he continues to be a pioneer in medical research into this beneficial phenomenon. I have chosen not to use Dr. Benson's term for one reason: to many panic-prone people, relaxation tends to imply "letting go" or "losing control." Because of this, they resist learning skills that promote relaxation. The word also is associated with meditative practices: not moving, emptying the mind, not thinking. The truth of the matter is that relaxation exercises and meditation do work. They are excellent tools to produce the Calming (or parasympathetic) Response. But these techniques of calming the mind and body must be modified to help you as you begin to face panic.

During the actual moment of panic you need skills that clear your head of extraneous thoughts, that sharpen your mind, and that keep you actively alert. You need the ability immediately to confront panic and regain control of your body on short notice. This chapter and the next two chapters explain how to elicit the Calming Response through formal exercise. Later chapters will teach you how to apply this skill at the moment of panic.

MEMORIES AND IMAGES

Before you learn the techniques for producing the Calming Response directly, reflect for a moment on times when you have naturally felt at ease, peaceful and calm inside. Perhaps you can remember walking into a church when it was completely empty. A church can be awe-inspiring: huge stained-glass windows, ceilings that seem to touch the sky, a peaceful quietness that invites you to sit and empty your mind. Imagine sitting alone in a church, repeating a simple prayer or letting your mind drift easily. There are no crowds to contend with, just you alone with your peaceful thoughts.

The process of prayer itself invites a calming of the body and mind. In addition to renewing our relationship with God, we quiet ourselves. And as we become calm and quiet we gain perspective on troubled times. Anyone who has successfully turned to prayer during a crisis knows this feeling. I am not advocating any religious undertaking. But if you are religious, I promise you that by letting yourself *calmly, slowly,* and *meaningfully* pray during a stressful time, you will literally relax the major muscles of the body and significantly reduce any current anxiety.

Other situations can produce this same sensation for you. When I sit by an open fire, watching the flames flickering, skipping from log to log, changing size and shape and color, I become pleasantly mesmerized by those flames. My worries and problems seem to drift away as my attention is consumed by the fire, its crackling sounds, its sweet smell.

Remember as a child lying in a field and watching the clouds slowly take shape? First comes a clear impression of Lincoln's face. Three or four minutes later it's a long train, slowly ambling across the sky. Without effort the clouds freely drift into pleasant patterns, allowing your eyes to relax their gaze.

Imagine fisherman sitting on the shore or in a boat, as still as their lines in the water, hour after hour. Their tranquil faces express a relaxed and easy quietness. Think of your own times of stillness and calm in the past. Have they ever come from rocking gently on the porch, back and forth, back and forth . . . no real effort, no pressures, just sitting and drifting? Or perhaps that peacefulness has come when you have risen early in the morning or stayed up alone late at night for some private time.

FOCUSING THE MIND

When we focus on neutral or comforting thoughts and images, clear and measurable physiological changes take place in the body. As an experiment, read again the "Memories and Images" section you just read. This time, read slowly while you let yourself imagine each scene as I describe it. Try that now. If that experience begins to produce the Calming Response within you, here is what may be changing:

Your oxygen consumption is decreasing.
Your breathing is slowing.
Your heart rate is decreasing.
Your blood pressure is lessening.
Your muscle tension is reducing.

There is a growing sense of ease in the body and calmness in the mind.

You can contrast this with how you felt when you were reading earlier chapters, in which I described anxiety-provoking times. *Our images have tremendous influence over our bodies.*

I am not describing to you some simplistic idea like "Just relax and you'll feel better." I am identifying the opposite and equally powerful capacity of the nervous system—the parasympathetic response, or Calming Response—which is essential to counterbalance the Emergency Response and all anxiety. And it is a capacity you already use. Anytime you feel comfortable and at ease, it is because of this Calming Response. Each time you fall asleep, it is because your Calming Response has quieted down the body and mind enough to allow sleep. What science has gradually discovered in the past twenty years is that we actually can activate the Calming Response through conscious effort. In the field of psychology, this discovery is as important as the achievement of NASA in placing the first humans on the moon. Our mental processes can alter the biochemistry of the body. An entirely new frontier is now open to us.

Taking Conscious Control

Typically the responsibility for tensing and calming the body has been left to the unconscious mind. You probably are not aware of it when the muscles of your body become tense. I am not consciously aware of the number of muscles in my neck, my back, my arms, or my hands, which are contracting in order to help me write this sentence on my notepad. My unconscious does that detailed work for me so that I can consciously consider how to express my thoughts to you.

But muscle tension is a major component of anxiety and panic attacks, and if you are not aware of it, it works against your progress. It is during these times of difficulty that we need to become skilled at consciously noticing and changing our muscle tension.

When you become anxious, your muscles automatically tense; that is the rule. The reverse is also true: when the muscles are not tensing, your mind cannot become anxious. In fact, to loosen and relax the muscles is an excellent method of activating the Calming Response. By the way, muscles don't actually "relax"; they are either not contracting or contracting to some degree. When I teach people calming techniques, I speak of "relaxing" the muscles to mean "letting go" of any muscle tension they notice.

Unfortunately, most people who are afraid of a panic attack will physically tense their muscles and psychologically become anxious as a means of "remaining in control." They consider their tension to be a necessary way to stay on guard. But whenever you are highly tense and anxious, your ability to think logically is greatly diminished. The "solution" of bracing yourself contributes to the problem. Reducing your muscle tension automatically reduces anxiety and invites the Calming Response. Your mind gets rid of all those useless negative thoughts so that you can concentrate on the situation at hand. Any of the relaxation techniques and meditations that are being taught these days actually increase your ability to think clearly and therefore increase your self-control.

Much has been written about such relaxation techniques over the past twenty years. The first popular movement began in the mid-1960s, when Transcendental Meditation (TM) was introduced into the United States. In 1975 Dr. Herbert Benson's bestseller *The Relaxation Response* brought scientific and medical credence to TM and other relaxation/meditation techniques. But, much earlier, in 1938, Dr. Edmund Jacobson created a medically sound method for reducing tension. He described his design to the professional community in his book *You Must Relax*. Dr. Jacobson's "progressive relaxation" technique continues to serve as one of the cornerstones for behavior therapy today. Teaching relaxation or meditative techniques to persons with anxiety disorders and a broad range of physical disorders is now a standard practice within behavioral medicine and psychology.

In the Western world, these practices were "discovered" within the last fifty years and have yet to become an integral part of our culture. However, the true beginnings of the discovery of the meditations and breathing patterns that elicit the Calming Response date back thousands of years and have since that time served as the principal techniques of all major Eastern religions to achieve peace, clarity, and oneness with God. In those times, the practice of religious exercises was widespread, since religion served as the psychology, the philosophy, and the science of each culture. Yet the "new" techniques that are slowly receiving scientific validation and credibility in the 1980s and '90s in the Western world are the centuries-old methods from India, Tibet, China, and Japan that are encountered in Buddhism and Zen Buddhism, Hinduism, yoga, pranayama, Taoism, and T'ai Chi Ch'uan. The skills presented in the chapters that follow are based on the scientific complexity of Western medicine, research, and psychology and at the same time reflect the simplicity so often found in Eastern philosophy.

In the next chapter you will learn of the pervasive physiological effects of one of our body's simplest functions: breathing. Breathing is so instinctual that we have long taken it for granted. To control panic, however, breathing is our most powerful somatic tool. Without its help we can fall prey to over twenty-five symptoms; with its help, we can calm the body and clear the mind. Our breathing patterns are always involved in panic; they are either part of the solution or part of the problem.

11

The Breath of Life

Breathing is an essential function of the body. With each inhalation, oxygen is delivered to the bronchial tubes of your lungs. Passing through the millions of tiny air sacs, the oxygen moves into your arteries, where it is captured by your blood cells. When blood circulates out of the lung area, it is bright red because of its high oxygen content. The oxygen-rich blood is pumped through the heart to all parts of the body. All the cells throughout the body then exchange their waste products for oxygen. The blood returning to the heart is duller in color because of its diminished oxygen content. The heart pumps the waste-filled blood back to the lungs. As you inhale more fresh air, a form of combustion takes place, in which the blood cells absorb oxygen and release carbon dioxide. And the cycle begins again.

If your lungs do not take in enough air, your blood will not be oxygenated or properly cleaned. Your complexion will be pale, since blood vessels with low oxygen content are dark blue. (If you look at your hands now, you can probably see some blue blood vessels. This is the normal color of your veins, which are returning blood to the lungs for a fresh supply of oxygen.) In addition, your digestion is impaired from too little oxygen, and your organs and tissues are not fully nourished. A lack of oxygen in the blood can contribute to anxiety, depression, and fatigue.

The respiratory system regulates breathing in order to maintain a balance of oxygen and carbon dioxide in the bloodstream. In normal circumstances, your rate of breathing is determined by the amount of carbon dioxide that must be expelled from you bloodstream and the amount of oxygen needed to satisfy the demands of your immediate activity.

Panic and breathing patterns are intimately related. The less you understand about the process of respiration, the greater the power of panic. This is so because changes in breathing alone can produce over two dozen sensations within the body. If you are unaware of your ongoing breathing patterns and you don't realize that the mechanics of respiration alone can be solely responsible for those uncomfortable feelings, then you will become frightened.

If your fear includes being uncertain whether your heart or lungs are functioning properly, your alarm will take on panic proportions. People who have heart or lung damage, such as from a myocardial infarction or a chronic obstructive pulmonary disease (see chapter 6), may experience this kind of panic when they begin to have trouble breathing or think that they are having another heart attack. Other panic-prone people, who notice symptoms and interpret them as "I can't breathe" or "I'm having a heart attack, I'm going to die," will immediately feel the effects of panic. These thoughts automatically and instantly switch on the body's Emergency Response.

The most important task during those moments is to stay rational. Panic can cause you to become so emotionally tangled up in your fearful expectations that you fail to take supportive action. Your mind becomes cloudy, your symptoms escalate, and your thoughts run in seven different directions. At the same time the symptoms in your body continue to grow in strength, often for two reasons. First, you continue to frighten yourself by your thoughts. And second, you ignore the changes in your breathing and instead focus on your symptoms. Mastering your thoughts is a target of later chapters. In this chapter you will learn just how extensively you can control your symptoms by the way you breathe.

I want to give you some details about the mechanics of respiration. At first glance, this information may seem too technical to be useful, but nothing could be further from the truth. Actually, the contribution that respiratory patterns play in the cause and cure of panic has been virtually ignored by sufferers and health professionals alike. My professional experience has taught me to use the respiration process as a central focus of treatment. Once a client of mine can control his breathing patterns in a variety of situations, I believe he is 50 percent along on the road to success. For some people, identifying and mastering breathing patterns will completely end their symptoms and resolve their problem.

SIGNALS OF CHANGE

When it comes to taking a breath, our lungs don't have much say in the process. As a basic life-sustaining force in all mammals, breathing has evolved as a relatively simple function controlled neurologically by the respiratory center in our hindbrain, located just above the spinal cord. When a signal arrives from the brain stem, the muscles around the lungs contract, which increases the space within the chest. This diminishes the pressure within the lungs relative to that outside the body. The lungs now are "forced" to inhale in order to equalize their internal pressure with that of the environment. A second signal is then sent to instruct those muscles to stop contracting. As the muscles relax, pressure increases in the lungs and air is forced out. This basic mechanical process is the typical method of breathing. Only in special situations does our breathing fall under the control of our more evolved, or higher, brain centers.

The brain makes all its executive decisions on the basis of the information it's currently gathering. What information should it pay attention to as it selects a breathing pattern for any given moment? You might expect that it simply attends to how much oxygen we need. In reality, adjustment of respiration is based more on the amount of carbon dioxide in the body than on the amount of oxygen needed. This is in part because carbon dioxide plays such an important role in maintaining a proper acid base balance (or pH balance) in the body and in producing energy through metabolism.

To understand the relationship between breathing and panic, we need to look closely at all the factors that relate to increased respiration. The brain will signal the respiratory system to increase its rate and depth of inhalation in response to specific chemical and neurological signals, including those that indicate an excessive amount of carbon dioxide in the blood, not enough oxygen in the blood, reflexes from our joints and muscles as they begin to move, an increase in body heat caused by metabolism and emotional arousal. As the breathing rate increases, the excess carbon dioxide is deposited in the lungs and exhaled, more oxygen is passed into the bloodstream from the air sacs in the lungs to assist in metabolism, and body heat is lowered by increased evaporation of water through the lungs. When the brain and the chemical receptors in the arteries find that "things are back in balance," the brain signals a return to a normal breathing pattern.

This balancing process becomes a little more complex when we introduce the other influences on breathing patterns. This first is the body's autonomic nervous system. You have already read about this in the previous chapters, the sections on the Emergency Response and the Calming Response. An increased breathing rate is one of the many automatic and instant responses of the body's alarm system. It can take place independently or as a component of the mass action of the Emergency Response.

The second influence on breathing patterns is conscious thought or emotion. If you stand at the edge of a pool and contemplate swimming a lap, your breathing will automatically increase in anticipation of the activity. If you think about arguing with your boss at work when you are standing in the kitchen washing the dishes, you will also increase your rate of breathing, and usually without any conscious awareness. Any of the "active" emotions—anger, fear, joy, or excitement—require energy from the body and therefore stimulate faster breathing. Conversely, when you feel sad or depressed, less carbon dioxide must be expelled, less oxygen is needed, and breathing slows.

The third influence on breathing is the tension of stress. Studies consistently show that during episodes of stress, people breathe more rapidly and consequently levels of carbon dioxide in the blood drop significantly.

TWO TYPES OF BREATHING

Studies have revealed another important phenomenon that plays a significant role in mastering panic. It appears that people under stress not only begin to increase their respiration rate, but they also shift from breathing into the lower parts of their lungs to breathing into the upper parts. Figure 4 illustrates these two kinds of breathing, upper-chest (thoracic) and lower-chest (diaphragmatic). In upper-chest breathing the chest lifts upward and outward. The breathing is shallow and rapid. In lower-chest breathing, each inhalation is deeper and slower. Below the lungs is a sheetlike muscle, the diaphragm, which separates the chest from the abdomen. When you fill your lower lungs with air, the lungs push down on the diaphragm and cause your abdominal region to protrude. Your stomach looks as though it is expanding and contracting with each diaphragmatic breath.

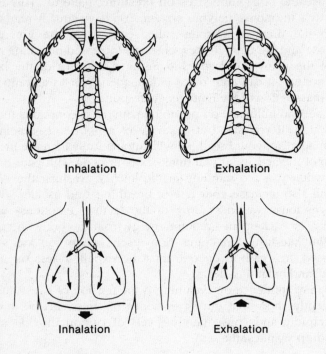

FIGURE 4. *Two kinds of breathing, upper-chest (thoracic) above, and lower-chest (diaphragmatic) below.*

As research continues, we are learning more and more about the importance of these two breathing patterns. One study of 160 men and women found that those whose typical breathing pattern was slow and deep were more confident, emotionally stable, and physically and intellectually active. Those whose habitual breathing pattern was rapid and shallow were more passive, dependent, fearful, and shy.

Rapid upper-chest breathing is a normal, brief response to any threatening or anxiety-provoking situation. It now appears that this kind of breathing is a rather stable ongoing feature of people who are chronically anxious or phobic. In studies where chronically anxious subjects were specifically asked to begin breathing in their upper chest, they reported increased psychological and physical symptoms.

Slow deep breathers, on the other hand, have a slower resting heart rate and a less "trigger-happy" Emergency Response. The habit of slow, easy, diaphragmatic breathing invites the Calming Response, promotes good health, and provides long-term protection for the heart.

These studies tell us that both short-term and long-term breathing patterns are directly related to psychological strength and the subjective experience of anxiety. By changing your habitual breathing pattern you can increase your defenses against panic. By changing your breathing pattern during an anxious episode you can reverse your body's panic-provoking symptoms.

THE HYPERVENTILATION SYNDROME

Changing your long-term breathing patterns will be beneficial to you generally—but your most important ally will be your breathing during the moment of panic. As mentioned earlier, a change in your breathing should directly correspond to your activity level. For instance, if I am out running for exercise, it won't be long before I am breathing rapidly from my upper chest. My body is now demanding more oxygen, and my metabolism is producing larger amounts of carbon dioxide, which must be exhaled. I can keep that breathing pattern up for as long as I'm running.

What happens if I stop running but force myself to continue breathing at that accelerated rate? I continue to exhale large quantities of carbon dioxide (CO_2), but no longer am depositing that amount of carbon dioxide into my bloodstream. Immediately my blood CO_2 level drops. When that takes place, CO2 begins to leave my nerve cells, raising the pH level in the cells and making them more excitable. Because of this I may begin to feel nervous and jittery. Changes in the pH level remove calcium salts in my blood, which increases the excitability of my peripheral nerve endings, causing tingling around my mouth and fingers and toes. At the same time, this diminished level of CO_2 suppresses my Calming Response: my pupils dilate, my hands and feet begin to feel cold, my heart continues to race, lights seem brighter and sounds louder.

Simultaneously, the blood vessels in my brain constrict, which lowers the amount and the rate of oxygen transferred into those tissues. This produces most of my uncomfortable symptoms: dizziness, faintness, distortions in vision, difficulty concentrating, and a sense of separateness from my body (depersonalization).

Most of these symptoms will develop in under a minute of this type of breathing, called hyperventilation. All these changes are reversed by slowing the rate of breathing. Although uncomfortable, none of these short-term changes in the body's chemistry can cause lasting harm.

Most people who hyperventilate never realize they are doing so. They don't report that they are having a problem with their breathing. Instead, they complain of various specific or vague symptoms throughout their body. Specialist after specialist will search for thyroid, cardiac, gastrointestinal, respiratory, or central nervous system problems. Misdiagnosis, which is common, can lead to operations on the spine, the abdomen, or other organs. Just as likely, though, the patient will be labeled anxious or neurotic by the physician and referred to a mental-health professional, who will also fail to identify hyperventilation as the culprit. It is true that many people who are prone to hyperventilate are also anxious. But I would be anxious, too, if I continued to spontaneously experience such dramatic and undiagnosed symptoms!

PHYSICAL AND PSYCHOLOGICAL COMPLAINTS CAUSED BY HYPERVENTILATION

Cardiovascular

Uncomfortable awareness of the heart (palpitations)
Racing heart (tachycardia)
Heartburn

Neurological

Dizziness and light-headedness
Poor concentration
Blurred vision
Numbness or tingling of the mouth, hands, and feet

Gastrointestinal

Lump in the throat

Difficulty swallowing
Stomach pain
"Swallowing air"
Nausea

Musculoskeletal

Muscle pains
Shaking
Muscle spasms

Respiratory

Shortness of breath
"Asthma"
Chest pain
Choking sensation

General

Tension, anxiety
Fatigue, weakness
Poor sleep, nightmares
Sweating

Figure 5 shows how hyperventilation can be part of the vicious circle of panic. The process is as follows: (1) Any kind of emotional or physical disturbance can stimulate (2) hyperventilation, without the person's being consciously aware of the change. (3) The symptoms of hyperventilation develop rapidly. (4) As soon as the person notices enough uncomfortable symptoms (5) he becomes panicky ("I can't breathe!" or "I'm going to faint!"). Before these thoughts are even completely registered in the mind, (6) the body has reacted to this interpretation with its Emergency Response (to face whatever is threatening the body). This further supports rapid upper-chest breathing and the cycle is re-created, with an increase in the number or intensity of symptoms. (See Figure 5.)

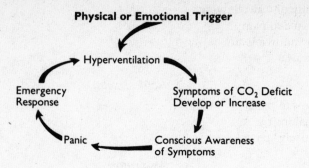

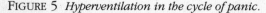

FIGURE 5 *Hyperventilation in the cycle of panic.*

Only minor degrees of hyperventilation are necessary to initiate its effects of increased heart rate, constriction of blood vessels, and a shifting of the acid base balance in the blood toward alkalosis (a high pH level in the blood, causing light-headedness). If you want to see how quickly these changes occur, try this: breathe in and out as rapidly as your can for no more than fifteen seconds. Then sit back and notice the sensations in your body.

People who tend to hyperventilate appear to develop a general sensitivity to breathing patterns. The amount of carbon dioxide in their lungs at any time can change considerably relative to people who don't tend to overbreathe. Carbon dioxide levels drop markedly with any deep sigh, and recovery to normal levels takes longer. This instability, combined with the habit of upper-chest breathing, makes them even more susceptible to panic.

Once the problem is identified, recovery and control can be just as dramatic. In one study, more than one thousand patients diagnosed as hyperventilators were taught breathing and relaxation skills. For most of the patients all symptoms were gone within one to six months. Seventy-five percent were completely free of symptoms at a twelve-month follow-up, and 20 percent experienced only occasional mild symptoms, which were no longer troublesome.

THE FOUNDATION SKILLS

There are two important things you need to learn about your breathing in order to conquer panic. First, you should learn how to breathe from your diaphragm and make that breathing pattern a part of your daily life. Old habits die hard, so you will have to work at this one. But by shifting to this slow, diaphragmatic breathing you will over time bring your blood carbon dioxide level back to a more stable position, and it will be less sensitive to brief respiratory changes.

Second, you will need to become skilled at shifting to this kind of breathing whenever you begin to feel panicky. During panic, one goal is to turn off the Emergency Response and encourage your body's Calming Response. Proper breathing will promote this shift.

All methods of eliciting the Calming Response will require one or both of two types of breathing: what I call "natural" breathing, and "deep" breathing. A simple exercise will teach you both of these breathing techniques.

1. Lie down on a rug or on your bed, with your legs relaxed and straight and your hands by your sides.

2. Let yourself breathe normal, easy breaths. Notice what part of your upper body rises and falls with each breath. Rest a hand on that spot. If that place is your chest, you are not taking full advantage of your lungs. If your stomach region (abdomen) is moving instead, you are doing fine.

3. If your hand is on your chest, place your other hand on your stomach region. Practice breathing into that area, without producing a rise in the chest. If you need help in accomplishing this, consciously protrude your stomach region each time you inhale.

By breathing into your lower lungs, you are using your respiratory system to its full potential. This is what I mean when I use the term *natural breathing:* gentle, slow, easy breathing into your lower lungs and not your upper chest. It is the method you should use throughout your normal daily activities.

4. *Deep breathing* is an extension of this normal process. With one hand on your chest and one on your abdomen, take a slow, deep breath, first filling your lower lungs, then your upper lungs. When you exhale, let your upper lungs go first (causing your upper hand to drop), then your lower lungs (causing your lower hand to drop). This deep breathing is used at the start of the Deep Muscle Relaxation exercise in chapter 12 and also in exercises later in the book.

5. Practice the natural slow breathing and the deep slow breathing several times, until you become familiar with each process. Remind yourself to practice the natural breathing technique often throughout each day. No matter how awkward it feels now, with practice it will eventually come naturally and automatically.

These are very important techniques. Just like the relaxation exercises, they are foundation skills that will later assist you in managing your symptoms. Soon you can incorporate them into relaxation exercises. But don't overload your circuits by trying to remember too many things at once. For a while, simply practice natural breathing several times each day.

NATURAL BREATHING

Give this exercise your full attention.

1. Gently and slowly inhale a normal amount of air through your nose, filling only your lower lungs.
2. Exhale easily.
3. Continue this slow, gentle breathing with a relaxed attitude, concentrating on filling only the lower lungs.

One reminder: if you take too many deep-breathing breaths in a row instead of slow, gentle breaths, you will produce a sensation of light-headedness—the same feeling people get when they hyperventilate. It means you have just reduced the body's level of carbon dioxide. This is not harmful in the short run, only uncomfortable if you are not expecting it or don't know why it is occurring. All you have to do is return to *natural breathing* and that symptom will disappear,

You may have heard someone suggest breathing into a paper bag when you hyperventilate. That is logical: when you breathe into the bag, you use up all the oxygen in that small area. Less oxygen goes into your bloodstream, more carbon dioxide is added, and your symptoms disappear. Breathing in the natural manner described in this exercise will accomplish the same goal. In fact, some persons who have suffered from hyperventilation-type panics have completely cured themselves by learning one skill: natural breathing.

If clinical studies are accurate, your body's physical improvement will begin long before you consciously recognize any change. Therefore, you will probably need to have faith that a change in breathing habits will help you. Your breathing pattern is one of the foundation skills upon which everything else in this book is built. Unless it is in place, other attempts to control your symptoms will not get the physiological support they require.

If you have never had the opportunity to learn a formal method of producing the Calming Response, now is an excellent time to begin. In chapter 12 you will find a description of four techniques. If you have never learned a formal relaxation or meditation exercise, take the time to read through chapter 12. Choose one of the four methods, or experiment with each of them. Begin as soon as you are ready, since the techniques I will present in later chapters presume a basic understanding of and proficiency in at least one of these methods. If you have learned formal relaxation or meditation in the past, yet still have problems succeeding at some of the new techniques in this book, you may choose to practice them again. Many of my clients who have successfully controlled panic attacks make formal relaxation or meditation time a continuing part of their daily activities. They consider it "preventative medicine," just like getting regular exercise or eating a proper diet. Some follow the motto, "If you are too busy to meditate, you're too busy."

12
Releasing Tensions

When a person thinks about a situation related to her anxiety, mental images activate the muscles into particular patterns of tension, as though bracing for a blow to the body. Dr. Edmund Jacobson was the first to propose that physical relaxation and anxiety are mutually exclusive. In other words, if a person learns how to recognize which muscle groups are tense and can physically let go of that tension, then she will lower her emotional anxiety at that moment.

I have designed an audiotape program and instruction manual that will help you practice certain skills described in this book (see Resources, p. 367). Three of those tapes help you learn formal relaxation skills outlined in this chapter. The first exercise in this chapter gives you an opportunity to learn how you personally experience tension. Called Cue-Controlled Deep Muscle Relaxation, it is based on well-researched and time-tested methods for training your mind to notice the subtle cues of muscle tension—and to release that tension.

Some people find that a passive technique to quiet the mind and relax the body is more suited to their personal style than Cue-Controlled Deep Muscle Relaxation. You will have two choices if you prefer a technique of this nature. One is called Generalized Relaxation and Imagery, and the second is a meditation practice. All three of these methods are useful in learning the general skills of clearing the mind and calming the body.

CUE-CONTROLLED DEEP MUSCLE RELAXATION

This exercise, which takes approximately twenty minutes, trains your body's large muscles to respond to the cues you give. Your task is consciously to notice what muscle tension feels like in specific areas of your body and consciously to release that tension. Learning this particular technique is not essential to conquering panic. It is, however, one of the best ways to learn about your tension and how to alter it. If you have learned a different technique that produces these results, or if you have already mastered this skill, feel free to move on to the next sections of the book.

I suggest that my clients practice this exercise once a day every day for five weeks. Why so often for so long? Because this is a straightforward, mechanical exercise that physically trains the muscles to release their tension. At certain intervals during the exercise, you are asked to repeat a cue word, such as "loosen" or "relax." It seems to take about five weeks of practice before the physical loosening of the muscles becomes associated with that cue word. You will be creating new "circuits" between your brain and your muscles, as I described in chapter 10.) Once the learning has taken place, the muscles will be prepared to release their tensions rapidly when that cue word is spoken (along with several other cues that I will mention later).

GENERALIZED RELAXATION AND IMAGERY

In Cue-Controlled Deep Muscle Relaxation, you rely on tensing the muscles first as a way to experience relaxation. As an option, or for an occasional change of pace, you may want to try the twenty-minute Generalized Relaxation and Imagery exercise. In this practice you will focus only on relaxing—not tensing—your muscles. In addition, several new visual images are added to help you increase your sense of comfort and well-being as you enjoy peace and quiet.

MEDITATION

After considering all three methods, you may prefer meditation instead of a relaxation technique as a way to release tensions. Meditation is a family of mental exercises that generally involve sitting quietly and comfortably while focusing on some simple internal or external stimulus, such as a word, one's breathing pattern, or a visual object. In relaxation, the individual engages in a number of mental, and sometimes physical, activities. In meditation, the person is physically still and has a much narrower focus of attention.

There are a number of potential benefits to learning meditation, and I will explain them later in this chapter. These benefits fall within two general categories. First, meditation helps you to gain control of your physical tension by eliciting the Calming Response. Studies show that during meditation, as well as during relaxation, the heart rate and respiration rate slow down and blood pressure diminishes. Over time, meditators report feeling less daily anxiety, and they tend to recover more quickly after highly anxious times. Thus, meditation and relaxation provide similar gains for controlling physical tension.

The second category of benefits offers the greatest distinct contribution to those who experience panic. Learning the skills of meditation can dramatically increase your ability to control your fearful thinking by teaching you new ways to respond to your automatic thoughts, emotions, and images. The typical panic-prone person dwells on her worries, pays close attention to fearful thoughts, and responds emotionally to her negative images. Instead of being in control of these experiences, she is controlled by them.

To learn to meditate is to learn how to step away from these experiences to become a detached, quiet observer of your thoughts, emotions, and images, as though you were watching them from the outside. Anyone who has experienced panic knows that the negative thinking during panic is so powerful that you can't simply say to yourself, "These thoughts are ridiculous. I am not about to die." That only invites a mental argument that increases panic: "Yes, I am about to die! My heart's racing a mile a minute. People die under this kind of stress."

Any type of self-change strategy requires as a first step the skill of self-observation. To reduce your anxiety reaction and halt your negative thinking, you must be capable of stepping back from them far enough to put them in perspective. Chapters 13 through 16 will teach you how to gain that perspective and use it to control panic. This chapter gives you the foundation skills needed to implement those techniques.

There are two types of meditation to choose from. Since both accomplish similar goals, you can practice either or both of them. The first is concentration meditation.

Concentration Meditation

The four essential prerequisites for doing this meditation are (1) a quiet place, (2) a comfortable position, (3) an object to dwell on, and (4) a passive attitude.

Just as with the relaxation techniques, you should use a quiet place in your home or elsewhere to practice. Then, assume a comfortable body posture and begin to invite a passive attitude within your mind, meaning that you don't need to worry about or become critical of distracting thoughts. You just note them, let them go, and return to the object you are dwelling on. The difference is that during meditation you select one object to focus on continually during the twenty minutes. You may choose a word (such as "calm," "love," "peace"), a religious phrase ("Let go and let God"), a short sound (such as "ahh" or "omm"), a feeling, or a thought. You gently repeat that word or phrase silently at an easy pace. (For instance, if it is a one-syllable sound, you might say it once on the inhale and once on the exhale.) Or you may use your breathing pattern as the focus of your attention.

Both in meditation and in relaxation you are attempting to quiet your mind and to pay attention to only one thing at a time. An especially important skill to develop is that passive attitude. There should be no effort involved in the meditation. You pay attention to instructions, but you don't struggle to achieve any goal. You don't have to work to create any images; you don't have to put any effort into feeling any sensations in your body. All you have to do is remain aware, be in a comfortable position, dwell on the phrase, and easily let go of any distracting thoughts until those twenty minutes are over. That is the passive attitude.

A modification to this traditional concentration meditation, called "One Hundred Counts," is presented on pages 224–25 in chapter 15. It can help you remain mentally focused if you continue to be bothered by irrelevant thoughts. A second modification of this technique is a tape called "Acoustic Meditation," which provides pleasant sounds, patterns, and rhythms to enhance your ability to concentrate. See "Resources" (page 367) for information.

Awareness Meditation

The second meditative technique is awareness meditation. In concentration meditation, you dwell on one object and consider all other awareness as distractions. In awareness meditation, each new event that arises (including thoughts, fantasies, and emotions), becomes the meditative object. Nothing that rises up independent of your direction is distraction. The only distractions are the comments that you begin to have about what you see, hear or feel.

The process is as follows. Find a quiet place to sit comfortably for twenty minutes. Begin by focusing on your natural breathing pattern. Mentally follow each gentle inhalation and exhalation, without judgment and without comment. (Those who become anxious when attending to their breath may focus on a single word or sound instead.) After a few minutes, allow your attention to shift easily among any perceptions that rise up. As each new thought or sensation registers in your mind, observe it in a detached manner. As you observe it, give that perception a name.

In the first few minutes of meditation you focus your awareness on each breath. As you loosen your attention you soon notice the tension you are holding in your forehead muscles. Without effort or struggle, subvocalize a name of the experience—perhaps "tension" or "forehead tension"—and continue observing. Eventually, your perception will shift. As your detached observing mind follows your awareness, you take notice of a mental image of a man's face with the corners of his mouth turned downward. Do not become involved with the image: don't analyze its meaning or wonder why it appears. Simply notice it and name it—"frown" or "man, sad face"—while you maintain your uncritical perspective. When you lose your detachment or become involved in emotions or focused on a decision, return your full concentration to your breathing pattern until you regain your detached observer. Everyone gets caught up in their experiences from time to time during meditation. Don't be self-critical if you continually drift off and fail to expel those perceptions. In concentration meditation you merely relax, let go, and focus back on your meditative word. In awareness meditation you relax, let go, and follow the flow of your perceptions from a distance. *What* you observe is not important. *How* you observe is the key: without evaluation and without involved comments.

What You Can Learn from Meditation

You needn't become a skilled meditator to gain benefits from meditative practice. In fact, highly anxious people will find that the two relaxation techniques are easier to follow, and they may wish to choose one of those as a long-term method to relax their muscles and quiet their mind. However, it is the process of *practicing* meditation that provides the valuable understanding that you can directly apply to controlling panic, even if you only practice the technique for several weeks.

Consider that during panic we become consumed by our momentary experience. We notice the unpleasant sensations in our body and become frightened by our interpretation of their meaning ("I'm going to faint," or "I won't be able to breathe.") We notice our surroundings and become frightened by how we interpret what we see ("There's no support here for me. This is a dangerous place right now.") We reinforce these sensations and thoughts by conjuring up terrifying images of ourselves not surviving the experience. Most of our thoughts, emotions, and images are out of proportion to reality. To gain control of these moments we must become skilled at disengaging from our personal distortions.

We will not develop this skill by waiting until our next panic to practice. By then it's too late, because panic has control. The best time to learn a basic skill is during nonanxious periods. Then, we introduce that new skill gradually, over time, into the problem situation.

Here are the valuable learnings you can glean from meditative practice:

1. Meditation is a form of relaxation training. You learn to sit in a comfortable position and breathe in a calm, effortless way.

2. You learn to quiet your mind, to slow down the racing thoughts, and to tune in to more subtle internal cues. You acquire the ability to self-observe.

3. You practice the skill of focusing your attention on one thing at a time and doing so in a relaxed, deliberate fashion. By reducing the number of thoughts and images that enter your mind during a brief period, you are able to think with greater clarity and simplicity about whatever task you wish to accomplish.

4. You master the ability to notice when your mind wanders from a task, to direct your mind back to the task, and to hold it there, at least for brief periods. At first there may be a longer interval between when your mind wanders and when you notice it. With continued practice, you learn to catch yourself closer and

closer to the moment in which you lose track of your task.

5. Through meditation you desensitize yourself to whatever is on your mind. You are able to notice your personal fears, concerns, or worries and at the same time step back and become detached from them. In this manner you can learn about your problems instead of being consumed by them.

6. If you regularly practice meditation and are able to feel more relaxed during that time, you gain the experience of mastery: your voluntary actions produce pleasurable changes in your body and mind.

7. As you acquire the knowledge of how you feel when you are calm, then you can use that feeling as a reference point during your day. For instance, if you feel calm after meditation in the morning, you will have a greater chance of noticing the subtle cues of tension later in the day. In other words, meditation (as well as relaxation) helps you become more alert to what circumstances are stressful in your life. You then have time to intervene in your circumstances before your tension builds to uncomfortable proportions.

8. In the upcoming chapters you will learn the importance of noticing your thought process leading up to and during panic. You must develop the sensitivity (1) to notice those thoughts, (2) to then let those thoughts go, and finally, (3) to turn your attention to some specific supportive tasks. That is no simple feat! By practicing meditation you practice those three steps without simultaneously struggling with the frightening experience of panic.

9. Some people attempt to overcome the anxious thoughts leading up to panic by replacing them with positive thoughts. For instance, if they are thinking, "I'm about to lose control and go crazy," they will begin to simultaneously tell themselves, "No, I won't. I've never gone crazy before. I'll calm down soon." Sometimes this is quite a successful strategy. At other times, though, it can backfire by producing an internal quarrel. In arguments, we tend to "dig in" to defend our position, and that's what can happen here: the fearful thoughts only get stronger. A central strategy you will learn in the coming chapters is first to stop those fearful comments completely by shifting your attention to some neutral task. Then, after disrupting your fearful thoughts for a few seconds or a few minutes, you will be better able to introduce positive, supportive suggestions without risking the internal battle. The

two meditative techniques in this chapter teach you this basic skill. In chapter 15 you will learn two of these interrupting processes— Calming Breath and Calming Counts—which are similar to brief forms of meditation.

WHICH METHOD IS BEST FOR YOU?

One essential purpose of practicing formal relaxation or meditation is to give your mind and body the peaceful rest that comes when- ever you elicit the Calming Response. By practicing one of these methods daily for a number of weeks, you learn how you feel when you calm down. You discover that you don't "lose control" as you let go of your tensions; you actually *gain* control. Choose whichever method interests you, then give yourself time to catch on to the technique.

I have outlined a number of benefits that can come from medita- tion. If you are a person who is plagued with many anxious thoughts, you will probably have an easier time with concentration meditation rather than awareness meditation, since it provides you with a specific mental focus. Research suggests that people who experience predominantly physical symptoms of anxiety can dimin- ish these tensions best through regular practice of active techniques such as Deep Muscle Relaxation. Engaging in some form of regular physical exercise—such as walking, dancing, or active sports—can also help control anxiety that you express physically. If you want a variety of suggestions during your relaxation practice and also want the pleasure of sitting quietly without having to move your muscle groups, then you will like Generalized Relaxation and Imagery. Even if you prefer one of the two formal relaxation methods, I sug- gest that you spend some time with meditative practice. Use medi- tation to teach yourself how to interrupt your intrusive thoughts while you use relaxation to gain a sense of calmness.

Whichever approach you choose, your initial concentration will take serious effort. Invest your time, and don't be self-critical if you notice few immediate positive results. Use the time as practice, not as a test. Even the simple task of sitting quietly for twenty minutes each day can bring rewards.

13

How to Inoculate Yourself Against Panic: The Eight Attitudes of Recovery

We've covered a lot of ground together. And there is certainly much information in these pages for you to absorb! How are you feeling about this project? Some people can feel that the task of controlling panic is daunting. When you consider the need to remember so many facts, suggestions, and techniques along the way, you can feel downright overwhelmed.

This chapter will help you feel more in control by giving you the Big Picture of how to handle panic. It will offer a way to organize all that you are learning into several common points of view. My intention from the beginning has been to give you as much information as you could possibly use, because you must become a student of panic to really take control of it. On top of that knowledge base you need to have many tricks and maneuvers to help with your anxiety. Yet every year that I work with people having panic attacks I become more convinced that you have one *primary* task. That is to manage your attitude. *Attitude* means your basic view of your relationship with panic and anxiety, your judgment of panic, your belief about how you should act in the face of anxiety.

As we approach any task, our attitudes and beliefs influence the degree to which we are willing to try to solve problems, our determination to persist in the face of obstacles, and the amount of time and energy we devote to the endeavor. So, pay attention to all the skills in this book, and practice those skills regularly. Review the facts on any special areas of interest to you. Follow the step-by-step guidelines in the last chapter. But when you are ready to take on panic, focus *primarily* on your attitude. That will be the driving force of your healing.

Few self-help books put most of their marbles on "attitude." Typically they will direct you to make lists of your strengths, prioritize your goals, experiment with new behaviors, and record your changes. These are excellent suggestions for a self-help approach, but it is the nature of *panic* that requires you to go beyond technique to modifying your attitude. I firmly believe—after talking with thousands of people in treatment sessions, training programs and public lectures—that it is attitude, not technique, that will take you across the finish line.

Consider the possibility that you can "inoculate" yourself with these eight statements. One of the greatest achievements in medicine began when William Jenner discovered that fluid from cowpox sores could immunize people against the deadly disease of smallpox. Physicians can now inoculate against dozens of illnesses, from polio, rubella, and yellow fever to tetanus, hepatitis B and rabies.

A vaccine consists of a dead or modified form of a disease-causing microbe. Once injected, it stimulates the body's production of antibodies to the microbe. If the microbe should subsequently enter the body, the antibodies help neutralize and remove the microbe from the body before it can multiply and cause disease.

You inoculate yourself by taking in some of the causative agent in order to experiment with it or to become immune to it. Therefore, inoculations are paradoxical treatments: they take you close to what you want to avoid. That's how you can use this chapter. *Stop* doing the activities that seem instinctual in the face of panic. Instead, go directly *toward* panic, drop your guard and let it touch you. Clearly you will be "experimenting" when you apply these inoculating attitudes. I predict that you also will become immune to panic, which means "not affected by or responsive to panic."

How valuable can your attitude be? I know some people who have applied *no* techniques—they didn't control their breathing, they didn't learn relaxation skills, they didn't plan strategies for coping with symptoms—and they still brought their panic under control in a matter of weeks. They did that by focusing strictly on the eight attitudes presented in this chapter.

The reverse is not true. I have known many more people who have attempted to apply techniques without a shift in their attitude. They used the techniques while simultaneously thinking, "This better work! I can't stand this anxiety. I shouldn't be feeling this way." Unfortunately, they continued to struggle with symptoms of anxiety and panic.

So, the point is this: *especially* when things aren't working for you, when you follow suggestions and they just don't seem to help, *that* is an important time to return to this chapter and check on your attitude. Anytime you begin to experience a few symptoms of anxiety returning, again pay attention to applying these attitudes to your symptoms.

Have I grabbed your attention? I hope so, because it's easy for one chapter—no matter how important it is—to get lost among twenty others.

THE EIGHT ATTITUDES OF RECOVERY

Expected Attitudes	Healing Attitudes
"I can't let anyone know." →	"I am not ashamed."
"Panic is evil, bad, the enemy." →	"What can I learn as a student of panic?"
"I want to avoid the symptoms." →	"I want to face the symptoms to gain skills."
"I *must* relax *right now*." →	"It's O.K. to be anxious here."
"I must stay on guard." →	"I won't guard myself against anxiety."
"This is a test." →	"This is practice."
"I must be certain that there is no risk." →	"I can tolerate uncertainty."
"This had better work." →	"It's O.K. if it doesn't work."

As you practice your skills to overcome panic, take a look at your basic attitudes and consider any changes that might make you more determined and committed to solving this problem. The kinds of statements people make about themselves or their behaviors often represent their attitudes.

In this chapter, two contrasting statements reflect each of these eight attitude shifts. The first self-statement in each pair reflects a personal position that undermines the task of controlling panic. It is the most likely way that any of us would think about such a difficulty, so it's no surprise if you think this way. It comes *quite naturally*. The problem is, it doesn't work. When put into action, it works against your desired goal of healing. The motto I go by is this: if what you are doing isn't working, try *anything* else.

The second self-statement in each pair reflects the attitude I encourage you to explore. It moves you away from being a victim of anxiety and toward the freedom of panic-free living. But I must warn you, it might feel *quite unnatural* to hold these attitudes in the face of panic or anxiety.

1. "I can't let anyone know." ⟶ "I am not ashamed."

It's hard to let others know of our problems. First, we can feel embarrassed to admit that we don't have our lives together as well as (we fantasize) they have theirs. Then, if our problems are lasting awhile, we don't want others to get fed up with our complaints. Or we might explain what's bothering us only to have others say, "I don't get it. I don't know what you mean." Or, worse yet, "What's the big deal?" In addition, people can start giving us advice on how to fix it and expect us to take action soon. Speaking to someone about a problem doesn't mean that we are feeling courageous enough to try to fix it. These possible reactions can be good reasons to keep our problems to ourselves.

There are at least two other reasons to be secretive when the problem is panic attacks. The first is the stigma around mental-health problems. Think how easy it is for employees to call in sick because they have the flu, or even a migraine headache. But who's willing to say, "I'm having a bout of depression that's going to keep me out for a couple of days"? You can tell your boss you have to miss that cross-country trip tomorrow because your grandmother died. It takes more strength to admit you are afraid of flying. A mental-health problem can be seen as a mark of disgrace.

Second, failure to control panic can heighten our own feelings of shame and low self-esteem. Not being able to travel in the same circles as our peers, or perform tasks that seem so simple to others and were once simple for us—it's easy to see how that wears down our sense of self-worth. And as our sense of self-worth diminishes, we become even more susceptible to the influence of panic. For instance, if you believe you are not worth much as a human being, then you will be less likely to try to help yourself. If you believe that this panic simply reflects your lack of basic skills necessary to cope with the world, then you will be more likely to face the stressful events of your life.

I think it is best to address all of these fears—social embarrassment, lack of understanding, stigma—by first addressing our beliefs about our own worth. This will help us touch our guilt and shame, and any feelings of personal inadequacy. I don't expect to do a complete makeover of your personality in a few pages. However, I do want to instill in you the attitude that you deserve to feel self-respect.

Panic requires that you work on building up your self-worth, self-confidence, and self-love, because panic has the powerful ability to wear away at your psychological vulnerabilities, to weaken your resolve. When you feel you have to hide your problem, then every time panic arises, you will begin to tighten up inside. You will try to contain it, not let it spill out, not let it be seen. When you attempt to contain panic, it grows. When you respect yourself, you can begin to make decisions based on what will help you heal, not what will protect you from others' scrutiny. When you make that change, you starve panic by supporting yourself and letting others support you through this tough time.

Look over this list and see whether any of the statements reflect your beliefs about yourself:

I am inferior to others.
I'm not worth much.
I'm disgusted with myself.
I don't fit in with others.
I'm just no good as a person.
There's something wrong with me, or inherently flawed about
    me.
I'm weak. I should be stronger.
I shouldn't be feeling this way.

There's no reason for all this anxiety I'm feeling.
I shouldn't be having these crazy thoughts.
I should already be better.
I'm hopeless.
I've had this problem too long.
I've tried everything; I'm not going to improve.
My problems are too ingrained.

Such self-critical attitudes support the first stages of restricting our options. We start to limit the way we act around others. If we feel as though we don't fit in, or that we are not worth much to those around us, we tend to protect ourselves from rejection. We think of others first and ourselves second:

I can't tell anyone.
I can't bother other people with my problems.
I have to take care of others.
I can't let people see me this way.
People won't think I'm O.K. if they know I'm anxious.
I must hide my anxiety, hold it all in, not let anyone know my
    feelings, fight it.

This chapter focuses on the influences of our beliefs on our daily lives. These include the belief that we are worthy of success and happiness and the belief that we have a variety of positive choices available to us in our lives. These are attitudes that help us solve problems. They are convictions that affirm us.

An affirmation is a positive thought that supports us as we move toward our desired goals. Your greatest internal strength will come from the ways you affirm your worth as a person. There are two kinds of affirmations to explore. The first are beliefs concerning who you are, and the second are beliefs about what you need to do in this life to succeed. Consider the following statements. How might you change your approach to your life if you believed these words?

Accepting Who I Am

I'm O.K. just the way I am.
I am lovable and capable.

I am an important person.
I'm already a worthy person; I don't have to prove myself.
My feelings and needs are important.
I deserve to be supported by those who care about me.
I deserve to be respected, nurtured, and cared for.
I deserve to feel free and safe.
I'm strong enough to handle whatever comes along.

No one expects you to change a long-standing attitude overnight. But if you can continue to reflect on these attitudes until you begin to believe them, you will be on your way to overcoming panic. Building up our sense of self-worth increases our ability to confront the obstacles to our freedom.

The second kind of affirmation has to do with our expectations about how we must act around others. It reminds us that we don't have to please everyone else and ignore our own wants and needs, that we all get to make mistakes as we are learning, and that we don't need to view every task as a test of our competence or worth.

Supporting What I Do

It's O.K. to say no to others.
It's good for me to take time for myself.
It's O.K. to think about what I need.
The more I get what I need, the more I'll have to give others.
I don't have to take care of everyone else.
I don't have to be perfect to be loved.
I can make mistakes and still be O.K.
Everything is practice; I don't have to test myself.
I am not ashamed.

These attitudes give us permission to take the time we need to feel healthy, rested, and excited about life. They insulate us against the paralyzing poison of shame.

Explore what obstacles stand in the way of these affirmations for you. Perhaps you will find some clues in chapter 4's discussion of the panic-prone personality. Sometimes discussing these issues with a close friend or a self-help group helps. Other times the causes of these blocks are not so clear or easily removed. If you feel stuck, consider turning to a mental-health professional for insight and guidance.

Once you address the issues that block your willingness to support yourself, pay attention to these affirmations. Find ways to accept these kinds of statements, then let your actions reflect these beliefs. (You may have to begin by *acting* as though you believe them—even when you don't—before you discover how well they will serve you.) In addition to the support of friends and a mental-health professional, look for courses in your community on assertiveness training. Such course teach you how to turn your positive beliefs into actions.

2. "Panic is evil,   ⟶   "What can I learn as
   bad, the enemy."   a student of panic?"

Who wouldn't be angry and rejecting toward something that produces such chaos in your life? Seeing panic as the enemy is a natural response. I assume that up to now you have had plenty of practice viewing panic as the villain. Now try something new—consider panic your teacher.

The martial arts, developed in Asia, teach self-discipline, physical combat technique, and a philosophy, or attitude, about life. All but one are ancient schools. Aikido, a twentieth-century martial art based on love and dedicated to peace, puts a different spin on the art of self-defense. And "spin" is an appropriate expression. In the Western world, we use boxing as the prototype for fighting. If someone punches, you punch back. You meet force with opposing force. By contrast, the traditional martial arts axiom is "Push when pulled and pull when pushed."

As the attacker approaches you to push or punch, you learn to grab the forward moving hand and pull it. You don't oppose the challenger with equal force. You take the attacker's movement and energy and use it against him. For instance, as he pushes, you pull him past you and onto the ground.

In Aikido the axiom "Push when pulled and pull when pushed" becomes "turn when pushed and enter when pulled." You accept, join, and move with the challenger's energy flow in the direction it is going. You offer nothing for the challenger to resist. You turn and spin with the attacker instead of moving past him.

Imagine teaching an American the art of Aikido. It requires *sincerely welcoming* the attack and struggle, *truly understanding* the attacker's intentions, *loving* the attacker. The moment the challenger begins to approach with an attack, the Aikido student shifts her position. She stands with open arms and open palms, "welcoming" the challenger. If you try it for a moment, holding your arms out by your side with your palms open to the front, you will notice how vulnerable you feel.

I will leave the details of other Aikido moves to the masters. It is the basic attitude that I want to address. The attitudinal stance in Aikido is that each challenge is an opportunity to learn and practice, not something dangerous or frightening. The student views the challenge as a gift of energy, a creative system of joining rather than one of conflict. This view eliminates the notion of "enemy."

Let's apply this to your relationship with panic. First of all, please know that I realize how frightening a panic attack is. You can't simply "relax" in the face of panic, because your body is flowing with adrenaline-produced anxiety. This is a given: you begin with the normal human reaction of fear. What we are doing with this attitude shift is taking that state of fear and changing it. We are moving from an *automatic* reaction toward a *designed* reaction, one that brings you freedom and personal choice. The way we will change fear is by *adding* something to it, not by taking your fear away.

As you enter that restaurant, drive across that bridge, sit down in the middle aisle at the movies, or walk up to that group at the party, be curious about your anxiety. How is it expressing itself right now? What is it inviting you to be afraid of? What skills is it encouraging you to practice at this moment?

If you suffer from panic attacks, your best stance will be "Panic, anxiety, you have something to teach me. What is it? Help me understand myself."

Perhaps over time panic will teach you to stand up for yourself and be more assertive. Maybe it will lead you to be more self-revealing and vulnerable around those who love you. Or it might help you express your deeper desires for what is important in life, to take you out of the trap of playing the role of good mother, wife, employee. While I don't know what you, in particular, will learn, I do know that *every* student learns once she focuses on her desire to learn.

I am not saying that panic *always* comes into people's lives because they are missing some basic learning (although sometimes it does). Taking the stance of a student who truly wants to learn is a way to *stop* taking a resistant stance toward panic. The focus of our attention right now is how to get better. Choose to become a student of panic because it is the attitude that best moves you toward health. If you are paying attention to how you can learn from panic, then you will stop fighting *against* panic. As you reduce your fear and defensiveness, you influence the entire dynamic of your relationship with panic, and it can no longer rule your body.

3. "I want to avoid" ➞ "I want to face the symptoms the symptoms. to gain skills."

Another common expression in the martial arts is "Love the mat." During the learning process you'll find yourself again and again lying flat out on the mat after your opponent gets the best of you. By embracing challenging experiences as a necessary part of your training, you reduce your resistance to the learning process. "Love the mat" is a winning attitude of the student who knows that she doesn't always get to be in control.

The only way to get the best of panic is to face the symptoms directly and practice your skills. Many people make the error of designing practice sessions in which they enter the fearful situations *until the point* that they feel discomfort. Then they retreat. This approach makes their recovery process long and arduous.

The task of provoking your symptoms requires courage. Think of courage as "being scared and doing it anyway." This way, as you face panic, you don't have to *get rid* of fear, you need to *add* courage. In fact, you only need courage in fearful situations!

Provoking your symptoms is exactly what I encourage you to do. Don't wait until your weekly schedule puts you into a panicky situation. Set up events that will provoke your distress. Some would say that this goes beyond courage to stupidity. It's like being in the jungle and running *toward* the lion's roar. But that *is* the move, and the expression "run toward the roar" will be a useful reminder.

If your symptoms suddenly end without any effort on your part, that will be a wonderful experience. However, you will still be open to blackmail by panic because you have yet to learn how to respond to the symptoms when they come. If at any point in the future the symptoms return, you'll be back at ground zero: reacting to panic with many of the eight expected attitudes. Although it is difficult to push yourself into situations that make you anxious, those efforts will help inoculate you against panic's control of your future.

Your job here is to be proactive, not reactive. Don't wait for the anxiety-provoking situations to arrive. Look around your world for ways to stir up trouble. Ask yourself, "What can I do to get myself anxious today?"

I can still remember Mary B.'s words: "Come on, panic, give me your best shot." Here's how she set the scene. "I was at the library gathering some research for a paper. After about twenty or thirty minutes I suddenly started feeling quite anxious and confined. I really wanted to run out of there. My body started shaking, I felt light-headed and I lost all concentration on my work. Then, I don't know how it came to me, but I decided to take the bull by the horns. I walked to the end of the row of shelves and sat down cross-legged on the floor. (I didn't want to crack my head open if I fainted.) Then I said, 'Come on, panic, give me your best shot.' And I just sat there. I sat there and took it. Within two or three minutes all the symptoms stopped. I got up and finished my work, which required about three more hours in the library."

That was quite a learning experience for Mary B. Before that night she would have left the building immediately upon noticing her symptoms, gone straight home, never finished that research, and mentally kicked herself over the next two or three weeks for having failed at her task.

The nature of panic is that it produces *involuntary* symptoms in your body. By voluntarily seeking out those symptoms you begin to change panic. You take away its involuntary nature, and start to shift the control over to you. So as you accept this challenge of "I want to face the symptoms to gain skills," remember to *love the mat* and *run toward the roar.*

4. "I *must* relax *right now.* ➡ "It's O.K. to be anxious here."

Continuing our theme, once you choose to face your symptoms, then what do you do? I have spent so much time in this book emphasizing ways to calm down. These are important skills. But equal to them is your willingness to *stay anxious.* You simply cannot escape this paradox: calm down, and let yourself stay anxious.

When anxiety hits, your instincts tell you to get rid of it. It's the American way: "Don't just stand there, do something!" But a more powerful intervention is "Don't just do something, stand there."

Although you will train yourself to respond to anxiety using coping skills that include calming your breath and quieting your thoughts, do not make relaxation a demand. When you require yourself to relax, you add another demand to an already stressful situation. That will only add to your stress.

Instead, take the more permissive attitude of, "It's O.K. that I'm anxious right now." Accepting your anxiety in the moment when it occurs will reduce the anxiety. It takes away the internal demand and helps you build your tolerance.

Your accepting inner voice may go something like this: "It is really no surprise that I am anxious right now. This is my first flight since I got scared during the trip to Orlando. I don't like to feel trapped and out of control. This is harder than driving because I can pull off the highway when I need to. I can't get off this plane whenever I want. So I'm going to practice all the skills I've brought on board with me. If I'm still anxious, that's O.K. I can handle those feelings, and as I do, I won't be so worried on the next flight."

So, shop in that mall, give that speech, go to that dinner, or climb that ladder . . . and use all your many skills to help you stay cooled out. Just add to those skills the important attitude of "It's O.K. to be anxious here."

5. "I must stay on guard." ⟶ "I won't guard myself against anxiety."

Panic leads people to become vigilant. A panic attack hits suddenly, catches you by surprise, and causes you pain. Our bodies and minds have been trained over hundreds of thousands of years to guard against pain. A toddler doesn't have to burn himself on a stove too many times before his built-in instinct trains him to watch out for stovetops. In that same way, when you've been "burned" several times by panic, your mind searches rapidly for danger signals anytime you approach a panic-provoking situation. You are watching, listening, feeling with great attention, on guard in case something "goes wrong" in your body or your surroundings. Unfortunately, all this vigilance only contributes to your distress.

You are tensing yourself up in anticipation of a problem. This is the definition of anticipatory anxiety.

What about when a panic attack begins? Think about what you say to yourself. Even *during* panic, almost all your communications are anticipatory in nature: "I'm really feeling bad right now. *What if this gets worse?*" "I'm light-headed and dizzy. What if I faint *in a moment?*" "My face feels flushed. *What if people start seeing this?*" On and on it goes. "I can't let myself *get any worse*." "I can't let the symptoms *increase*."

This natural, instinctual response to threat works against you. When you stay on guard as you approach events, you increase your tension and become more vulnerable to a panic attack. When you warn yourself to stay on guard in the *midst* of panic, you secrete even greater amounts of adrenaline into your bloodstream, causing more intense symptoms. You can't remain anxiously on guard and simultaneously learn to control panic.

The well-respected psychologist-writer, Dr. Daniel Goldman once said, "A person prevails over anxiety by sacrificing attention." To come out on top you must let down your guard. You must not pay such close attention to what might happen next. You must clear your head of its constant and frantic analysis.

Now if you do this—if you stop being so vigilant—you run the risk that something might slip past your conscious attention. Some little twinge in your body might go unnoticed. You might not see that four cars are waiting in line ahead of you in the left turn lane at the stop light. So, as usual, here is an intervention into your problem that can at first make you *more* anxious, not less. When in the past you have kept your guard up as a way to stay in control, I am suggesting that you now let down your guard. Now, you may feel that you are not protecting yourself. If you feel vulnerable, you'll probably feel a little anxious in response. (This is another reason to become a student of the attitude, "It's O.K. to be anxious here.")

There are two further considerations here. The first is a paradoxical one (no surprise): when you are considering the possibility of confronting an anxiety-provoking situation, it is fine to plan out how you will take care of yourself. In chapter 18 I will walk you through such preparations. But make those plans with the expectation that you may become a bit anxious, and *not* with the fearful dread that panic might strike. Include in those plans your decision to accept any anxiety as it arises, without holding yourself in a death grip waiting for its arrival. The paradox to play with is *plan, and don't stay on guard*.

Second, let's consider where you *can* place your attention when you pull it away from your anxious anticipation. If you will reflect for a moment, I think you can appreciate just how much time and attention you devote to dreaded anticipation. There are so many valuable things to be doing with your attention. The world outside you offers beautiful, warm, sunny days in the summer and the soft glow of a fire in the winter, the embraces and laughter shared with those who love you, the challenges of solving problems at work and home, the stimulating interest of conversation, music, study. When you are anxious, turn your attention *outside* yourself. Become connected to life, and allow that rich healing contact to influence your feelings. Stop trying to figure yourself out! Be anxious and *simultaneously* become interested in your surroundings.

There is a second choice for your attention when you stop focusing on what terrible things might happen in the future. Pay loving, caring attention to *yourself* in *this moment*. By asking, "How am I feeling *right now?*" and "What do I need *right now?*" you will contribute to your self-control far more than by asking, "What will I do if that terrible thing happens next?" Start supporting yourself on the basis of what you need at this moment, instead of becoming anxious about what will happen thirty seconds from now. The upcoming chapters will suggest what actions to take. Apply those skills with the attitude "I don't need to stay on guard against panic."

6. "This is a test." ⟶ "This is practice."

I hope that I will never take another exam to receive another certification within my profession, even though every month I set aside special time to study. At forty-three, I'm no longer interested in jumping through hoops to prove to someone else that I can do my job as a psychologist.

I can remember what it was like preparing for my last licensing exam: four months of studying fifteen hours per week, plus holding down a job. If I failed the exam, I'd have to take it again in six months, and eventually I'd have to pass it to be a psychologist. I worried going in, because only a certain percentage of psychologists can pass; many people *must* fail each test, on the basis not of their score, but of the ranking of their score. I passed that exam. But during the months, days, and especially hours before it, I had to work on handling my worry as well as my knowledge areas.

It seems that people who are prone to panic attacks turn many experiences into tests. When you decide to enter a previously difficult situation, do you say, "This will be a test of how well these new skills work"? As soon as you declare it a test, your body is going to secrete adrenaline, because you will be saying to yourself, "Uh-oh, I'd better do well," while you simultaneously imagine yourself failing. When you say, "Uh-oh," you secrete adrenaline through your body, and you feel anxious. The more you set up future events as tests, the more you are going to feel anxious.

People declare, "This is a test" before an event, and they declare, "I failed that test" after the event. I have watched clients improve steadily week after week. Then, one week, they inevitably have a small setback in their progress. From this one episode they become dejected, depressed, and demoralized. They are full of self-critical and hopeless thoughts. They don't simply say, "I failed"; they then say, "And I shouldn't have" or "And that means I should quit trying" or "What's the point?" or "And that proves I'll never change."

As you begin taking action, your attitude about the task will be an important factor in your progress. I instruct my clients to consider any activity they engage in as *practice*. I take a firm stand on this point. Never view a future task as a *test* of your progress or of your ability to overcome panic. Never look back at an attempted task in order to label your efforts a failure. Never invest your sense of self-worth in the positive or negative outcome of your plans. I recommend this attitude not only for people who want to master panic, but also for all of my clients, regardless of their problem, and I attempt to support this attitude in my own life with my son and daughter.

When you decide that all your experiences are practice, you are in effect saying that you are both willing and able to learn from each of those experiences. You might fail to meet a certain goal by a certain time, but your *intentions* aren't a failure, and your *efforts* aren't a failure. They are the successful ways that people learn: setting goals and applying effort. No one knows everything about any particular subject. Our greatest scientists continually create new questions to ask about their fields of expertise. These brilliant men and women would be the first to defend the importance of maintaining the open, curious, exploratory mind of a student.

When you test yourself during every activity, you inhibit your learning. If you say to yourself, "That action I took yesterday proves that I'm never going to make it," you essentially have said, "Don't bother learning from yesterday; it's too late for you." Of course, the truth of the matter is that making mistakes and studying them are among our best learning tools.

Since everyone who takes on a challenge has setbacks, you can assume you will too. When you hear your self-critical or hopeless comments rise up, let them go. They will only distract you from learning.

It's true that if you set a goal of remaining at a party until eleven P.M. but your discomfort caused you to leave at nine-thirty, you failed to meet your goal. That is like throwing a dart at the bull's eye from fifteen feet and missing it by three rings. Let that experience be feedback to you as you take corrective action. What can you adjust for your next throw? Can you take aim at a different spot on the target? Give the dart more arc on the throw? Concentrate on your follow-through? Step closer to the target?

As you approach events, concentrate on what you can do to improve your outcome. Experiencing some worry and anxiety about the outcome is understandable. Just don't let it consume your creative thinking. There are two important focal points for your attention when you leave a scene without meeting your goal. The first is "What can I learn from my experience in that situation that I can apply next time?" The second is "How can I take care of myself now that I am leaving this difficult situation?" Practice the skill of supporting yourself in the face of a disappointment. If your goal is improving your performance next time, how do you want to treat yourself after your difficulty this time? Stop being critical of yourself and begin developing a supportive voice within you.

7. "I must be certain that ➝ "I can tolerate uncertainty."
there is no risk."

Most problems with anxiety relate to a fear of uncertainty. My educated guess is that the brain chemistry of about 20 percent of the population leads them to have a more difficult time than the average person in tolerating *uncertainty regarding risk*. Of course, this can put them at a serious disadvantage, since living demands risk. It is no wonder, then, that so many people develop anxiety problems. They worry because their brain is demanding closure on a specific issue. Their mind says, "This is how it *must* turn out for me to feel secure. And I *must* feel secure. Do I know *for certain* it will turn out this way?" It is as though they require a 100 percent guarantee that they will encounter zero risk. That is simply too much to ask of life. If you intend to go up against one of the most powerful forces of the natural world—continual change—you will have a tough time winning. Listen to these expectations of life and you will see what I mean. The person with panic attacks, phobias, or social anxieties asks such questions as:

"Can I know for certain that I won't have any symptoms?"
"Can I know for certain that I won't have to leave?"
"Can I know for certain that I won't feel trapped?"
"Can I know for certain that this isn't a heart attack?"
"Can I know for certain that I won't die on that plane?"
"Can I know for certain that I won't cause an embarrassing scene?"
"Can I know for certain that people won't stare at me?"
"Can I know for certain that I won't have a panic attack?"

If we look at a different anxiety problem, obsessive-compulsive disorder, we find the same kinds of questions:

"Can I know for certain that this object is clean?"
"Can I know for certain that I won't get contaminated if I touch the ground?"
"Can I know for certain that my family will be safe?"
"Can I know for certain that I didn't run someone over?"
"Can I know for certain that I unplugged that iron?"
"Can I know for certain that I won't kill my child?"

If it is true that some people's brains cause them to feel a strong yet inappropriate need for certainty, confronting that problem involves disrupting those demanding thoughts. It involves confronting them consistently and directly *every day* to produce the change we want. This is where your new attitude comes in. You must find ways to accept risk and tolerate uncertainty.

Stay with me as I explain how this works, because this stance doesn't seem very attractive at first glance. Whatever outcome you fear, work to find a way to *accept that outcome as a possibility.* For example, imagine that sometimes when you begin to have panicky symptoms you feel a pain in your chest that runs down one arm. Each time it happens, your first thought is, "This could be a heart attack!" Of course you have had one or more medical evaluations by a specialist. Let's also say that all physicians you consult declare that you have a strong heart, take good care of yourself, and are not at risk of a heart attack.

Nonetheless, as soon as that pain shoots down your arm, you say, "This time it really *could* be my heart! How do I know? There's no guarantee that this is only panic. And if it is a heart attack, I need help now!"

Let's also say that you've been learning to reassure yourself as a way to get some perspective on panic. "Look, guy, you've been to the emergency room twelve times in the last two years. One hundred percent of those visits have been false alarms. You know you suffer from panic attacks, and this is what *they* feel like, too. Take a few Calming Breaths, relax, wait a few minutes. You'll begin to feel better."

The reassurance lasts all of five seconds. Then you start again. "But I don't *know.* I don't know *for certain.* If this is a heart attack I could *die! *Right *now!* There's always a chance."

It's the same with people's fear of dying on a plane. Commercial flight is the safest mode of transportation we have. On average, about 100 people die on a plane per year, while 47,000 motorists die on the highways and 8,000 pedestrians die each year. If you are looking for a risk-free environment, don't stay at home; 22,000 people die of accidents a year without even leaving their houses!

Even though your odds of dying on a plane are one in 7.5 million, the dialogue goes like this, "There's still a chance I might die. And if I do, that will be the most horrible, terrifying death I can imagine." You reassure yourself, "Planes are safe. You'll be fine. The pilot has gray hair; he has twenty-five years' experience."

"Yes, but how do I *know?* How can I be *certain?*"

This is what you do to yourself, in your own unique areas of worry. You ask, "How can I be certain someone won't criticize me?" or "How can I be certain I won't have to leave the concert?" You might as well give it up, because you can never satisfy the demand for absolute confidence. No amount of reassurance will ever be enough.

Here, instead, is the attitude to strive for: "I accept the possibility of a heart attack [plane crash/panic attack] happening."

For fear of heart attacks: "I accept the possibility that this time it could actually be a heart attack. I'm going to respond to it as though it is a panic attack. I accept the risk that I might be wrong."

For fear of dying on a plane: "I accept the possibility that this plane could crash. I'm going to think and feel and act as though this plane is one hundred percent safe. I accept the risk that I might be wrong."

For fear of having to leave an event: "I accept the possibility that I might have to leave the restaurant. I imagine I'd feel embarrassed, but I'm willing to tolerate that now."

By making the decision to accept the possibility of a negative outcome, you circumvent the requirement for absolute certainty of your future comfort and safety. There's always a chance you will have a heart attack, regardless of your health. There's always a chance you could die in a plane crash, regardless of the relative safety of air travel. There's always a chance you will leave the restaurant and become embarrassed.

If you want to lower your chances of panicking and raise your chances of flying comfortably or feeling more at ease at the restaurant, you have work to do. Your job is to lower your risk of problems as much as makes common sense, then accept the remaining risk that is not under your control. You only have two other basic options. You can keep worrying about the risk while you continue with these behaviors. That leads to anxiety and the increased likelihood of panic. Or you can withdraw from these activities. The world can get by with you never flying again. The world can get by if you never enter another restaurant. There are consequences to these behaviors, of course. (It may take longer to travel to your friends or relatives, and so forth.) But it's your choice.

I encourage you, instead, to practice this idea of accepting uncertainty.

There is an interesting thing about many therapeutic interventions designed to help you control anxiety. Most actually make you more anxious at first. This one—giving up the requirement for complete confidence in the outcome—is a good example. For instance, you begin to feel that pain in your chest that shoots down you arm. Now you are saying, "I'm going to apply all my skills as though this is a panic attack. I'm not going to act as though this is a heart attack." Do you think 100 percent of you is going to agree to this plan? No way! Some part of your mind is still going to feel scared, because, try as you might, some part of you will *still* be worried about a heart attack.

If worrying, or fearful monitoring, is one of our most common ways to stay in control, then if you practice letting go of your worries, your mind and body will feel out of control. That will make you anxious. This anxiety is the distress of positive experimentation and change. It's a good kind of anxiety. Remember what Daniel Goldman said: "A person prevails over anxiety by sacrificing attention." But expect it to be uncomfortable at first anyway! Have faith that over time, this anxiety will diminish.

Reading about the next attitude shift will give you a better understanding of the value in accepting uncertainty.

8. "This had better work. ➞ "It's O.K. if it doesn't work."

Thinking out loud with Camille helped me put a bigger piece of the puzzle together.

Camille N. called me from Florida four years ago. She said she had suffered from panic attacks for many years and found the first edition of *Don't Panic* in the library last year. She was wondering if, on her trip back to New York in a month, she could stop in for a consultation. We set up the appointment, and Camille arrived as scheduled.

Camille turned out to be similar to many of the people who see me from out of state. She was an impeccable student of the techniques. She practiced formal relaxation daily. She had her breathing skills down pat. She planned her practice sessions in the anxiety-provoking situations and knew the most supportive self-talk during panicky times. But she kept having trouble.

"Like last week, for instance. I was driving down the boulevard about four-thirty, and the traffic was moderate. I needed to take a left so at the stop light I moved over into the turn lane, three lanes from the right curb, and pulled up behind four cars. Immediately three more cars pulled in behind me and the other two lanes filled with traffic. These lights are notoriously slow, and I've always hated getting trapped like that.

"When I felt my stomach get tense, I knew I had to work with my skills. First I reassured myself that I could handle this. If I needed to, I could even get out of the car, leave it right there at the light. I took a nice big Calming Breath, then started Natural Breathing. I dropped my hands from the steering wheel and let them relax in my lap. Nothing seemed to help!"

Outwardly I was attentive and positive, but inwardly I was frustrated, thinking, "Why? Why wasn't that helping? That should be working!" I felt like the Wizard of Oz. This woman has driven so far in anticipation of this specifically arranged meeting with the expert who wrote the book she depends on to get well. Now here we are, face to face, and I'm about to say, "Hmm, I'm not sure what else to suggest."

I'd love to be able to say, "Then it dawned on me . . . " In reality it took another thirty minutes of struggle to see the new opening. Both Camille and I were making the same error, and you can see it in our self-talk. She says, "Nothing seemed to help!" I said, "Why wasn't that helping? That should be working!" Despite all our combined years of study, we were unknowingly committing a basic mistake. Our immediate goal was for Camille to stop being anxious. We thought if she applied enough technique—handle your negative talk, get your breathing straight, be willing to tolerate symptoms, wait—she would get "results" of diminished anxiety.

"What's wrong with that?" you say.

Here's the answer, which may be tough to accept. While the long-term goal is to diminish your anxiety, the immediate goal is to continually monitor your attitude—to *accept exactly what you are experiencing, as you experience it*. As soon as you say, "This had better work," you are moving against this important task. It is fine to observe, study, and learn from your current experience, but don't declare that your feelings must change on demand. Our bodies and minds simply don't work that way.

This is paradox in its purest form. The attitude to aim for is, "It's O.K. that I'm anxious right now. I'm also going to fool around with getting rid of this anxiety. I'm going to try every trick and gimmick I know. I'm going to apply all my concentration, my tenacity, and my commitment to the task of getting rid of this anxiety. I'm going to use what I believe is the best combination of skills and attitudes for this specific type of anxiety. If it works, that'll be great. And if it doesn't work—if I'm still anxious—*that'll be O.K. too*."

This is the attitude that even the best students of panic tend to miss. You must step up onto the platform of acceptance. Apply your skills from there. Maintain that stance through all the good and bad responses you get to your skills. And end up standing there in the end—accepting exactly what you are experiencing— regardless of the outcome.

The most important point here is that this position—"It's O.K. if it doesn't work out"—is not about passive resignation to the status quo. It is not surrendering to the fact that "you have panic attacks and you better get used to it." Instead, it is a part of an active, dynamic process of healing. Think of this attitude as a technique that you apply throughout the moments you are either anticipating or having trouble. When you say, "This had better work," you are testing yourself and you will respond by emotionally and physically tightening up. When you tighten up, you feed panic. By saying, "It's O.K. if it doesn't work," you pull yourself out of this testing environment. Crazy as it sounds, this action of removing the demand for success actually *increases* the likelihood of your success.

Someone once said that if you want to hit the bull's eye every time, throw the dart first and then draw the circles around it. Say yes to every experience; that's where you start. There will be plenty of hardships coming your way before the final curtain. You might as well get on friendly terms with them. Say yes to them when they arrive. Then begin to manipulate them actively and creatively. The fear of being trapped is a common concern for people with panic. Freedom comes by saying yes to whatever trap life puts you in, then doing something to get yourself out. Whenever one of your attempts fails, begin immediately to do the really hard work: accept that you are still stuck in discomfort. Take time to complete that task—of accepting the dissatisfying outcome—first. Then redouble your efforts to change that outcome next time.

These eight attitudes are not simply philosophical underpinnings. They are active workhorses in your healing process. Think of attitudes in a new way; think of them as technique.

To find out their benefits for you, don't wait until you are having a panic attack. Write these eight statements on an index card and carry them with you throughout the day. Pull them out when you're feeling uncomfortable and stuck. Use them to influence what you do (or don't do) next. That's a good way to begin to learn of their benefits. It is also consistent with the metaphor of inoculation: you start by learning to accept a small amount of discomfort, and build your confidence on that experience. Nobody learns to drive by entering the Indianapolis 500. A much easier place to begin is the mall parking lot on Sunday morning, with your supportive parent sitting next to you. Master these attitudes gradually by giving them a chance in lower-risk situations. Then gradually turn your attention to those panic-provoking situations.

Who knows? Maybe these are the only "techniques" you'll need.

14

Your Mind's Observer

In the first nine chapters you learned about the complexity of panic. Now we will begin to apply that information to a specific task: controlling an actual panic episode. To do so we must first make the complex simple. When you face panic you will want to rid yourself of unnecessary worries or questions and replace them with a few simple thoughts. In order to think clearly during panic, you must understand how panic attacks take place.

You are already familiar with your physical symptoms, and I have discussed them in chapters 1, 8, and 11. But panic is not those symptoms alone. If it were only the physical discomforts, panic could disappear from your life as rapidly as it enters. In chapter 7 I identified the manner in which panic becomes more than just the physical. It invades your mental processes as well. In fact, a panic episode often begins *in reaction to* your thoughts ("I wonder how I'll feel today? I wonder if I'll feel nervous again?").

For a panic attack to grow in intensity, you must do two things:

1. You must closely observe your current experience.
2. You must comment on those observations.

To reduce panic you can change either one of these acts. Let's look at each of them more closely.

Imagine that you are interested in buying a house. To begin your search you are spending a Saturday with a realtor, viewing four different houses within your size, location, and price range. At each site you will probably spend thirty to forty-five minutes walking through the rooms and around the yard. What are you doing during that time? What is your mental process?

The first thing you do is *observe*. Your eyes are scanning each room slowly: you are noticing the layout of the kitchen, the size of the bedrooms, the number of baths, and so forth. You look for moisture in the basement, insulation in the attic, and check the condition of the exterior.

Let's call this part of us—which objectively gathers information—our Observer. When you take a first look through a house, it is best to simply "flip on" the Observer within you. In that way you can gather much more information about each potential home. You may even take a notebook to record the facts you need to make an intelligent decision.

That's Step 1. Step 2 is to begin to *comment* about the data you have collected, to consider your personal preferences as to size, design, location. You analyze each house according to your needs and desires. Here is what might go through your mind as you view a house for the first time. Notice how the thoughts come in two stages:

OBSERVER: [As you drive up the driveway.] The drive is concrete; there's a two-car open garage. The house is Colonial style, and the yard is manicured. COMMENT: Looks good. We could use a carport. Maybe we could even enclose it one day. The outside looks well cared for. Colonials aren't my favorite, though.

[As you enter the kitchen.] This is bigger than mine, with an island in the middle. Open entry into a breakfast nook. No windows in the kitchen. Also opens into the living room/dining room combo. Walk-in pantry. And lots of cabinet space. COMMENT: Wow! This is what I'm looking for! Plenty of space to spread out, plus we can eat most meals without lugging things into the dining room. And lots of storage would be a treat. Major drawback is the lack of natural light. It's so nice to be able to look outside from the kitchen. But I think I can live with it. Let's see if the rest of the house is as nice.

There is a clear and distinct difference between the Observer statements and the Comments. The Observer simply notices and reports objectively any data it receives. It is like the attitude of the judge in a courtroom: "Just the facts please, ma'am." The Observer applies no biases, preferences, personal desires, or judgments to the facts.

In Step 2 we comment on our observations. Now we *are* influenced by our desires, beliefs, values, hopes, fears, and judgments. ("I love it/hate it/am afraid of it/don't care for it/want it/want to change it/doubt I can have it/wish it never happened/hope it works," and so forth.)

NEGATIVE OBSERVERS

It is when we comment on our observations prematurely that our problems begin. Imagine that as you drove up to that house you said, "It's a Colonial. Colonials aren't my favorite. That's a strike against this house already; the inside probably won't do, either. Why don't we go on to the next one." Your quick judgment would prevent you from continuing to gather information. In this case, you would have missed the opportunity of seeing your ideal kitchen. And the quality of that kitchen might have offset the exterior design. When we are quick to judge, we lose valuable information.

Prejudice is judging people, situations, or experiences prior to objectively observing them. One of the greatest tragedies of racism, sexism, and ageism is that so many talented people are arbitrarily dismissed without regard to their unique qualities and talents. The same process occurs during panic. Our beliefs or fears are so predominant that we never objectively observe the situation. With only a minimal amount of data, we quickly interpret the situation as an emergency and begin our panic routine. We blend a two-step process into one step. We no longer take time to take advantage of our detached, objective, data-gathering Observer. We instantly analyze and interpret each new piece of information as though we were certain of its meaning.

The interpretation of events is the mental process that produces the panic response. As I discussed in chapter 9, during a panic-provoking time the brain lacks relevant information about exactly what is going on, and it doesn't know a more appropriate way to respond. Consequently it selects the same old response it used in the past to handle a similar situation. The brain pushes the panic button because we withhold new information from it. We do not slow down enough to collect current information; we fall back to our preconceived notion that we are "out of control." By using the skills of your Observer at the moment of panic, however, you will gather current, relevant information about your body and your surroundings. This vital data will guide you toward gaining control of your anxiety attack.

You already have an excellent capacity to observe. In fact, panic happens only to those who are capable of paying close attention to small details. It is important to renew your acquaintance with this skill, so that you may begin to use it during panic-provoking times.

Instead of taking the time to observe the threatening situation, the panic-prone person will quickly observe and interpret the situation in one swift moment. In my work with clients over the years, I have found three primary ways in which they "contaminate" the responsibilities of the Observer by adding negative comments during this important first step. I call the three Negative Observers the Worried Observer, the Critical Observer, and the Hopeless Observer. Here are some examples of these Negative Observers' comments.

The Worried Observer

"My heart rate has increased . . . Oh no, what does that mean? Am I starting to have a heart attack? I must be."

"My speech is scheduled for next week . . . I know I'm going to start stammering. Then everyone will watch me shake in my boots. I'll be so embarrassed."

"There are a lot of people shopping here today . . . That means that the checkout lines are going to be endlessly long. I'll have to stand there forever. I'll probably start to get dizzy again. I might even faint on the spot."

THE WORRIED OBSERVER

- Anticipates the worst
- Fears the future
- Creates grandiose images of potential problems
- Expects and braces for catastrophe
- Watches with uneasy apprehension for any small signs of trouble

Over time, the Worried Observer creates anxiety.

The Critical Observer

"Last week when I drove to the store I had no symptoms. This morning I became anxious and never made it to the store . . . I'm doing terribly! I'm so angry I failed! I'm such a weak person."

"Tonight is the Webers' party, and I'm afraid about going . . . Well, that's typical. Every little thing bothers me! I feel like a two-year-old. When am I going to grow up and face the world!"

"They're thinking of having the family reunion in Florida . . . Oh, great. Guess who's going to spoil everything again. I'm too afraid to fly, I won't shop by myself, I don't like highways. What am I doing to this family!"

THE CRITICAL OBSERVER

- Makes certain you understand how helpless and hopeless you are
- Doesn't hesitate to remind you of the mistakes you have made and that you are lucky to have anything or anyone in your life
- Points out each of your flaws regularly, in case you might have forgotten them
- Uses any mistake to remind you of what a failure you are

Over time the Critical Observer produces low self-esteem and low motivation.

The Hopeless Observer

"Susan wants me to go out to lunch with her . . . There's no way I can survive a restaurant. I just can't handle it. What's the point I'll never be in control."

"I used to be so outgoing. Now I hardly leave the house unless I'm taking the kids somewhere . . . I've dug myself into a hole, and I'll be here for years."

"I feel physically drained today, and I wanted to get some work done around here . . . Why bother?"

THE HOPELESS OBSERVER

- Suffers over your present experience
- Believes there is something inherently wrong with you
- Believes that you are deprived, defective, or unworthy, that you are missing what it takes to succeed
- Expects that you will fail in the future just as you have failed in the past
- Expects that you will continue to be deprived and frustrated
- Believes that there are insurmountable obstacles between you and your goals

Over time the Hopeless Observer creates depression.

All three of these ways of negative commenting contaminate your natural ability to observe. They distort information about your life in a hurtful way. They don't encourage your progress, your independence, or your self-esteem. Instead, they invite you to surrender your efforts and give in to failure.

If we study the experiences of people who have significantly restricted their lives out of fear of panic, we can see more clearly the destructive patterns of these Negative Observer comments. Listen to the statements of each of these clients during one of our first sessions. Imagine how these thinking patterns literally halt their progress.

ANN: I watch myself. I'm always trying to keep this grip on myself. I'm monitoring every little thing that I do, and in the final analysis I decide that I'm not in control.

Ann tells us that she has the skill to observe herself. But she takes that ability and moves it to a Worried Observer extreme. She becomes the Detective, watching her every move to discover clues that will prove she is out of control. Since she is completely focused on herself, since she notices every small change, and since she *expects* the worst, sure enough, she always concludes, "I'm not in control."

DONNA: I judge my level of success in recovery by how well I get through a bad feeling. If I stay out of bad feelings and keep going, then I feel like I'm almost healed. But if I lie down or quit, then I'm very negative about myself. I only support myself when I've been successful.

Notice that Donna, too, has that Observer skill. But she makes extreme interpretations of the facts. When she has a great day, she is certain her problems are over forever. Her standards are so high, however, that if she has any kind of setback she labels herself a "failure." She views her actions through Critical Observer eyes, and she can never be good enough. The Critical Observer allows no room for mistakes.

KAREN: I started to feel physically sick today, like an allergic reaction. Then I said to myself, "How much is physical and how much is psychological?" I started arguing in my mind, "Should I drive myself to therapy or not? I don't think I can." Finally I gave in to myself and asked my husband to drive me. I just didn't think I could handle it, and I didn't want to struggle anymore. Now that I'm here, a part of me doesn't really care, but another part of me feels disgusted with myself for not fighting.

Karen's statements reflect all three of the Negative Observer contaminants. Her Worried Observer questions, "How much is physical and how much is psychological?" Her Hopeless Observer surrenders, "I can't handle it. I don't want to struggle anymore." Then her Critical Observer delivers the final blow, "I'm disgusted with myself for not fighting." Can you imagine what it is like to treat yourself this way on a daily basis? This is how anxiety, low self-esteem, low motivation, and depression can become central parts of a panic-prone person's life.

SHERYLL: In my own case I'm too keen an observer, in a negative way. I'm observing myself constantly, but it's always with fear. Like Claire Weekes says, "Headphones on your feelings."*

*Dr. Claire Weekes is a pioneer in the study of anxiety and panic. She has written three books on these topics.

Sheryll's Worried Observer amplifies any minor change in her feelings: "Oh, no, what was that?" "Is it still there?" "Is it getting worse?" "Will I be ready to handle it?" Why is she fearful? Not because she is having uncomfortable physical symptoms, and not because she is paying attention to her body. It is because her Worried Observer is saying to her, "Any moment now you might be overwhelmed with a severe anxiety attack. Stay on guard!" To the Worried Observer, your current experience is irrelevant. Instead, it remembers how bad the past has been and imagines how frightening the future will soon be. Your Worried Observer can actually supersede any rational thoughts. If the Worried Observer is thinking of past trauma and imagining future danger, your brain has no choice but to interpret these fantasies instead of interpreting your current reality. The brain then responds to the presumed danger by automatically shifting into emergency gear. *To stop the physical symptoms of panic you must stop the Worried Observer.*

   DONNA: I know I get angry with myself whenever I get tense for no reason.

There is usually some reason why we get tense or anxious during a time when there is no actual threat. Either the events of the past remain with us, or we are anticipating events in the future. Using the Observer, we can objectively review those events and our reactions to them. Based on that information, we can choose the most supportive action to take. Donna's Critical Observer, however, prevents her from thinking in a caring manner about her needs. Instead it says, "There's no reason to be tense! What the hell is wrong with you!" Because her Critical Observer is so strongly embedded within her belief system, it prevents any current facts from entering into the picture.

Each of these contaminated Observers operates on a pre-existing negative belief system. Each one of them, therefore, keeps the mind closed and prevents intelligent decision making.

   ANN: When I begin to notice symptoms I become paralyzed and I start listening in on my body. And my immediate reaction is to run away from it. I have tried to sit, or to "handle" it, but physically it depletes me so much that I have to run. I'm feeling symptoms now, and my immediate reaction is to get out of here. I don't feel I have the energy, the physical or the emotional energy, to see it through, because I've been like this for twelve years. I feel like I'm going to drop dead next week because of the effects, because of the toll this has taken on my health.

Ann's comments reflect the stance of the Hopeless Observer. She becomes "paralyzed" and completely absorbed by the symptoms she notices. She feels so "depleted" of energy that she can't imagine surviving her symptoms. Since she has been this way for twelve years, she has decided that nothing will ever change this pattern. Every anxious episode seems to pile on top of the last one, and her burden gets heavier and heavier. Eventually, she imagines, she will collapse from the toll. This is the type of contamination that leads to depression.

Since our actions are based on our interpretation of the facts and not the facts themselves, all of these Worried, Critical, or Hopeless Observer comments prevent us from taking positive action. Turn back to the three Worried Observer examples on page 198. Read each one, then imagine what kind of action these interpretations might produce. Do the same for the Critical and Hopeless Observer statements. See if you notice any pattern among the nine examples. (Try it now.)

Most likely you saw that these kinds of conclusions were drawn:

I'd better go lie down.
I think I'd better cancel.
I ought to leave while I can.
I'm not going to keep trying.
I might as well not be around people anyway.
I'll tell them to go without me.
I quit.

In other words, these contaminated Observers lead to passivity and inaction. They invite you to surrender to helplessness, to stop trying, to wave the white flag.

The Worried Observer, which is usually present just before or during physical symptoms, goes one step further. It provides a distorted interpretation of events for the brain. Take the first example:

"My heart has increased its rate. Oh, no, what does that mean? Am I starting to have a heart attack? I must be." The brain makes this interpretation: "I'm losing control." The brain then responds appropriately to an inappropriate interpretation: "All systems to Emergency Response!"

That is why sometimes immediately after you ask whether symptoms are developing, those symptoms become stronger, almost magically. After such an experience you tell yourself, "Good job. I was paying close attention and caught myself before the panic snuck up on me. I'd better stay on guard more often."

But there is nothing magical about it. Do you see the vicious circle? Your "solution" creates your problem:

1. You pay close attention to your physical sensations.
2. You become suspicious of a minor sensation.
3. You interpret that sensation to mean the beginning of an anxiety attack or other serious disturbance.
4. Your brain turns on the Emergency Response to "save" you.
5. You vow to be even more sensitive next time.
6. Back to Step 1.

THE INDEPENDENT OBSERVER

What is the alternative to this passive, fearful, guarded cycle? How does one get out of these old, repetitive patterns? Three general tasks are required at panic-prone moments:

Step 1. Think with your Observer.
Step 2. Calmly interpret the facts.
Step 3. Choose an appropriate action.

By eliminating the Worried, Critical, and Hopeless comments, your Observer instantly becomes one of your strongest resources.

THE INDEPENDENT OBSERVER

- Takes times to collect all the relevant information
- Is detached from strong emotions
- May feel concern, yet thinks calmly

- Is devoid of prejudices
- Gains a perspective on the situation
- Sees problems in a different light
- Is objective

Who can possibly face a challenging situation with confidence while mentally reciting a litany of fears, criticisms, or doubts? The Observer dismisses such comments and focuses on the important information at the moment: "What is taking place in my body right now? What is special about my current situation? (Have I been afraid here before? Is it reminding me of a past or future fear?) What sense can I make of my current reaction?" These types of questions can be asked and answered based on a momentary reflection, as though you are stepping back from the scene for a short time. ("Hmmm . . . I'm starting to get tense again. How come? Nothing special is bothering me; I'm just sitting here watching TV. [Pause for reflection.] Oh, yeah, that character on the show was just fighting with her husband. I think that's when I started getting tense.")

The ability to slowly and objectively size up a situation is a crucial first step, because this information determines what action you will take next. If, in the above example, you quickly think, "Oh, my gosh, I'm starting to have an anxiety attack. How bad will this one be?" you become a powerless victim of panic by not pausing for even a moment before surrendering to the symptoms. But if instead you stop to think, "I'm reacting to the fighting on TV," now you have something you can grasp, something that seems plausible.

Gathering the facts and interpreting the facts are two different steps and should be treated as such during panic-prone times. In Step 1 ("Think with your Observer"), your Observer is concentrating on your present experience. It doesn't get emotional or excited. It is unattached to the facts that it gathers. Even looking around for a cause of the current tension can be done in a detached manner. Not a frantic rush of thought, such as, "Oh, I feel a little jumpy right now. I've just woken up. Why do I feel so jumpy? Oh, no, I probably didn't sleep well, or I had bad dreams. Oh, damn, here it comes, the start of another terrible day." You must remember that you have time to think methodically, "This is not an emergency." In fact, the more time you give yourself to think, the greater chance you have of using your Observer's skills.

In this example, if you are thinking more slowly, your Observer might say, "Hmmm . . . I'm feeling a little jumpy right now. I've just woken up. [Pause for reflection.] There is probably some logical reason why I'm feeling this way, even though I'm not certain what it is." This example raises an important point. Notice that the Observer didn't come up with the exact cause of the tension. Sometimes the cause isn't obvious or immediately known. At those times the Observer makes a new factual statement: "There is some logical cause for my sensations, even though I can't put my finger on it immediately." It does not say (as the Worried Observer might), "I've *got* to know what's causing this, *now!*" Instead, it carries out its responsibility, which is to calmly collect and report information.

Your body may be shaking, your legs may be weak, your breathing may be fast. But your Observer can separate itself from those symptoms. It can report, in a detached manner, the facts that it gathers. It notices them but does not get preoccupied with them. *To become preoccupied with the symptoms is to encourage the symptoms.*

The Observer does not try to fix the problem. Instead, it observes the action without disturbing it. All of us who have had to react to a sudden physical emergency in the home or on the highway have first-hand experience with the skills of the Observer. After the crisis has passed, most people will be able to report in great detail everything that they saw or thought. It is as though time slowed down and every second during the crisis lasted a minute. This detailed memory is produced by our Observer. Like a video camera, it records, objectively every single piece of relevant information. During the moment of panic, your first task will be to watch and listen through that Observer's camera.

Step 2 is to calmly interpret the facts that your Observer has reported. Now you are determining the relationships among the facts you have gathered. In response to the observation about the TV show ("Oh, yeah, that character was just fighting with her husband. I think that's when I started getting tense"): "Since I have trouble facing conflicts in my own life, I bet that's why I'm overreacting to this scene. I don't need to become so involved in these feelings right now."

In the second example ("Hmmm . . . I'm feeling a little jumpy right now. I've just woken up"): "It won't be helpful to focus on these symptoms right now."

In other words, Step 2 ("Calmly interpret the facts") answers this question: "Based on what I now know from observing, what do I seem to need?" Again, you take a calm moment to explore that thought.

In the early stages of learning this skill, I recommend that you slow down your thinking during Step 1 and Step 2. I suggest that you take at least ten times (!) longer than you do now, simply to gather your information. That sounds like forever, but "slow down" is a relative term in this situation. The panic-prone person probably takes less than two seconds before concluding that she is losing control. *No* objective thinking takes place. In most panic-provoking moments all you need is less than twenty seconds of observing in order to realistically assess the situation. Another ten seconds will often be enough time for you to interpret the information. At that point you are ready for Step 3: "Choose an appropriate action." The following chapters are dedicated to helping you make this choice. This suggestion of thirty seconds is only to give you a general sense of the time needed. Of course, each situation and each person require varying degrees of time. Some of my clients can accomplish these steps in less than five seconds:

OBSERVER: I'm tense.

INTERPRETATION: I don't need to be.

ACTION: Take a deep breath, sigh out loud on the exhale, let go of tense muscles.

In an example requiring a little more time, our thoughts might run like this:

OBSERVER: I'm feeling anxious right now. How come? Hmmm . . . maybe it's because Jim's going on a business trip for three days. I've been nervous during those times in the past.

INTERPRETATION: I need to find a way to reassure myself these next few days.

ACTION: Why don't I talk about my concerns to Jim before he leaves. Who knows, maybe it'll help. Plus, I'll talk with Judith. Her husband travels a lot, and she'll probably have some advice. I want to have some ideas before Jim leaves on Wednesday.

To further illustrate these two steps, let's review the nine hypothetical situations on pages 000–000. This time I will remove the
Negative Observer comments, leaving simple Observer statements
(Step 1), followed by possible interpretations (Step 2). Remember
that Step 2 answers the question, "On the basis of what I now
know, what do I seem to need?" Specific action to take in each scenario is not presented yet; that will be Step 3.

OBSERVER: My heart rate has increased. I'm starting to worry
what that means.

INTERPRETATION: This is *not* an emergency. I can calm my
worries and calm my body.

OBSERVER: My speech is scheduled for next week. Right now
I'm afraid I might perform poorly.

INTERPRETATION: It's O.K. to be concerned about my talk. I
also probably need to gain some confidence in my ability
before then.

OBSERVER: There are a lot of people shopping here today. That
means the lines will probably be long. I've been uncomfortable in lines before.

INTERPRETATION: This is *not* an emergency. I need to pace myself
while I'm here. I want to leave here later with at least a few groceries, and I don't need to rush myself. I'll do the best I can.

OBSERVER: Last week when I drove to the store I had no symptoms. This morning I became anxious and never made it to
the store.

INTERPRETATION: When I don't meet my goals, I tend to
become harsh on myself. That's not helpful. I need to support
myself and set a new goal.

OBSERVER: Tonight's the Webers' party, and I'm afraid about
going.

INTERPRETATION: It's O.K. to be afraid about the party. Social events are usually tough for me, so this is normal. But it would be best if I stayed calm and busy until it is time to get ready.

OBSERVER: They're thinking of having the family reunion in Florida. I've been so afraid of flying that I haven't been on a plane in six years.

INTERPRETATION: Nothing is going to be decided immediately. I have time to think about my options.

OBSERVER: Susan wants me to go out to lunch with her. I often feel trapped in a restaurant.

INTERPRETATION: I need to believe that Susan will be supportive of me if we go. And I need some control over the logistics of lunch.

OBSERVER: I used to be so outgoing. Now I hardly leave the house unless I'm taking the kids somewhere.

INTERPRETATION: This pattern is hurtful to me. I need to find some activities that will help me feel better about myself.

OBSERVER: I feel physically drained today, and I wanted to get some work done around here.

INTERPRETATION: If I do nothing all day I'll end up angry with myself. I need to start by accomplishing some very small, brief tasks. I need to take one step at a time.

15

Finding Your Observer

In chapter 10 I described the Calming Response, which can counter-balance the symptoms of panic. In chapter 14 I introduced the concept of the Observer, which can give you needed perspective during anxious times. This chapter will detail for you specific methods for producing the Calming Response and eliciting your Observer at the same time. During a panic-provoking moment, that is exactly what you want to do. By calming the body and clearing the mind of negative comments, you will become mentally sharp and alert, ready to take care of yourself within seconds.

THE FIRST IMPORTANT STEPS

The best way to master a new skill is to break it down into learn-able chunks. For instance, when you learn to type, you begin by repeatedly typing a few letters in order to master the proper finger movements. Again and again you repeat those patterns until your confidence builds. You then practice typing more letters in a row, then more complex sets of letters. You are always instructed to type slowly at first so that you may concentrate better; speed will come later. The process then continues in gradual stages: two-letter words, three-letter words, five-letter words, phrases, and finally, full, punctuated sentences.

You need the same diligence and patience here. If you have never mastered a formal relaxation or meditation technique, daily practice will build your skill and confidence. Slowly you will be better able to recognize when your mind and body are tense and when they are comfortable. Mastering any of the techniques in this chapter requires time. Remember when you first learned to ride a bike or to roller-skate? During your early attempts you probably said, "I'll never catch on. I'm so clumsy." But you persisted, and you learned.

Some people may feel these methods won't be powerful enough to affect their panic attacks, which are overwhelming. I say to these people what I have said to my clients over the years: if you commit yourself to controlling anxiety attacks, you can do it. If you want to learn these new behaviors to conquer your anxiety attacks, then practice, practice, and practice some more. No one needs to be continually devastated by this problem.

In the Deep Muscle Relaxation technique, by allowing your muscles to rehearse again and again those contractions and relaxations you are giving them a chance to create new pathways in the brain. Soon those pathways will be strong enough to operate without practice. By repeating the structured experiences in this chapter again and again, you will create new pathways for these needed skills as well. Anyone who plays a musical instrument knows how much time and effort is required to learn those first hand movements. After persistent practice, those same movements come reflexively, without conscious thought.

Remember that your primary goal is to find a long-lasting method for regaining control over panic. This is a one-step-at-a-time process. It is easiest to learn a new skill during low-anxiety times, when you are not feeling under stress. Once you have mastered the skill, then begin to apply it to the panic-provoking times. No one learns to type after they have been hired as a typist. And no one should expect these methods to work as effectively at first as they will after practice.

Let me begin with a few brief experiences. For the first one I would like you to follow these guidelines:

CALMING COUNTS (PRACTICE VERSION)

- Sit comfortably.
- Take a nice, long, deep breath and exhale it slowly while saying the word "relax" under your breath.
- Then simply close your eyes.
- With your eyes closed, let yourself take ten natural, easy

breaths. Purposely count each exhale, starting with "ten," until you reach "one."

- When you reach "one," open your eyes again.Practice this experience now, and as you begin to read the words again, let yourself read them slowly, as though you have shifted into a more gentle, quiet state. Let your natural breathing remain calm, gently inhaling into your abdomen as described in chapter 11.

I would now like you to try this same process a second time, with one additional step:

CALMING COUNTS

1. Sit comfortably.
2. Take a long, deep breath and exhale it slowly while saying the word "relax" under your breath.
3. Close your eyes.
4. Let yourself take ten natural, easy breaths. Count down with each exhale, starting with "ten."
5. This time, while you are breathing comfortably, notice any tensions, perhaps in your jaw or forehead or stomach. Imagine those tensions loosening.
6. When you reach "one," open your eyes again.

Practice this now, starting with a deep breath.

Now please try the experience a third time, this time taking twenty breaths and counting each exhalation, from "twenty" to "one." Practice this now.

As you open your eyes and before you become active again, take a moment to mentally scan your body. What do you notice? What has changed? How do you feel in general right now? If your body is feeling a pleasant kind of heaviness, lightness, or tingling, if you felt some of your muscles unwind, if your breathing seems calmer, then you are learning first hand about the Calming Response.

Did you have trouble keeping track of the numbers? Did you become distracted by other thoughts? Did you make any Worried, Critical, or Hopeless comments during the three exercises? Usually, the better able you are to passively concentrate on the counting, the calmer your body and mind become. The more you work at trying to concentrate, the harder this task becomes. Your job is to *not* focus intently on how your breathing is changing; to *not* evaluate how the exercise is progressing while you are in the middle of the experience. It is simply to let each exhale be a "marker" of the next number in your mind—inhale . . . exhale . . . "twenty" . . . inhale . . . exhale . . . "nineteen" . . . and so forth. When some other thought comes into your mind, gently dismiss it and return to the counting.

Your Observer and the Calming Response

Whenever your breathing settles down and your mind focuses on a few simple thoughts, you are inviting the Calming Response. During Calming Counts, when you notice your breathing just enough to count each exhalation, and notice and gently let go of any unnecessary comments, you are using your Observer. This exercise is an excellent way to teach yourself about your Observer and the Calming Response.

You can apply Calming Counts specifically to controlling panic attacks. One way is to incorporate them within relaxation or meditative techniques to help you concentrate more completely. We know from experience that if you structure a period of private time to quiet your mind and relax your body on a daily basis, panic will find less and less opportunity to intrude into your life. The more rested you are physically and psychologically, the better protected you become. If you are having difficulty concentrating during these structured quiet times, Calming Counts can be helpful.

Cue-Controlled Deep Muscle Relaxation, described in chapter 12, is one method of developing the Calming Response by using your Observer. At the same time it prevents the tensions of the day from piling up. If you practice this method, you will notice Worried, Critical, or Hopeless Observer comments rising up from time to time during the twenty minutes (which you should acknowledge and gently dismiss). The final portion, in which you are instructed to "go to your safe place" in your mind, requires the greatest skill in passive concentration. If you find that you have difficulty maintaining an easy, quiet concentration during that time, use the following counting exercise in place of your visual image: instead of "going to your safe place," begin counting silently with each exhalation, from "one hundred" to "one." Follow the Calming Count instructions.

ONE HUNDRED COUNTS

1. Sit comfortably.
2. Take a deep breath, exhale slowly, and silently say "relax."
3. Breathing in a relaxed, natural manner, count silently from one hundred to one, using each exhale as one count.
4. If you happen to notice any tension in your face, jaw, stomach, or other areas, easily suggest in your mind that they relax.
5. As you notice any irrelevant thoughts, easily let them go and return to your counting.
6. If you lose track of your counting, simply return to some number close to where you were.
7. When you reach "one," gradually open your eyes as you think about feeling refreshed and alert.

If you enjoy private time to unwind from the tensions of each day, I suggest that you also experiment with meditation, which is the sister to relaxation exercises. As I described in chapter 12, the four essential features of meditation are a quiet place, a comfortable position, an object to dwell on, and a passive attitude.

Here is a modification of concentration meditation that uses Calming Counts. I have designed it especially for my panic-prone clients, because it offers two distinct advantages over traditional meditation. First, it gives you a stronger sense of being in control, since you must consciously keep track of the descending numbers. Second, it reduces the number of irrelevant thoughts that drift into your mind. This is most helpful during the times when you become flooded with Negative Observer comments. Calming Counts give you a specific and neutral task: to count with each exhale until you reach "one." This task will be in direct competition with your Negative Observer comments, therefore your mind will become less involved with such self-destructive thoughts.

MEDITATION OF ONE HUNDRED COUNTS

1. Sit in a comfortable quiet place.
2. Take a deep breath, exhale slowly, and say "relax" silently.
3. Begin counting at "one hundred" while breathing naturally. Use each exhalation to mark the next number, until you reach "one."
4. When extraneous thoughts enter your mind, simply note them and let them go. Return to your focused counting.
5. When you reach "one," begin counting again at "one hundred."
6. When you reach "one" the second time, count forward with each breath, from "one" to "ten." During this final ten-count sequence, suggest to yourself that you will open your eyes at "ten" feeling alert and refreshed.

When you finish this or any other exercise in this book, do not immediately begin to evaluate how well or how poorly you performed. There are many variables that determine our responses to any particular exercise. For instance, on certain days when you are more anxious, your concentration may not be strong. Nonetheless, practicing the structured experience that day, difficult as it is, may give you greater benefits than if you had a "good" practice during a less pressured day. Anytime you consciously choose to quiet your mind and relax your body, you are promoting your health.

As you become more skilled in producing the Calming Response through daily formal practice of relaxation or meditation, you may begin to use a briefer technique, which I call the Calming Breath.

THE CALMING BREATH

1. Take a deep breath, filling first your lower lungs, then your upper lungs.
2. *Slowly* exhale, saying "relax" (or a similar word) under your breath.
3. Let your muscles go limp and warm; loosen your face and jaw muscles.
4. Remain in this "resting" position physically and mentally for a few seconds, or for a couple of natural breaths.

If you need or want to have your eyes open because of your circumstances (you are driving a car or are with a group of people), feel free to do so. During your early weeks of learning, however, find opportunities to practice this exercise with your eyes closed. This will improve your body's chances of responding to your suggestions.

During the Calming Breath you will be taking advantage of the "cues" you have developed in practicing the formal relaxation or meditative techniques: you are repeating a special word, breathing in a special manner, and giving the body a chance to develop the same pleasant sensations it has during the Calming Response.

This is another skill, like Calming Counts, that you should practice throughout your day, whether or not you are feeling tense. Even if you have never practiced any lengthy relaxation exercises, you can immediately begin using Calming Counts and the Calming Breath. Such techniques, used several times each day, can help you reduce the buildup of normal everyday tensions. If you begin to use it regularly during noncrisis times, you will create new pathways in the brain that promote mental calmness and muscle relaxation. Then, when you need this skill during a panic-provoking moment, it will almost be second nature. (A guided practice tape of these breathing skills is available. See "Resources," page 00.)

YOUR OBSERVER AND PHYSICAL TENSION

Sometimes it is best to focus your attention first on releasing your tense muscles, and then on quieting your mind. When you notice yourself tense as well as anxious, you might benefit from one of these two brief techniques to relax muscles. After you complete either process, you should be better able to slow your thoughts and begin other supportive activities.

Brief Muscle Relaxation

This is a simple five-minute muscle relaxation technique. One by one you tighten and relax four groups of muscles in your body, much as you do for Cue-Controlled Deep Muscle Relaxation. You'll squeeze them tightly for about ten seconds and relax them for about ten or fifteen seconds. Here are the groups. Try them as I describe them.

UPPER BODY

The first group is in your upper body: your arms, shoulders, chest, and neck. Tense this particular group by bending your arms, then crossing them in front of your chest. Your elbows will be pointing down, your fists will be pointing up. Now tighten your fists, arms, shoulders, chest and back. Lift your shoulders up to your ears as you tense them, and hold that position *while you're breathing*. Continue breathing, and keep those muscles tense for about ten seconds. Now let them go—drop your arms to your lap and loosen them. Take some calm gentle breaths, and with each exhalation, let yourself relax those muscles a little more.

THE FACE

Let's look at that second group, the face. Squeeze the muscles of your face together as though you've just bitten into a lemon. Purse your lips, bite down on your teeth to tense your jaw, crunch your face up, wrinkle your nose and squint your eyes. Hold this position for about ten seconds while you breathe through your nose. Now let go, allowing those muscles of your face to relax and loosen.

STOMACH AND LOWER BACK

The third group is your stomach and lower back. Take a deep breath and pull in your stomach as far as you can. Tense the muscles in your lower back. Hold your breath while you are in this position six seconds as you silently count to "six, one thousand." Now slowly exhale and let these muscles loosen and relax for about fifteen or twenty seconds. Just let them go.

LEGS

Group four is your legs. Extend your legs straight out in front of you. Tense all your leg muscles as you point your toes toward your head. Hold this position for ten seconds as you continue to breathe gently. Now allow these muscles to relax as you drop your legs to the floor.

Now loosen and relax your whole body for about fifteen to twenty seconds. Let any tensions drain away. You can invite quietness to come into your mind as well as your muscles.

BRIEF MUSCLE RELAXATION

1. Close your eyes and sit quietly, letting go of any distracting thoughts. (20 seconds)
2. Bend your arms, then cross them in front of your chest. Tighten your fists, arms, shoulders, chest and back, and lift your shoulders up to your ears, while you're breathing. (10 seconds) Now relax. (15–20 seconds)
3. Crunch your face up, wrinkle your nose, squint your eyes, purse your lips and bite down on your teeth. (10 seconds) Now relax. (15–20 seconds)
4. Take a deep breath, pull in your stomach and tense your lower back. Hold your breath while counting to six. Then exhale SLOWLY. Now relax. (15–20 seconds)
5. Extend your legs and tense them, while pointing your toes toward your head. (10 seconds) Now relax. (15–20 seconds)
6. Repeat Steps 2–5.
7. Sit quietly, clearing your mind and focusing on your gentle breathing or on a pleasant scene in your mind as you invite your body to feel relaxed, warm, and heavy. (60 seconds)
8. Open your eyes, feeling refreshed and at ease.

These are the four major groups. You can use any one of these, depending on where your tension is located, or do all of them in sequential order as a way to begin to let go of general muscle tension.

When you finish tightening and relaxing those four muscle groups, let your whole body become limp and loose, and your mind quiet. You can also visualize yourself in a pleasant, relaxing scene, such as the beach, floating on a cloud, or enjoying a stroll in a peaceful environment. Let your body loosen. Remain in this quiet, relaxed state for about a minute before you slowly open your eyes.

The Ten-Second Grip

With this technique, the only prop you need is the arms of your chair. (I first designed this for those needing to loosen their physical tensions while on commercial flights.) Grab the armrests of your chair and squeeze them as hard as you can, making your lower and upper arms contract. Tense your stomach and leg muscles as well. Hold the tension for about ten seconds, while you continue to breathe. Then let go with a gentle long Calming Breath. Repeat two more times. Then shift around in your seat, shaking loose your arms, shoulders, and legs and gently rolling your head a few times. Finish off by closing your eyes and breathing gently for about thirty seconds. Let your body feel warm, relaxed and heavy during that time.

THE TEN-SECOND GRIP

1. Grab and squeeze the arm rests of your chair, tensing your upper and lower arms. Tense your stomach and leg muscles as well. Hold that position about ten seconds while you continue to breathe.
2. Let go and take a Calming Breath.
3. Repeat two more times.
4. Shift around in your seat, shaking loose your arms, shoulders, and legs and gently rolling your head a few times.
5. Close your eyes and breathe gently for about thirty seconds. Let your body feel warm, relaxed and heavy during that time.

Along with releasing tensions, all the structured experiences in this chapter will teach you how to rid yourself of unhelpful thoughts by first noticing them and then dropping them. Almost every time you practice one of these techniques, you will experience random thoughts floating up in your mind. The more you practice letting go of them, the greater skill you will develop, so that during actual problem times you will apply this new skill easily. Then, instead of noticing a stray thought during a Calming Counts practice, you will be disarming negative thoughts that are producing tension within you. That is why you should never become discouraged about your progress on these techniques. The more difficulty you face while learning these skills, the better prepared you will be for the problem times. I cannot stress enough that repetitive practice will reward you tenfold over time. These methods need to become as automatic as your panic response is, because in the moment of panic you will want to focus on only a few simple thoughts. The more these skills become second nature to you, the better they will serve you during troubled times.

16

Taking a New Stance: The Supportive Observer

For most of us, the world is full of decisions to be made, choices to consider, options to select. Every day we must discriminate dozens of times among an array of alternatives, from selecting the right combination of clothes in the morning to choosing what to eat at each meal to deciding which projects to tackle for the day. How do we make these decisions?

Within each of these arenas we develop, over time and through trial and error, our individual tastes. If I were to ask you to describe your favorite foods, the music you enjoy most, or your ideal vacation spot, you would probably describe the qualities you look for in making your choice. For instance, "I like a vacation spot with lots of sun but that's not too hot. Somewhere that isn't too crowded. And it would have to have water, either a pool, a lake, or the ocean." We discriminate among actual vacation spots on the basis of the characteristics we value.

Becoming aware of our general tastes and preferences makes each specific decision easier. I don't stand in the kitchen every morning, stupefied over whether I should have cereal, eggs, pancakes, French toast, oatmeal, granola, or just a glass of juice for breakfast. Since I am by now quite familiar with my likes and dislikes, I can choose in a few minutes—usually cereal and coffee.

FILTERING THE FACTS

It is the same with any of our decisions. The more we develop our sense of taste, our preferences, our values, our leanings, the less time we need to spend picking from an array of choices. Imagine how annoying it would be to have to spend a half hour reviewing each selection on a restaurant menu before picking an entrée. At some point we must trust our judgment. We must take a stand.

To make a decision we move through three stages. First, we observe and register the information available to us ("This menu has steak, pasta, and fish"). Second, we interpret that information on the basis of our knowledge, experience, and preferences ("I had steak last night, and I'm not in the mood for pasta; I think I would like the stuffed flounder"). Finally, we take action that is based on our interpretation (we order the flounder). In other words, during the interpretation phase, we screen the information through our personal inclinations before we choose an action.

This discrimination process doesn't always work in our favor. When the panic-prone person screens all collected information through one of the Negative Observers, he reduces his options in a self-defeating manner. Each of the Negative Observers has its own special attitude about the world.

Here is a typical stance of the Worried Observer: "In all likelihood, things are going to turn out badly. I should be extremely careful before taking any action. What choice will keep me from experiencing any discomfort whatsoever? I must avoid problems. I need to feel completely comfortable. I'm willing to give up a lot if it will ensure that I'll feel safe. If I make the wrong choice, it could prove catastrophic."

The Hopeless Observer might filter all choices through this attitude: "I've always been uncomfortable in these situations, and I probably always will. Nothing's going to help. The same problems I have had in the past will continue tomorrow, next week, and next year. I'll never feel better. Things are just too difficult."

The Critical Observer may screen choices in this manner: "You'd better not make another mistake. The chances are that if you try anything new or bold, you'll screw it up and embarrass yourself again. You don't have what it takes to change. You are only good at failing."

Our minds are always interpreting and commenting on our experience of the world. To control panic you need to recognize your Negative Observer comments and interrupt them. If you don't interrupt these negative attitudes about yourself and the world, you will continue to feel controlled by panic, since these attitudes will prevent you from taking successful action.

Let me give you a model with which to consider this idea, illustrated by Figures 6 and 7. During every moment of the waking day our minds are observing the environment through our senses. Everything that we see, hear, touch, smell, and taste is a stimulus that is recorded by what I call our Observer. If our minds allowed this vast array of sensations to register fully in the brain, we could not make sense of the world. It would just be one confusing, overwhelming mess. Therefore, all stimuli that the Observer records go through a filtering process so that we can choose an appropriate response. That filter reduces the stimuli to a few simple ones, which we then interpret. On the basis of our interpretation of this filtered-down, simplified version of what we have observed, we decide how to respond (see Figure 6).

For instance, you have decided to go out to lunch today. You drive into the parking lot of a restaurant. At that moment your Observer records all of your impressions: the color, size, and shape of the building, the number and kind of cars in the lot, and so forth. In the next instance you filter all that data down to a few concepts and interpret them: "This is the restaurant that I wanted. It doesn't seem too crowded, either." On the basis of all the various stimuli but on your filtered interpretation of them, you choose a response: "I'll eat here."

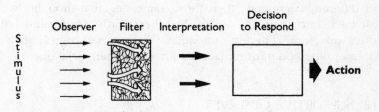

FIGURE 6. *Simple decision-making process.*

Now, suppose instead that sometime in the recent past you had had a panic attack in a restaurant. Today you decide to go out to lunch with a friend. You drive up to the restaurant and observe the same stimuli as in the above example: the size, shape, and color of the building, the number of cars in the lot. Perhaps you even see people eating in booths by the window. Only this time you filter all that identical data through your Worried Observer (see Figure 7).

Now your interpretation completely changes: "This is a frightening scene! I'll be out of control here! It's not safe!" Now your decision changes, because our decisions are always based on our interpretation of the facts, not the facts themselves. This time you decide, "I'm going to become a nervous wreck if I stay here. I'd better avoid this place. How do I get out of here?"

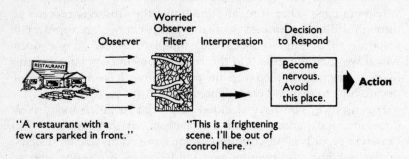

FIGURE 7. *Decision making with Worried Observer filter.*

This is why I say that to control panic you will have to learn to disrupt your Negative Observer comments. But, as they say in physics, nature abhors a vacuum. Your mind must always comment on your observations. If you disrupt worried comments during a panic-provoking moment but neglect to replace them with new and different comments, then those same negative thoughts will float back into your awareness. In other words, your mind will always use some filtering system; if you remove your Negative Observer filter you must replace it with a more beneficial one.

THE SUPPORTIVE OBSERVER

What qualities must this new filter have? During panic-provoking moments, the typical person needs several important resources:

1. *A sense of choice.* You need to feel free to move, free to change your direction. You want to know that you won't be trapped and won't be controlled by someone else or by some event. The greater the freedom you sense, the more comfortable you feel.

2. *A sense of safety.* You need to feel protected from harm, safe to pursue your task. You need to feel secure in your surroundings. As you feel increasingly safe, you feel more at ease.

3. *A sense of support.* You need to feel stable and secure. You need to feel respected, nurtured, and cared for. You need to feel good about the choice you make. The more supported you feel, the easier it is to try new activities.

4. *A sense of confidence.* You need to believe in yourself, have faith that you will make it. You need to hope for and expect the best. You need to trust in your own abilities, to believe that you will succeed. The more confident you feel, the more power you have over your actions.

In essence, you need to develop within you a new Observer—a supportive, confident part of you that offers you a number of safe choices. I call this part the Supportive Observer.

I am not suggesting that you can completely erase all the worried comments you make when facing panic. For many people, those comments come reflexively, automatically, whenever they consider facing a panic-provoking situation. Instead, I am suggesting that you add another perspective that will support your healthy, positive intentions, a perspective that can come into play as a new filter during panicky times. To do so will take some time and much practice. One of the best ways to start is to regard the Supportive Observer as a new attitude that you can instill within yourself. That attitude has a particular manner of thinking about things. And it has a distinct voice.

THE SUPPORTIVE OBSERVER

- Reminds you of your freedoms and choices
- Gives you permission to feel safe
- Supports all your efforts
- Invites you to feel confident
- Trusts you and lets you trust yourself
- Expects a positive future
- Points out your successes
- Looks around you for support
- Believes that you can change

- Knows that there is always more than one option in decisions
- Focuses more on solutions than on problems

"I CAN ... IT'S O.K. ..."

The voice of the Negative Observer within us is usually harsh, dramatic, and extreme: "I *can't* let myself feel this way." "This is going to be *terrible*." "I'll be the *laughingstock* of the company." "I'm being *ridiculous*." "*Nothing* will work." Too often we believe that to control panic we must be strict and rigid with ourselves. We must suppress our symptoms ("I can't let this anxiety continue"), contain our feelings ("I can't let anyone find out"), or limit our options ("A person should never walk out during a meeting"). This restrictive attitude ends up increasing panic's ability to control our lives. If one of the central fears in panic is the sense of feeling trapped, confined, or out of control, then the more messages we give ourselves that limit our options, the more we feel trapped by those limitations and the more discomfort we will feel.

Suppose I begin to feel a twinge of tension in my stomach just before I am to give a lecture, and I immediately think, "I can't let myself feel any anxiety." That thought alone is powerful enough to increase my anxiety. If instead I respond by saying, "I can handle a little anxiety here; it's normal to feel this way just before I begin talking," then I am not making myself feel trapped. By permitting the symptoms to exist, I am not supporting the increase of those symptoms.

See if these statements reflect any of your attitudes:

TYPICAL NEGATIVE OBSERVER STATEMENTS

- I can't let myself feel *any* anxiety. There is no acceptable level of anxiety.
- I can't experience any anxiety if I go there.
- I can't let these symptoms continue.
- I can't let these symptoms increase.
- I can't handle these feelings.
- If I don't control these feelings they will run wild.
- I can't take the risk. I can only handle it this way! I can't change my routine.

- I've got to prove to myself that I'm better. (This is a test.)
- I know I'm going to get anxious as soon as I walk in there.
- I must stay on guard at all times to feel safe.
- The only way to feel safe is to avoid all uncomfortable situations.

We put so many expectations and restrictions on our performance every time we attempt to actively engage in our world! It is no wonder that at the first sign of discomfort we tend to retreat, to avoid, or to run away. To face anxiety-provoking situations and succeed, we must give ourselves an easier task, one that allows for a greater number of acceptable options. As we adopt a more permissive, self-accepting attitude, we increase our sense of freedom and comfort.

The Supportive Observer is permissive, accepting, and flexible. It gives you more freedom and more options. It is constantly working to keep you from feeling trapped while at the same time helping you move forward toward your goals. That is the gift of the Supportive Observer: it helps you feel safer while it helps you take action.

The Worried Observer mislabels your emotions. When you begin to feel symptoms of anxiety, your Worried Observer filter says, "I'm terrified!" By this knee-jerk reaction it prevents you from noticing any gradual improvement in your ability to cope. The Supportive Observer gives you time to notice your emotions. It helps you label feelings more realistically. When you notice some anxiety, it keeps those sensations in check: "I'm beginning to feel a little afraid right now." It can notice the subtle changes in your tension level, when it increases and when it decreases.

The Hopeless Observer underestimates your capacity to cope: "I can't. It's impossible." The Supportive Observer says, "I'm not ready, yet. Let me back up a step and try a safer task." It reminds you that you can be in control and that you can master your problems.

Two introductory phrases most aptly express the Supportive Observer attitude: "I can . . . " and "It's O.K. . . . " Listen to how the Supportive Observer within you might think as you drive into that restaurant parking lot.

Well, here we are in the parking lot of the restaurant. I'm starting to feel nervous. Last time I ate out I had that panic attack.

I don't have to do this if I don't want to. It's O.K. to tell Susan that I'm just not feeling up to it. She really will understand. I don't have to keep this a secret from her.

I can also go inside and see how I do. I don't have to have the same reaction I had last time. I can feel safe in there. If I need to, I can get up and leave. Or, I can tell Susan that I'm nervous and get her support. There's no reason I have to stay through the whole meal if I don't want to. The worst that could happen is that I won't finish what's on my plate. I can handle that. So can Susan; I don't have to take care of her. In fact, she'll probably support me.

But I'm starting to breathe fast . . . This is *not* an emergency. It's O.K. to think about what I need right now . . . Let me just take a few Calming Breaths. I can let my muscles loosen a little. I can take time to calm down.

I think I'd like to go in, just to practice my skills of managing this scene.

Notice how permissive that voice is. It knows that the more freedom you offer yourself, the better you will feel. It doesn't demand that you perform. You can stop whenever you want. It also reminds you that you can seek the support of others; you don't have to go through all this alone. In fact, you will find that when you give yourself permission to tell others, you will feel a great relief. However, the more you force yourself to contain all your thoughts and feelings, the more trapped you feel and the stronger your symptoms become.

Until you establish a sense of free choice within yourself, your primary need will be to escape. Once you establish that sense of freedom, you can consider moving closer to your goal. In this example, you will feel more comfortable about entering the restaurant. This is because the greater sense we have that we can comfortably *escape* a place, the easier it is for us to *enter*. And with every step forward you again offer yourself support and choice. So the more you develop an attitude that permits you to have freedom of choice, the more you will be able to make healthy choices.

You also offer permission to reduce your symptoms. "This is not an emergency. It's O.K. to calm down a bit." It is also O.K. if you remain somewhat nervous. There is no reason for you to have to feel perfectly calm while you are trying a new behavior. If you panicked in a restaurant recently, it is normal to feel a little uncomfortable. You can expect that and accept it, because eventually you won't be frightened. Eventually you will have managed this situation enough times to trust that you won't lose control and fall apart, go crazy, or humiliate yourself.

The most restricting attitude is one that limits your behavior because of the possible opinions of others ("I can't leave the restaurant . . . because what would people think!"). Developing your sense of self-esteem will improve your chances to use these kinds of messages effectively. ("I would only leave the restaurant as a way to increase my comfort. I deserve to feel comfort and a sense of freedom of movement when I go out to eat. That's more important than worrying about other people's opinions.")

Figure 8 illustrates how you can use the Supportive Observer to replace the Negative Observer filter. Through a permissive, supportive attitude about your actions, the general interpretation of the scene changes from "This is a frightening scene—I'll be out of control here," to "It's O.K. to take a chance here—this is a place to practice my skills." Instead of deciding to become nervous and run away, you can then decide to move ahead, one step at a time, just for practice.

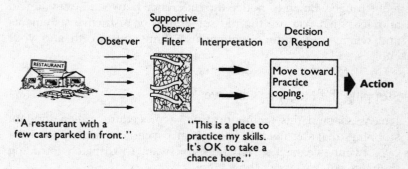

FIGURE 8. *Decision making with Supportive Observer filter.*

Here are some more examples of this permissive attitude:

SUPPORTIVE OBSERVER STATEMENTS
- It's O.K. to take a chance here. This is a place to practice my skills.
- I can be a little anxious and still perform my task.
- I don't have to let these feelings stop me.

- I can handle these symptoms.
- I am free to come and go according to my comfort.
- I always have options, no matter what.
- Regardless of what I'm doing or where I'm going, I can have freedom of choice.
- This is *not* an emergency; I can think about what I need.
- I can be relaxed and in control at the same time.
- It's O.K. to feel safe here.
- I deserve to feel comfortable here.
- I can slow down and think.
- I can trust my body.
- As I learn to trust my body I will have even more control of it.

Write down some statements that can support you in your goal of controlling panic. Choose ones I've mentioned or design some of your own, then spend time reviewing them. You can even put them on your bathroom mirror or refrigerator. Practice using them in the course of each day and in any situation where you want to feel stronger. Begin to notice the difference between how you feel and act when you use the old self-critical or restrictive statements and when your attitude statements affirm your worth and your choices.

Stopping the Negative Observer

I have adapted this technique from a procedure, called thought stopping, that the field of behavioral psychology has applied for over twenty years. Use it when you want to dispatch intruding thoughts quickly. This is how it goes.

To break a pattern of negative thoughts first you must begin to notice the moments when you are focusing on Negative Observer comments. Often we are not aware that our minds are rushing through negative thoughts. As you begin to pay attention to such thoughts you will start to notice these moments more frequently.

The most straightforward way to stop your doubts and worries is to do it as quickly and powerfully as possible, before they get your mind caught up in them. Once those worries strike—when you become aware of repetitive, unproductive, negative thoughts—mentally step back and observe them. Are your worries a signal of something you should pay attention to right now? Or are they just more noise in your day?

Ask yourself, "Are these thoughts helpful to me right now?" This is a *great* question; it will help you in a powerful way by confronting your automatic, negative thinking. Please don't ignore it! Simply by *asking* the question, you have momentarily interrupted your negative thinking, which is a good move. This is your Supportive Observer in action: it notices what you are thinking and decides if those thoughts are supporting you.

If the thoughts are not helpful—if they are noise—then consciously decide that you want to stop the racket. These thoughts are powerful and will draw you to them. They are drama, and your brain seeks out drama. Let your Supportive Observer reinforce your decision with statements such as "I'm in control of my thoughts. I don't need to be run by these ideas. It's O.K. to stop focusing on this."

You must make a firm decision of "not now." One way is to yell, "Stop!" inside your mind. I know that sounds like a silly thing to do. But yelling "Stop!" is a way to disrupt the drama of your worries. You fight fire with fire. It derails your current thought process and permits you to begin a new one.

If you need a little more stimulus to draw your attention, then wear a rubber band on your wrist. When you yell "Stop!" snap that rubber band at the same time. "Ouch!" Exactly! Now what are you paying attention to? That stinging wrist. For a split second you have left your worries and shifted to some other experience. You have created a space for a new focus of your attention.

Take advantage of that moment! Fill that space by practicing Calming Counts (the breathing technique of one deep breath and ten gentle breaths). This will be the most effective part of your intervention, because Calming Counts will accomplish two important goals. First, it will disrupt your typical pattern of worry. Instead of continuing to worry, you have to stop and think about how to do this highly specific breathing technique. You have to exhale all the way, take a deep breath, exhale again as slowly as possible, loosen and relax your face. Then you have to follow the next ten exhalations, counting each one, but counting *backward,* and seeing that number in your mind. Boy, that's busy work! And that's exactly what we are looking for: something to keep your mind so busy that it doesn't drift back to your worries. Calming Counts takes about a minute and a half. That's a wedge of ninety seconds between you and your noisy worries.

Second, you will be busy performing a technique that actually calms down your body. Calming Counts can help reverse any anxiety that starts to build in response to your worried thoughts. As you get physically calmer and as time passes, you will gain perspective on your worries and have a much easier time resisting them.

STOPPING NEGATIVE THOUGHTS

Listen for your worried, self-critical, or hopeless thoughts.
↓
Decide that you want to stop them. ("Are these thoughts helping me?")
↓
Reinforce your decision through supportive comments. ("I can let go of these thoughts.")
↓
Mentally yell, "Stop!" (Snap rubber band on wrist.)
↓
Begin the Calming Counts.

Even if your negative thoughts return a minute later, you have briefly disrupted them. This is a method of bringing your Observer to the foreground during a time of trouble. Several minutes later you may want to disrupt those negative thoughts again with a second set of Calming Counts. Slowly, you will begin to "step back" and see your worries from a new perspective. You will become less preoccupied, and your tension level will have a chance to decrease.

This technique is adaptable to many public situations. For instance, you can begin Calming Counts while waiting to give a speech. Instead of dwelling on negative thoughts such as "Everyone will notice that my hands are shaking" or "I know I'm going to make a fool of myself," you can preoccupy your mind by keeping track of your counts.

This same negative thinking process takes place when we anticipate facing our fears. Imagine you plan to attend your neighbor's party tonight. You usually avoid such parties because you become nervous in groups. But this week you decide you will fight your fears by attending this gathering of friends. It is now eleven-thirty A.M. You notice that you have spent the last thirty minutes repeating useless Worried Observer comments silently in your mind: "I can't do this. I'll never last. What if I get trapped there? I don't want to get trapped. I can't go. I just can't handle it. I'll never last." At this moment your Observer breaks in.

OBSERVER: I keep repeating the same thoughts in my head about tonight. I'm scared. I've decided to go, but I keep thinking about how to avoid it.

SUPPORTIVE OBSERVER: These thoughts are only making me more scared. They aren't helpful. I need to stop them.

ACTION: Mentally yells, "Stop!" Sits down for a minute and does ten Calming Counts.

OBSERVER: Now that I am quieter, I notice how tense my stomach is. I'm still scared.

SUPPORTIVE OBSERVER: Probably I'll be a little anxious all day. It's O.K. to be somewhat tense since I'm taking on a challenge tonight. I need to pace my day and keep myself fairly busy until it's time to get ready. That's a good way to take care of myself. I also want some support tonight so I don't feel like I'm going through this alone.

ACTION: Makes a list of a few worthwhile projects for the day that require some concentration. Shares concerns with a supportive person who will be attending the party. Monitors stomach tensions periodically through the day, using the Calming Breath to relax the stomach muscles when needed.

Notice what happened at the beginning of this example. I described the Observer as "breaking in" during your negative, obsessive thinking. This is probably something that already takes place within you now. You will become entangled in some negative thinking, then all of a sudden, some part of your mind will "step back" and comment on what you are doing. This is the moment you want to seize; this moment is the opportunity for change.

Begin to listen to your Observer rising up. When you notice it, *keep it!* Let yourself gather the facts of the moment objectively, then shift to some suggestion or plan that will take care of you and at the same time support your positive goals. If you begin criticizing yourself or making comments of hopelessness, simply notice them and then let them go ("Thinking that thought isn't helpful to me right now.")

INTERRUPTING THE PATTERN

Let's apply this concept of filters to the moment of panic. In a simple decision-making process, we move through three stages: (1) we observe relevant information, (2) we interpret that information, and (3) we choose an appropriate action (Figure 9). A panic attack occurs when that process becomes bogged down in the first two stages. First, we observe either our bodily sensations or our surroundings. Second, using our Worried Observer filter, we interpret our sensations as "panic" or our surroundings as "dangerous." Then we turn back and observe our bodily sensations again. We notice they are becoming increasingly uncomfortable. Next, we interpret these increased sensations as "panic," and so forth, in a continuing, escalating mental and physical crisis (Figure 10).

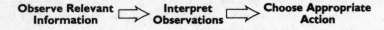

FIGURE 9. *Simple decision-making process.*

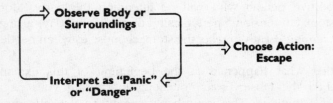

FIGURE 10. *Decision making during panic.*

This is how we create panic. We become stuck at the point of focusing on and reinforcing the idea that a problem exists. Our mind gives 100 percent of its attention to the problem and its potential repercussions instead of giving equal time to solutions. It fails to switch to Step 3, choosing an appropriate action, until it has enlarged the problem to monumental proportions. By the time it shifts to the take-action stage, the only solution to this self-imposed overwhelming crisis is to escape.

Panic is an automatic structured response, so you need to have an automatic structured response to it. The essential first step in a panic-provoking moment is to disrupt that pattern. If you do not consciously disrupt the pattern, it will follow its normal course automatically, which typically concludes with you "running away" from some situation to avoid what you interpret to be your "loss of control."

At some point during that process, you must stop long enough to notice what you are thinking. If you pay close attention, you will actually hear an Observer statement rise up spontaneously, reporting something about your current experience: "My heart's beating faster," or "I feel dizzy," or "I'm becoming afraid." *That is the moment to interrupt the pattern.* You must create a distraction from the negative thought pattern that typically follows such an Observer statement ("Oh, no! What terrible thing is about to happen to me?"). Your job is to drive a wedge between your symptoms and your negative, self-defeating thoughts.

Interrupt the pattern at the moment your Observer makes a comment, then seize that moment and instantly turn all responsibilities over to your Observer. Give your Observer some simple task to perform, one that requires no interpretations, no filters. By doing so you will also be inviting the Calming Response to compete with the rising Emergency Response.

There is a multitude of ways momentarily to disengage from the negative pattern and engage your Observer. Here is one major way: find something neutral or pleasant to do. I have listed a few examples below, some of which will sound silly, I'm sure. They all begin the same way.

FOCUSING YOUR OBSERVER DURING ANXIOUS TIMES

OBSERVER: "I'm starting to panic."

SUPPORTIVE OBSERVER: "This is not an emergency. I can care for myself by interrupting the pattern."

- Do a formal exercise, such as ten Calming Counts or a minute of repeating your meditative word with each breath.
- Take two or three Calming Breaths.
- If you are at your work desk, begin gently concentrating on some simple repetitive task. Don't bother trying to do the task well. Instead, concentrate on *doing it slowly*. For instance, open your file drawer and begin *slowly* counting the file folders. Or take out a piece of paper and write a few simple lists of any kind, *slowly* and methodically. If you are operating machinery, find some basic rhythm in your work and apply your breathing and counting to that rhythm.
- If you are walking down the street, begin *slowly* looking around while you continue to walk or as you stop and lean against a wall. Give yourself a minute or two of easy observing, such as deciding what color is predominant in the clothing of the people on that street, or any other simple task. Or pace your walking with your breathing: two steps while inhaling, three steps while exhaling, or any other easy rhythm.
- If you are in a restaurant, or are a passenger in a vehicle, take out your wallet or purse and reorganize your pictures and cards. Or, pull out all your dollar bills and order them by serial numbers.
- If you are at home, peel an apple or orange *slowly* and with concentration. Watch the light mist spray out each time you pull off a wedge of orange. Count each piece as it breaks off. Or reorganize the books on one shelf. Or make up a bed "army style," with attention to detail.
- If you are at a sporting event or a concert, begin studying the program in detail.

As I said, some of these suggestions do sound a little silly. But the point is to do something that requires simple concentration, that has relatively little importance, and that you can do slowly and methodically. You will also need to pay enough attention to distract you from holding down that emergency button. You are essentially calling "time out" on your negative thoughts. You are taking a chunk of time to do nothing but concentrate on your

Observer task. No checking back to monitor your physical symptoms, no evaluations of how poorly the interruption is working. Remember, this is Step 1, pure observing. Any interpretations ("This won't work") that float up during this time—thirty seconds to two minutes—should be gently dismissed.

Gaining control of these initial few moments will be a turning point. Once you have interrupted the pattern, even briefly, your mind makes room for positive, supportive thoughts about the problem. When you gain the edge of time, you gain perspective. Then, when you are ready, you can turn your Observer to your physical sensations, your negative thoughts, or your environment.

Imagine that you are driving down the freeway when you begin to feel anxious.

SUPPORTIVE OBSERVER: "I'm starting to get some panicky feelings; but I don't need to get all worked up. This is not an emergency. I need to interrupt the pattern."

ACTION: You start to notice the license plate and color of each car that passes in the outside lane.

OBSERVER: "O.K., here I am still driving the car. I've been paying attention to the license plates and car colors as a way of gaining perspective. I don't seem to be getting worse. I'm not losing control. What can I observe about my body? My heart isn't racing like it was. But I am squeezing the steering wheel really tightly with both hands, and my knuckles are white. I feel the knots in my shoulders. It feels like I am lifting my shoulders up to my ears."

SUPPORTIVE OBSERVER: "I'm in full control of my driving even though I am nervous. I can loosen my grip and still have control of the wheel. I can loosen my shoulders. I'm O.K."

ACTION: You take a deep breath, let out a sigh, loosen your hands on the wheel, and relax your shoulders. You concentrate on breathing calmly.

SUPPORTIVE OBSERVER: "My driving skills are good right now. I think I began to panic when I read that sign saying, 'Next exit 9 miles.' I need to reassure myself."

ACTION: You continue Supportive Observer comments. "I'm doing fine. I really caught myself early this time. I deserve a pat on the back. I can be nervous and still drive competently. I'll get where I'm going and back again."

TAKING CONTROL OF THE MOMENT OF PANIC

1. Listen for your worried, self-critical, or hopeless thoughts about your body and your circumstances.
2. Disrupt this negative pattern.

   - Use the Calming Breath or Calming Counts.
   - Find some neutral or pleasant task to occupy your conscious thoughts.

3. As you gain control of your thoughts and your breathing, observe your physical sensations, your negative comments, and your surroundings.
4. Answer the question "How can I support myself right now?"
5. Take supportive action on the basis of your answer.

In a panic-prone situation, you will not remain in your Observer or Supportive Observer role the entire time. Just as it does during you practice experiences, your mind will float away into Worried, Critical, and Hopeless Observer comments. You should expect that. As soon as you realize you are thinking negatively, disrupt that pattern. Return again to Observing, commenting with your Supportive Observer, and choosing an action. Whenever you feel in trouble, your first question should be, "How can I support myself right now?" Here is one way to view this dynamic. Don't expect that you are going to completely eliminate the negative chatter with a *replacement* voice. Instead, consider that you are bringing up a *parallel* voice that supports you and manages those negative thoughts. You will still hear that chatter, because part of your mind is still worried and believes you need to pay attention to its point of view. Your job is to incorporate that voice within your Supportive Observer comments, and not let it be a competing voice that you must argue with. When you hear yourself say, "This is too frightening for me," you can respond by saying, "I understand how scared I am, and I'll be able to do this anyway." You will most likely continue to feel scared and comment about your fear, but you can base your *actions* on your commitment to your goals. That is courage: you feel frightened, you acknowledge those feelings, and you move ahead anyway. As long as you can find your Supportive Observer, panic will never consume your life again.

17

Paradox in Action

How does one fight anxiety attacks?

I am sitting in Linda M.'s living room, listening to the story of her five-year battle with panic. The curtains are drawn, as if to keep out the fear. For six long years she has remained behind the doors of her home, too afraid to step outside.

> As soon as I consider taking a walk alone, my heart begins to pound and I get a tingling feeling from my upper body right down to my knees and toes. It feels as if my throat will close. I can't swallow. I try to fight all these symptoms at once, but that seems to bring on the panic. The more I fight it, the worse I become. I ask myself the same questions: "What's making me this way? Why does it continue? Why does it get worse?"

Donna B. is an agoraphobic who has suffered from anxiety attacks for over twenty-one years. During her worst months only her bedroom was a safe haven from the symptoms.

> When that panicky feeling starts, I want to fight it. But instead I almost always run from it. And it seems the faster I run, the faster it catches up to me. I've used the expression "quicksand": the more I struggle, the deeper I sink into it. After a while I almost feel the surrender: "O.K., fear, you've got me."

Linda and Donna fight the most devastating form of panic, the extreme case in which the individual becomes trapped inside her own home. Yet they illustrate the two primary ways each of us tends to battle our enemies. If we must face them, we gather our resources to fight them head to head. If we feel inadequately prepared to fight and win, we choose to steer clear of them, to avoid any kind of confrontation.

With panic these two strategies seem to fail. As Linda describes, the more you fight the symptoms directly, the stronger they seem to grow. The more you avoid panic-provoking situations, the more panic controls your life. The more you run from panic, the faster it seems to chase you.

In chapter 13 you learned about how our instinctual defenses fail to overcome panic. In fact, they actually support the recurrence of anxiety attacks. We encourage and strengthen the power of panic by treating it as our "enemy," to be avoided or to be battled. If we place ourselves on guard, waiting and watching for the next signs of trouble, we are inviting panic to return sooner. How? By establishing a special relationship with panic, a relationship of opposites. To take control of panic you need to understand this special relationship and then learn how to alter it. You also learned in chapter 13 about the Eight Attitudes of Recovery. Now we will look more closely at this paradoxical change in stance toward anxiety, and how to apply it during the moment of panic.

THE BALANCE OF POWER

First, let's look at this relationship of opposites. All the activities of our world are built around a dynamic tension between opposing forces. In chapter 8 I described the balance between rest and activity and between expansion and contraction, using the examples of the ocean tides, a pendulum, summer and winter, day and night, our patterns of work and rest, and the movements of our heart and lungs. I presented them as essential life-sustaining rhythms. The Emergency Response and the Calming Response also form a relationship between two equally powerful and opposing systems within the body that help to maintain our balance of health.

Polarity creates and maintains all types of activity. Every book, play, short story, movie, or TV show involves at least one basic polarity: antagonist versus protagonist, a detective missing the answers, a man wanting a woman, a teenager struggling between right and wrong, a poor family seeking food or shelter. Without this basic push-and-pull found in conflict, desire, struggle, decisions, or other differences, these dramas would not succeed. It is the tension of such unresolved problems that maintains our interest and involvement. In world politics, major activity is found only where a polarity exists, such as ideological differences between the United States and the Soviet Union from the 1960s through the 1980s, or one country's need to import what it is missing and another's need to export what the other needs.

On a more personal level, all parents have experienced this same dynamic when you take a toy away from a child; instantly the struggle begins, because now the child *wants* the toy. If you surrender and give the toy back, the child is soon bored with it and moves to some other activity.

Scientifically, opposites attract. Place the north end of a bar magnet next to another magnet. It will repel the other north end and attach itself to the south end. To make sure we continue to populate the earth, Mother Nature creates men and women as attractive opposites, producing desire.

In each of these examples there exists a complementary relationship between two opposites. Think of your own life and the lives of others around you. Whenever we set our minds to a goal, whether it is to graduate from school, achieve recognition, cook a meal, or take a vacation, we create this dynamic tension by choosing something we don't already have. We produce our positive, goal-oriented drive by distinguishing between what we have now and what we want. We are missing that degree, that recognition, that supper, or that vacation. And we seek out what we are missing. Once we reach that goal, we stop working and come to rest. Of course, moments later we have some new goal, large or small, because this process takes place constantly. These polarities, and the ensuing tensions they create, are not bad or wrong; in fact, they are the driving force of all action. If activity is taking place within a given field, you will find a basic tension between two opposites.

Now let's reverse the tables. How do you write a screenplay that will fail at the box office? Here is one way: make all your characters happy and content. Don't let any character worry, or set a tough goal for himself, or realize that he needs something more in his life. Let no one struggle to fulfill a dream. How will your audience react? Zzzzz.

How could we reduce the hostile tensions between two opposing countries? One way would be to devote a greater amount of media and government attention to our similarities instead of our differences, thus reducing the degree of polarization. Or we could discover a foe that is more powerful than either country alone (a worldwide disaster, another Hitler, or aliens from outer space). This would shift the dynamic tension toward a new polarity, a new "them versus us."

How can you make yourself depressed? By never setting any goals for yourself, by never striving toward the future. By not believing that things change or that you can change. By expecting that tomorrow will turn out just as badly as yesterday did. How could you deepen your depression? By creating a polarity in your mind between "everybody else" (who can change) and you (who can never be different).

HOW TO INVITE PANIC

In light of this principle of tension between opposites, how might panic attacks continue in someone's life? *Whenever you resist something, that something will persist,* because you have created a polarity. By resisting a panic attack, you support it, and the stronger your resistance, the greater your support. Here are several ways to prolong the existence of panic in your life:

- Fear panic.
- Actively fight against a panic attack.
- Avoid any panic-provoking situation.
- Set a goal of "never ever" having another anxiety attack.
- Worry about the next time you might feel the symptoms of panic.
- Try not to notice tensions.
- Expect to master panic before you face it again.
- Run away from panic symptoms.

Each of these actions invites anxiety attacks by creating a dynamic tension between you and panic. This tension takes on a life of its own and becomes the driving force behind an ongoing process. It provides the energy that sustains the process. You must interrupt this pattern if you are going to take control. Here is the paradox: to win against panic you must stop fighting it or running away from it.

Imagine that you are walking alone on an isolated dirt road in a foreign country. You are enjoying this beautiful peaceful day when in the distance you see a cloud of dust rising. You watch it curiously for quite some time. Soon you begin to make out the forms. Finally you see what faces you. Marching directly toward you are two hundred native warriors, each with battle attire and each carrying a long, sharp spear. They continue to advance, closer and closer. Now they are upon you. What do you do? Do you shove at them? Do you tell them to get out of your way? Do you begin to run away? Attacking and retreating both seem to be poor choices. Either one would provoke an aggressive response.

Take that same road and those same two hundred warriors. This time imagine that as you spot them approaching, you slowly move off the road, sit down, cross your legs, and simply observe them as they pass. What will they do?

Most likely the worst they will do is to jeer at you as they pass. What powerful warrior needs to prove himself by attacking someone who is sitting, passive and defenseless, off to the side? If you run or fight, you are producing just the polarity for which these warriors are prepared. If you do nothing but *passively observe,* you do not attract their attention.

"I Can't Catch My Breath!"

It is the same way with panic. To end your active, immediate resistance to the symptoms is the major first step. In some situations the best strategy is to go even one step further—do the very action that scares you the most. For instance, some people, when they get panicky, feel as though they can't get a full breath of air. This, of course, sets off their internal alarm, because everyone knows you need air to live. They begin gasping for a breath and becoming increasingly anxious.

What is the best maneuver when you can't catch your breath? Exhale all the way. But imagine suggesting that to someone in the middle of a panic. "What, are you insane? I'm on my last breath and you want me to let it all out?!" Paradoxical suggestions are always provocative. That's exactly what you want to do—provoke a confrontation with your ongoing ineffective strategy. Do the scary thing—let all that air out. Then you will discover that the lungs are relatively passive in the breathing process. As you exhale, the air pressure drops in the lungs relative to the outside air, the muscles around the rib cage contract, lifting the rib cage up, and air rushes into your lungs. Frightening as it seems, only through a full and complete exhale can you get a clear sense of a full, deep breath of fresh air.

GIVING UP THE STRUGGLE

Your most effective defense against anxiety attacks will involve the use of paradox. Dr. Claire Weekes, in her book *Simple, Effective Treatment of Agoraphobia,* recommends four methods of managing symptoms of anxiety: *face* the symptoms—do not run away; *accept* what is taking place—do not fight; *float* with your feelings—do not tense; *let time pass*—do not be impatient.

Each of these is a paradoxical response, one that seems contrary to logic. Logic tells us that in a threatening situation we should flip on our Emergency Response, tense the body, and immediately begin fighting. Or if we imagine we will lose, run like the devil before we get hurt.

Instead, what I am suggesting is that you flip on your Calming Response, relax the muscles of the body, don't fight your physical sensations, and don't run away. It's much like those Chinese finger cuffs we played with as kids. Do you remember them? They were made from a cylinder of thin woven bamboo, just large enough to fit the first finger of each hand into each end. You would give the finger cuffs to an unsuspecting friend and instruct him to place his fingers inside. That was the easy part. When he attempted to remove his fingers, the cuffs tightened. The more he tugged, the tighter the cuffs were. Those darn cuffs defy all logic because they are created paradoxically. To remove your fingers your need to *push* the bamboo together again with your free fingers, not pull them apart. It is the same with quicksand. If you struggle, you sink. If you remain very still—which goes against all your instincts—you have your best chance of remaining on the surface.

In chapter 7 you read about Michelle R., who became so fearful of panic that she stopped driving and avoided taking walks, staying home alone, or shopping alone. After a few sessions she realized that she was contributing to her panic symptoms by her Worried Observer thoughts. One morning, just prior to a business meeting, she caught herself thinking questions such as "What happens if you feel overwhelmed? Or if you get that panicky feeling?" While asking herself these questions she began to develop symptoms, and moments later she produced an anxiety attack. At that moment she recognized that her fearful thoughts of panic can lead directly to her actual panic symptoms.

From this awareness, Michelle made rapid progress. Several weeks later she began to practice driving alone and to take a few short walks. Her Worried Observer comments continued to hinder her:

> We agreed last week that I would return home from the session by driving on the freeway, and I did. Right before I got on the road I started to feel anxious. I thought, "What if I get a panic attack and I can't get off the highway?" I remained tense most of the drive, and my hands were perspiring. But I started thinking that I had an option to continue or to stop, and I really wanted to continue. I felt good that I made the progress. The worst part was anticipating the drive, not the drive itself.

Notice how Michelle succeeded in switching from her Worried Observer comments to a Supportive Observer stance. She said the worst part was before starting the drive, because that is when her Worried Observer typically runs through a series of negative fantasies about the future. She began by worrying about some catastrophic event that might take place if she kept driving. Once she began the drive she shifted into a permissive attitude, giving herself choice. "It's O.K. to stop driving if I need to. Or I can choose to keep going if I want." By always giving herself supportive options, she gained the confidence to continue. And she was able to follow through on her desire, which was to complete her task.

To fight panic paradoxically is to go against our basic instincts. I knew that Michelle needed to experience some success in managing her anxiety before she would be ready for my next instructions. Now that she was able to persist through mild symptoms and continued Worried Observer comments, I presented the idea of paradox: if you stop fighting panic, it will disappear. For the coming week I gave her the following instruction: "The next time you have fearful thoughts about panic, I want you to try, at that very moment, to have a full-blown panic attack. Tell yourself to increase your heart rate, to become dizzy. Try to produce all your symptoms."

As you can imagine, Michelle nervously laughed at my suggestion and questioned my seriousness. I explained the rationale behind this seemingly illogical advice. When we become afraid of symptoms we are supporting those same symptoms by establishing an oppositional relationship. The more fearful we become, the stronger they grow. By removing our fear we destroy this complementary relationship. We drain all the strength out of panic, because it requires our resistance in order to live.

In this same way, if you attempt to stop the symptoms or try to fight them, you are simply supporting and prolonging them. If you practice some kind of relaxation technique and then anxiously wait for it to reduce your symptoms, you will be disappointed. As I spelled out in chapter 13, techniques will not conquer panic; attitude will.

INVITING THE SYMPTOMS

In a paradoxical strategy your attitude must be this: "I want to bring these symptoms under voluntary control. I would like to increase all my symptoms right now." Then consider each symptom that typically bothers you. "I would like to start perspiring more. Let me see if I can become dizzy or make my legs shaky, right now." Through this attitude you accept your symptoms, and you permit them to exist. If you practice any relaxation techniques at that moment, you do so as a way to end your Emergency Response and reduce your Negative Observer comments so that you can continue to accept and encourage symptoms.

Listen to Michelle's description of her experience the following week.

> MICHELLE: I took a long walk on Saturday. First I walked to a shopping mall and bought a few things. That only took about half an hour, so I decided to walk down some residential streets. I felt a little panicky because there were no stores, no telephone booths to turn to for help—unfamiliar territory. I took a few Calming Breaths and reassured myself. Again, I found that my anticipation of trouble caused me more problems than any actual symptoms.

DR. W.: What kind of thoughts did you have?

MICHELLE: I would think, "Here I am . . . People don't know me . . . What if I faint? . . . No one would help me . . . I could start feeling dizzy." Then I would remember to do my breathing exercise and to say some positive things to support myself.

Remember the exercise you told me about last week, "Try to bring on the symptoms yourself"? I was surprised that the thought came to mind, but at one point I said, "Why don't you go ahead, feel like you're going to faint and see what happens?" And I sort of brought things back into perspective.

Dr. W.: How do you mean "brought things back into perspective"?

MICHELLE: Well, for a few moments *nothing* happened. Then I said to myself, "No, you know you're not going to faint. You know this happens to you all the time. You can walk through this neighborhood, and you are going to feel good about that when you are done." It was easy after that.

Something else seemed to change after Saturday. I've noticed an overall difference in my attitude . . . about myself. I seem to be staying away from criticizing myself. I'm not as down on myself. It's as though I started accepting my symptoms and accepting myself. Then Tuesday I spent the night alone for the first time in ages. That went well, no problems.

Michelle's experience with paradoxical intention is typical. When you completely and honestly request that your symptoms increase, they will usually diminish instead. It is important, however, that you don't make a pseudo-request, such as, "I'm beginning to become anxious. Now, I'd like this anxiety to increase . . . but I hope it doesn't, because then I'll never be able to handle it. So this trick had better work soon!" By fearing an increase in symptoms and trying to "trick" them into diminishing quickly, you fall back into the trap of opposing panic, and thereby encouraging and supporting those symptoms.

Here is how we might analyze Michelle's activity that Saturday through the experience of her Observer.

OBSERVER: [While walking throughout the shopping mall] I'm enjoying myself here today. I'm surprised and I'm pleased. I've been here a half hour. I want to walk around for at least another hour to build my confidence. I could walk down some residential streets, but I might start getting nervous.

SUPPORTIVE OBSERVER: It's time for me to take a little bigger risk. I need the practice.

WORRIED OBSERVER: [While walking through the neighborhood] Here I am in a strange place. People don't know me. What if I faint? No one would help me. I could start feeling faint.

OBSERVER: I'm starting to get worried and panicky. I can feel my heart beating.

SUPPORTIVE OBSERVER: I need to calm myself and feel reassured.

ACTION: Takes several slow, easy Calming Breaths. Tells herself, "This is not an emergency. It's O.K. to be somewhat anxious right now since I'm trying something new. I can be a little afraid and still take this walk. I am in control."

WORRIED OBSERVER: There aren't any stores around to turn to for help. There is no phone to use in case I have a panic attack. Oh no, I'll never make it.

OBSERVER: I'm starting to get upset again.

SUPPORTIVE OBSERVER: I need to take care of myself right now. I'll try what Dr. Wilson suggested last week.

ACTION: Tells herself, "Why don't I go ahead, feel like I'm going to faint, and see what happens, I'll increase my symptoms right now. I'll try to get dizzy and pass out on the sidewalk." She stops walking and tries to "will" herself into fainting.

OBSERVER: [After a couple of minutes] No, I can tell that I'm not going to faint. My symptoms aren't increasing even though I'm trying.

SUPPORTIVE OBSERVER: I can walk through this neighborhood, and I'm going to feel good when I'm done. [Her symptoms decrease, and she completes her walk.]

Fighting paradoxically is not only the instruction to increase your symptoms; it is an attitude and perspective to use whenever you face a panic-provoking situation. And it is a basic principle behind most of the practical skills in this book. For instance, in the Deep Muscle Relaxation exercise, you tense a muscle group to make it relax. In a panic-provoking situation, you calm your mind and relax your body. By calming yourself, you become more alert and better prepared to take control of panic than if you were to tense up for the fight.

USING PARADOX DURING PANIC

1. Take a Calming Breath, then begin natural breathing.
2. Don't fight your physical symptoms and don't run away.
3. Decide if you want to use paradox.
4. Observe your predominant physical symptom at this moment.
5. Say to yourself, "I would like to take voluntary control of these symptoms. I would like to increase my [name the predominant symptom]."
6. Consciously attempt to increase that symptom.
7. Now attempt to increase all the other symptoms you notice: "I would like to perspire more than this. Let me see if I can become very dizzy and make my legs into jelly, right now."
8. Continue natural breathing, while you consciously and fully attempt to increase all your symptoms of panic.
9. Do not get trapped in worried, critical, or hopeless comments such as "This had better start working soon! I certainly must be doing this wrong. It'll never work."

When you are controlled by panic you are run by your Negative Observer voice—"I can't . . . ": "I can't feel this way." "I can't get anxious, because someone will notice." "I can't handle this experience." As you begin to gain control over panic, you will notice that your voice shifts to that of the Supportive Observer—"It's O.K. . . . I can . . . ": "It's O.K. to feel this way." "I can be anxious and still perform my job." "I can manage these symptoms." Using paradox, you progress to the opposite end of the continuum. You take full responsibility for your symptoms by inviting them—"I want to . . . ": "I want to make my heart beat faster." "I'd like to see just how much I can perspire right now." "I want to increase all of these symptoms immediately." Keep in mind that this shift represents more than just a difference in semantics—it reflects a new attitude.

Negative Observer ⎯⎯⟶ **Supportive Observer** ⎯⎯⟶ **Paradox**
"I can't..." ⎯⎯⟶ "I can... It's OK..." ⎯⎯⟶ "I want to..."

FIGURE 11. *The shift in attitude toward one's panic symptoms.*

Start by practicing the use of paradox when you are feeling just a few minor symptoms. If you have trouble mastering the approach, look first at your attitude. Once your attitude is set—your complete willingness to embrace the symptoms in order to diminish their power—your skill will improve dramatically.

Experiment with using humor, because humor can put some distance between you and the symptoms. Try to prove to the world that you are a champion fainter. See if you can tie your stomach in knots so tightly that even the butterflies want out of there.

Don't be disappointed by early setbacks, because once this special attitude is in place, your entire perspective will have shifted. The goal of accepting and increasing anxiety is the object, rather than being free of anxiety. Panic comes when we try to control our anxiety and we fail. Since you are no longer trying to control your symptoms, it is much harder to experience a sense of failure. And when you don't think "I am failing right now," panic usually won't set in.

To win over panic, you stop fighting it. To rid yourself of panic, you let it exist. To conquer panic, you stop resisting. And that is the paradox.

18
Experience: The Greatest Teacher

Most people who are learning to handle panic seek ways to manage their symptoms when they appear. That is an understandable approach, but an insufficient one. To win over panic you must seek it out. All the new knowledge and skills regarding panic attacks that you have gathered so far prepare you for the important job of approaching the situations that you fear. This chapter attends directly to that job: to set up practice sessions that help you master this problem.

In previous chapters I have emphasized breathing skills and formal relaxation techniques. These play an important role in your program, which I have discussed. However, do not place too much emphasis on stopping panic by your breathing or abolishing panic by your formal relaxation skills. In the end, your strongest suit is to experience your negative sensations and learn to be unafraid of them. *Here is the best approach: use your breathing skills and relaxation skills in response to your uncomfortable physical sensations once they have started.* You can also use them before symptoms begin, but don't use them to *prevent* symptoms. You need to be willing to experience and to accept symptoms. Don't misdirect your attention toward strategies to avoid symptoms. These guidelines are for anyone who desires to control anxiety attacks, whether their episodes of panic occur within panic disorder, a phobia, asthma, premenstrual syndrome, depression, or any of the other physical or emotional difficulties mentioned in this book.

GUIDELINES FOR FACING PANIC

Find a Supportive Ally

We humans are social beings. We operate best when in communication with others. We change ourselves according to our relationship with others. When it comes to solving problems, there is no benefit to working in isolation and secrecy. You will make your most productive advances when you are supporting your own efforts and when you spend time with others who support you. It is essential that you develop a Supportive Observer within you as you face panic. One way to encourage your Supportive Observer is to develop relationships with people who have those qualities.

Find at least one ally: someone who cares about your well-being and values your worth, someone who respects and supports your goals. In choosing supportive allies, look for these traits: They remind you of your freedoms and choices. They give you permission to feel safe. They support all your efforts and invite you to feel confident. They trust you. They believe you can change, so they expect a positive future. They know there is always more than one option in any decision. They help you focus more on solutions than on problems.

An ally may be your spouse, some other family member, a close friend, someone who has struggled with these problems before, or a trained health professional. Often a person is willing to support us but doesn't know the best way to go about it. Most likely you will have to explain to your allies how they can help. For instance, you might want them to read this book so that they can better understand the problems you face. Or you might need to explain how the Supportive Observer sounds, as described in chapter 16.

This is not to imply that your allies must always be available to help you every step of the way. The most important role they play is to let you know you are not alone. When you know that someone in the world understands you, then you can feel you have a choice: you don't have to do this by yourself. You can feel safe: someone will be there to listen to you. You can feel supported: you don't have to be strong and independent 100 percent of the time. And you can feel confident: with the support of your allies you can learn to do most anything you desire.

When you have to depend totally on yourself, the pressures can be great. When you depend totally on someone else, you diminish your self-esteem and pride. But when you have someone in your life who is committed to a supportive relationship, then your personal power is greatly enhanced. Some days we are in no mood to pick ourselves up by the bootstraps, put on a smiling face, and meet the world head on. How nurturing it is to call someone and say, "Tell me everything's going to turn out O.K." Hearing that supportive voice can virtually be a life-saver. Over time, those supportive voices teach you how to talk to yourself in a sometimes gentle, sometimes firm voice that keeps this current problem in perspective as you explore solutions.

Always Fight For, Not Against

Taking control of panic is a positive process. We all have images of how we would like our lives to turn out. We consider tasks we wish to accomplish, pleasures we hope to enjoy, relationships we want to prosper. By gaining control over panic you get to turn your sights toward the positive future.

Panic, however, has other plans for you. It invites you to stop whatever else you are doing and fight against it. Panic would like you to halt your life and think of nothing else except your struggle with it. In a paradoxical way, panic lives off your willingness to fight it or run from it.

Don't fall for this trap. Never fight against this invisible enemy. Turn your eyes toward your positive goals, whether for today, this week, this year, or your life. Then fight forward, toward them. When you become anxious, tense or panicky, you then find ways of taking care of those feelings in order to continue moving forward. Always keep an eye on your positive future.

Let me illustrate this point with an analogy. Let's say that you have had a busy, active week. It's now Friday afternoon. Tomorrow, company will arrive for a weekend visit. You would like to prepare by cleaning the house and doing some laundry but at the same time you feel physically fatigued from the week.

What do you do? One choice is to focus on your fatigue. "I'm not going to let this exhaustion beat me. I'm going to fight that couch, because I want so much just to lie down and sleep." Notice how your attention now turns to the negative: how to stop exhaustion from setting in, how to keep yourself from taking a rest. You waste energy in this struggle.

Another choice is to look toward the positive future. "I would like my home to appear clean tomorrow. I also want to feel rested. Most important, I want to enjoy my guests over the next two days."

When you look forward to your desired goals, your attitude shifts. Perhaps in the long run it is best that you take that nap right now so that you will feel more like cleaning in a couple of hours. Or maybe doing a quick pickup and hiding that dirty laundry in a closet will give you more time to relax and enjoy your friends. Fighting exhaustion is no longer the issue. Straightening up a bit, feeling rested, and having a pleasurable weekend are much more important.

When anxiety or panic arrives, keep one eye on your positive goal while you respond. In essence, your attitude is "I am going to continue in this direction. Right now I need to see how I can support myself while I'm feeling uncomfortable. I'll take as long as I need to support myself so that I can continue heading toward my goal."

Face Panic Paradoxically

While you are moving forward toward your positive goals, assume that you will face panic along the way. When we set our sights on a challenging task we usually expect that we will work hard to achieve it. We make sacrifices and sometimes deny ourselves the easy way out of problems, because we know that is the cost we must pay. Struggle and effort, then, are part and parcel of working toward a positive goal. There are no surprises in that logic.

The twist comes when we face our anxieties along the way. During these moments, the needed work is often to *stop* working so hard. That's what the strategies described in this book are for: to help you *not* struggle with panic. You can use any one of the several Calming Response skills while facing panic, but not so that you can better "fight" panic or "banish" panic at that moment. Instead, consider them ways of passing the time while panic tries to pick a fight with you. By changing your attitude toward panic, you withhold its nourishment. It dies off from lack of attention. The same principle is involved when you purposely try to produce your symptoms, as explained in chapter 17. Whenever you permit panic to exist while you keep moving toward your positive goals, you weaken panic's grip on your life.

This, then, is the paradox. You must always work actively toward your goals. However, when panic stands in your way, you take control of it by not pushing or struggling. You slow down long enough to regain control, then continue on your way.

Set Your Long-term Goals

Panic exerts a force over you. It attempts to push you into a corner where you feel trapped and afraid: To confront this force you must place some target in front of you, some positive goal to reach.

Creating your own goal will give you a clear sense of purpose. When you feel lost or confused, this goal can remind you of your positive direction. Let's decide to divide your goals into Long-term and Short-term. Long-term Goals represent your final desired outcome regarding your basic difficulties with anxiety. Short-term Goals focus your attention for only several days, weeks, or months. Often there are several Short-term Goals for each Long-term Goal.

IDENTIFYING YOUR LONG-TERM GOALS

1. List all of the situations in which you have difficulty managing your anxiety and all the situations you avoid out of fear.
2. Rewrite each item to create a positive Long-term Goal.
3. If you have listed more than one Long-term Goal, rank order them two times:
   A. from the least difficult to the most difficult
   B. from your highest priority to your lowest priority

Start by identifying your Long-term Goals. Take time to follow these instructions, writing down each of your answers. First, list all of the situations in which you have difficulty managing your anxiety and all the situations you avoid out of fear. Then, rewrite each item to create a positive Long-term Goal. Here are several examples:

change "I don't want to be scared in restaurants."
  to "I will feel safe in restaurants and comfortably enjoy meals with friends."

change "I'm anxious on planes."
    to "I will be able to regularly fly in a plane across
         country."

change "I avoid parties or large groups."
    to "I will feel in control at parties and will enjoy
         myself without drinking alcohol."

change "I'm afraid to drive far alone."
    to "I will feel confident as I drive alone any distance I
         desire."

If you have listed more than one Long-term Goal, rank order them two times: first, from the least difficult to the most difficult; and second, from your highest priority to your lowest priority.

Set Your Short-term Goals

Mastering panic also requires a smaller Goal, which I call your Short-term Goal. This Short-term Goal will be your immediate task that moves you closer to your Long-term Goal.

To understand the difference between a Long-term Goal and a Short-term Goal, consider this example. Imagine that you are thirty years old and have worked as a typist for the past six years. After much soul-searching you feel a strong need to become more independent in your life's work. You decide to establish as your Long-term Goal greater job independence. Now what?

Your next step is to create a Short-term plan that will help move you toward independence. You ask yourself, "What can I do today, this week, or this month about that goal?" The answer to this question is your Short-term Goal: "This month I will investigate what kinds of jobs might give me greater independence." This Short-term Goal now gives you a concrete and specific set of tasks to accomplish in the immediate future. Once you set your Short-term Goal, you always have some positive tasks to direct your actions.

Let's say that after a month of exploring options, you take another step closer to your goal: "I think there is room in this city for a word-processing service. With my experience I know what it takes to provide quality typing to customers. I think I am capable of managing a small staff of typists. But I don't know much about business." You set your next Short-term Goal: "I'll take a 'small business' course at night this fall at the technical college." Now you have a distinct focus. You must select the best course, register, buy the materials, attend class each week, complete your homework assignments, and so forth.

It is far easier to motivate yourself when your goal is almost within reach. Small decisions can now seem important, because they influence your immediate-future goals. If you have difficulty applying yourself to your studies because owning your own business seems so far in the future, then set a Short-term Goal closer to your reach: "By the end of this course I want to be able to say that I applied myself every week to complete the assignments of that week. Therefore, I will start by finishing my paper due this Friday."

This is the process to use in overcoming panic. Someone might have the positive goal of "looking forward to the adventures of life without fearing panic." You will reach that goal by setting dozens of small goals, one after the other. As you accomplish one Short-term Goal you will set your sights on the next.

Don't be in a rush to reach your Long-term Goal. By focusing too much of your attention on the distant future, you can feel demoralized and frustrated, as though you will never arrive at your destination. Instead, create images of your positive future, but work actively on accomplishing immediate tasks.

Here's how to establish Short-term Goals. From your Long-term Goal list, pick the two goals ranked *least difficult,* and the two *highest-priority* goals. For each of these Long-term Goals, list up to five positive Short-term Goals. These should be stated in positive terms that represent what you want to be able to do within several days or several weeks. If you list more than one Short-term Goal, rank order them two times: first, from the least difficult to the most difficult, and second, from your highest priority to your lowest priority.

At any point in your day, you should be able to remind yourself of your Short-term Goal and create some task that moves you along. Do this not as a way to evaluate your progress, to point out your failures, or to criticize your weaknesses, but as a way to keep yourself motivated. Be careful of the Negative Observers, who are always just around the corner. The biggest troublemakers here are the Critical Observer and the Hopeless Observer.

SETTING SHORT-TERM GOALS

1. From your Long-term Goal list, pick the two *least difficult* goals and the two *highest-priority* goals.
2. For each of these Long-term Goals, list up to five positive Short-term Goals—what you want to be able to do within several days or several weeks, stated in positive terms.
3. If you have listed more than one Short-term Goal, rank order them two times:

   A. from the least difficult to the most difficult
   B. from your highest priority to your lowest priority

You can spot the Critical Observer by its tendency to talk about the past: "I said on Monday that I was going to get out of the house for an hour's walk each day. Here it is Thursday, and I haven't done it yet. *I'm doing terribly! I'm so lazy!*" These last two sentences are not only useless, they are damaging to your self-esteem. When working on the task of conquering panic, set your Short-term Goals with your Supportive Observer. Often the words will be similar, but your tone will reflect a supportive, future-oriented attitude. The Supportive Observer isn't interested in yesterday or even the last hour. It pays attention to the present and the near future, in this manner: "On Monday I decided to walk an hour a day. Now it's Tuesday, and I haven't started yet. *What do I need to do in order to take a walk today?*" Not fulfilling your agreement yesterday is unimportant. Don't waste time focusing on the past. You are not in control of yesterday, but you *are* in control of today.

Again, paradox comes into play as you set your Short-term Goals and work toward them. The paradox is this: you should set a concrete, specific immediate goal, with every intent to fulfill that goal. At the same time, it does not matter whether you actually reach your goal in the way you expected.

Let's say your Long-term Goal is to comfortably shop in stores again. You have been taking a number of steps to prepare, such as practicing the Calming Breath a dozen times each day, spending quiet, meditative time for twenty minutes each day, and learning to give yourself Supportive Observer comments during stressful times. Now you decide to set a new Short-term Goal: "to walk around inside South Square Mall today, looking in store windows with a friend, for thirty minutes." Once you commit yourself to that Short-term Goal, you take as many steps toward that goal as you can manage. It is unimportant whether you accomplish that goal today. Your task is to set a Short-term Goal and move toward it to the best of your ability. And no further. Tomorrow you will simply review your learning from today and set a new Short-term Goal if needed.

We all deserve to feel a sense of pride and success. Don't rob yourself of those good feelings by labeling yourself as a failure when you don't accomplish a task. Do not define your personal success in terms of reaching your Short-term Goal. In conquering panic, you are successful anytime you are actively moving toward your goal, regardless of whether you reach it.

Create Short-term Tasks

In this planning stage, the third step is to identify specific actions that will move you from your abilities today to the abilities needed to reach your goals. Practice this step now by picking one of your Short-term Goals. Think of and write down a list of related tasks that gradually move you closer to accomplishing that Short-Term Goal. The first item should be a low-risk experience that you can imagine accomplishing soon. Each successive item should include a little more risk-taking and should move you a little closer to your Short-term Goal.

Don't worry about creating the perfect schedule. Later, as you begin using this schedule, you will revise it on the basis of your experience. Simply outline a stepwise approach to accomplishing your Short-term Goal. Here is an example.

EXAMPLES OF SHORT-TERM TASK—DRIVING

SHORT-TERM GOAL

Comfortably drive a two-mile loop on the roads around my house.

SHORT-TERM TASKS

1. Map out a two-mile loop on the roads around my house.
2. With a supportive person driving, ride as a passenger on this loop, noticing all the opportunities to pull over to the side of the road or to turn off on a side road, all the gas stations, stores, driveways, and telephone booths that are accessible to me.
3. Drive this loop during a non-rush-hour time with a supportive person as passenger.
4. Drive this loop during a rush-hour time with a supportive person as passenger.
5. Drive this loop during a non-rush-hour time with a supportive person driving another car directly behind me.
6. Drive this loop during a non-rush-hour time with a supportive person driving another car several cars behind me.
7. Repeat step 5 during rush hour.
8. Repeat step 6 during rush hour.
9. Drive alone, with my support person waiting to meet me at a stopping point halfway along the route. Then have my support person leave before me and wait for me at the end of the loop.
10. Drive the entire loop alone while my support person waits at the finish.
11. Drive the entire loop alone while my support person waits by a telephone at another location.

FUTURE SHORT-TERM GOALS

Repeat all these steps for different loops and for longer distances, until I can confidently drive any distance I desire.

In order to look forward to the adventures of your life without fearing panic, one Short-term Goal must be to tolerate mild to moderate symptoms of anxiety. If you can accept those symptoms arising on occasion, and if you can trust in your ability to manage them, your fear of them will diminish.

Once you have set yourself this Short-term Goal of learning to tolerate symptoms, you can establish Short-term tasks. Practicing the breathing and Calming Response exercises in this book is a good start. During this early stage of learning you can begin listening for your Negative Observer comments. Once you discover how your thoughts consistently reinforce your sense of fear, you can begin to practice Supportive Observer comments or other disruptive techniques. In this way you slowly chip away at panic.

EXAMPLES OF SHORT-TERM TASK— TOLERATING ANXIETY

SHORT-TERM GOAL

Learn to tolerate symptoms of anxiety.

SHORT-TERM TASKS

In the next five days, I will

1. Practice breathing skills ten times a day.
2. Listen for and write down Negative Observer comments.
3. Practice Negative Thought Stopping daily.
4. Practice Supportive Observer comments whenever anxious.

Make Your Tasks Reachable

When my first child, my daughter, was about fifteen months old, I watched with amazement as she grew before my eyes. It seemed that each evening she showed me another "breakthrough" in her development. One day she learned how to stack one peg on top of another. I watched her face contort as she tried to send messages of control to her hand, sliding the top peg around on the surface until it finally dropped into position. She probably expended as much mental energy as the Apollo astronauts did in making the first lunar landing. Then, the expression of glee spread across her face as she heard my hollers and applause.

As hard as it was for me to imagine, in another couple of years Joanna was talking in sentences, picking out her own clothes, and eating with a fork and spoon. And I was able to stop washing diapers. To me, there is nothing more remarkable than the physical and intellectual development that takes place between conception and a child's fifth birthday. From just two cells comes the most incredible creation ever contemplated.

Child development is a slow, step-by-step process. One way that parents can negatively influence that process is by attempting to speed it up. A good parent is patient with the child, introducing just enough challenges to stimulate the child's growth, but not so much as to overwhelm. All good things come in time.

Many people who suffer from episodes of panic have been struggling for years and feel as though the struggles they face in the future will be too much to bear. To you I offer the same hopes and expectations parents have for their young children. The body is a phenomenal healing machine. It requires your faith, your commitment, your love, and your patience. With those qualities in place, it heals itself.

Just as your Critical Observer will focus on the past, your Hopeless Observer will think too far ahead. It looks at the distant goal and says, "I'll never get there. It is out of reach. I don't have what it takes to change." The Hopeless Observer has lost all curiosity; it never wonders about possibilities. Instead it uses your powerful skill of imagery to conjure up a picture of failure and concludes, "I can't."

Your Supportive Observer isn't wearing rose-colored glasses, looking through to impossible dreams; unrealistically imagining that you can do anything in the world. But its positive attitude is clearly distinct. The Hopeless Observer will look toward a distant goal and comment, "I can't." Your Supportive Observer will say, "I'm not ready for that, yet."

These two comments may appear to be quite similar, but they

aren't. When you say, "I can't," you are essentially closing the door on your ability to make a difference in your own life. When you say, "I'm not ready yet," you are presupposing that someday you will be ready. Your Supportive Observer keeps the door open for further growth and improvements, regardless of how long it takes.

There is always some step that is within your reach. If you feel incapable of accomplishing any of your tasks, you must create smaller and smaller steps until you find one to which you can say, "I wonder if I can do that? It seems within my reach." For instance, you don't begin learning public speaking skills by placing yourself at the podium in front of a thousand people. You learn by talking into a tape recorder and then listening to your voice, by telling more stories to your friends during dinner conversations, or by imagining yourself comfortably addressing a small group of friends.

If you fear panicking while you drive, the thought of taking a cross-country trip might be overwhelming. What can you imagine doing? Can you sit in the driver's seat of a car, with the ignition off, parked safely in the driveway, while you practice your Calming Response skills? If so, can you start the engine, back the car to the end of the driveway, then return it to its parked position, even if you feel somewhat anxious? Can you do that ten times? Once you feel in control of that step, can you drive around one block, with a supportive friend as a passenger? If not, practice driving to the corner and back. If that is not yet within your reach, let your friend drive the car to the corner, then exchange places and drive back yourself.

HIERARCHY OF TASKS FOR SHORT-TERM GOAL

For each Short-term Goal

1. Create a list of related tasks that gradually move you closer to accomplishing your Long-term Goal.
2. Review the list to ensure that
   A. The first item is the lowest-risk item on the list that you can imagine accomplishing soon.
   B. Each successive item includes a little more risk taking and moves you a little closer to your goal.

Regardless of what you fear, there is always a step small enough for you to take toward overcoming that fear. Whenever you run into difficulty, simply back up to a smaller step. The size of your step can never be too small. The Chinese philosopher Lao Tsu wrote in the sixth century B.C., "A tree as great as a man's embrace springs from a small shoot; a terrace nine stories high begins with a pile of earth; a journey of a thousand miles starts under one's feet."

Face Your Tasks One at a Time

Some of my clients tell me that they feel most comfortable with activities if they can wait until the last moment to decide to participate. Often this is true because these individuals let their negative images and thoughts run wild. If they commit themselves to an activity seven days in advance, they subject themselves to a week's worth of anxiety, fear, and grandiose negative fantasies.

To take control of panic you must take control of planning your safe, enjoyable future. As you learn again that you can indeed plan activities in your life, then you will also be able to pleasantly dream about your future. Our plans and dreams fill us with the sense of hope that we each deserve, no matter what our past may have been.

Unfortunately, part of this planning must now include facing difficult situations. You won't be able to get around anxiety, you'll need to learn to go through it. Begin now by committing yourself to daily practice of facing your discomforts.

Experience is the greatest teacher. All the reading and talking and analyzing and planning that you do will be worthless unless you translate them into action. You must act against your Negative Observer beliefs to overcome them. Without doubt, your actions will provide you with your most valuable experiences.

Don't let your fearful thoughts stop you. And don't wait for some magical day when you will have mastered panic before you have even faced it. To resolve this problem you must start doing those things that you usually avoid, even if you have some symptoms of anxiety. You must practice facing anxiety. So begin by dispensing with excuses that stall your positive physical progress. You can chip away a little bit at your goal each day, if you choose to do so, by practicing your skills.

Now you are ready to begin working on the tasks you outlined above, while applying the knowledge and skills from all of these chapters. The stages of this step are: preparing for practice, beginning practice, responding to worried thoughts, responding to uncomfortable physical sensations, and ending the practice.

As you begin your practice, remember to face tasks one at a time. Don't look back to your last practice unless it is to remind you of your skills and capabilities. And don't look ahead as a way to remind yourself how far you have to go. Continue to practice a specific task until you feel relatively comfortable then begin the next one. Never wait until you are *completely* comfortable. Don't measure your progress by how quickly you improve your skills. Measure your progress by how persistent you are in your determination to reach your Short-term and Long-term Goals. Shaping your positive attitude each day, and developing a consistent schedule for practice—these two intentions will pay off with success.

Choosing a Short-term Goal

You will be practicing the Short-term Tasks listed under one or more Short-term Goals, so your first decision is to choose a beginning Short-term Goal. There are no rules for selecting the perfect Short-term Goal to work on; use your best judgment to pick one. You have rank ordered your Goals in two ways: how difficult they seem and how important they are. Let those rankings help you make your decision. For instance, there may be a goal that is moderately hard on your difficulty list but is a high priority. Your desire to accomplish that goal may help motivate you to work on it now, even though there are easier items on the list.

You also can work on more than one Short-term Goal at a time. Perhaps you choose to focus both on the goal of driving comfortably to the mall and the goal of tolerating exercise that elevates your heart rate. You may have time in your week to practice driving skills every two days and practice cardiovascular workouts on the opposite days.

Preparing for Practice

There is a great array of options for practicing Short-term Tasks. In the beginning weeks, I suggest that you follow a structure similar to the one presented in this chapter. As you get more proficient at designing and implementing your practices, feel free to take short cuts. By the end, your practice can be as informal as this: "Hmm . . . I feel anxious about doing something like that. I think I'll try it!"

One of my clients is working on construction in an office building. One day last month his coworker reported that one of the elevators had been temporarily stuck between floors for a few minutes. Upon hearing that, Alan became anxious and worried about getting stuck himself. Within a few minutes he excused himself, walked to the bank of elevators and rode one to the top floor and back. He simply would not allow his fears to begin to take hold of him anymore.

Before practicing any Short-term Task that moves you closer to one of your Short-term Goals, consider each of these questions in detail. You will benefit from writing your answers down, making them concrete.

PLANNING EACH TASK

1. What is my Short-term Task?
2. When will I do this?
3. How long will I take?
4. What *worried* thoughts do I have about this Task?
5. What *self-critical* thoughts do I have about accomplishing this Task?
6. What *hopeless* thoughts do I have about this Task?
7. What can I say (in place of those negative thoughts) to support myself during this Task?
8. How can I increase my sense of commitment while working on this Task? (Your answer will be information about the setting or event, sense of options, willingness to take risks and feel uncomfortable, use of props such as a book or music, etc.
9. What support do I need from others?

DECIDING HOW LONG TO PRACTICE

Whenever possible, practice your task for forty-five minutes to ninety minutes at a time. It is true that shorter practices also will help your confidence, and some types of practices can only last a few minutes (such as looking people in the eye and smiling as you go through a reception line). However, from research we know that one of the most important purposes of task practice is to develop habituation: during prolonged exposure to an anxiety-provoking situation, intense anxiety gradually decreases. As your anxiety diminishes, you can think more clearly. In the future, when these situations occur again, you will react with some anxiety and some distress, but not with the terror that you once felt.

So when you can, design your sessions for this forty-five to ninety-minute length, which promotes habituation as well as confidence. You may have to repeat the same behavior several times: Forty-five minutes will afford you many elevator rides. An hour's shopping may require a trip to the grocery store, then a walk next door to the pharmacy. Ninety minutes of aerobic exercise can mean that you run in place five minutes, then spend the next fifteen minutes calming yourself down if you got too scared, then another five minutes of aerobics and ten minutes of calming yourself, and so forth, until the time is up. The definition of "practice" means anything that you do while still facing the anxiety-provoking situation. For instance, you might enter the grocery store and stay only five minutes, then have to leave because of your distress level. For the next thirty minutes you may need to sit in your car, practicing your breathing skills to calm down enough to reenter the store. Then you enter the store for another ten minutes before finishing your practice. That equals forty-five minutes of practice—even though most of it was in the car—because all of that time you were working.

CREATING SUPPORTIVE STATEMENTS

Study your answers to questions 4, 5, and 6, above. These Negative Observer statements are the most likely ways you will sabotage your efforts in the practice. Use them to design your supportive statements (question 7). Write these positive statements down on a card to carry with you during practice.

INCREASING YOUR COMMITMENT

As you plan your practice, consider what you can do to support your commitment. Certainly reviewing the eight attitudes in chapter 13 is a positive step, because they will remind you that taking risks is the smartest way to get stronger.

You may also feel safer and therefore more committed if you gather information about the setting or event. If you are attending a party, know what the appropriate attire will be. If you are driving a new route, check the map in advance or take the ride first as a passenger. If you are spending a night in an unfamiliar hotel, call ahead to learn about their facilities.

Bring along any props that can help you manage the situation. For instance, if you are practicing eating alone in a restaurant, you might carry a novel to read as you wait for your food. For a long drive, bring your favorite music or borrow a book-on-tape from the library.

RECEIVING SUPPORT FROM OTHERS

Decide if you would like one or more support persons to assist you in the practice. If so, choose people who believe in your worth and respect your efforts to improve yourself. They don't have to have an intimate knowledge of anxiety problems; in fact, they might even be confused about the subject. They do need to be willing to follow instructions. Tell support people exactly how you would like them to help. What should they say to you before and during the practice? What should they do?

VISUALIZING SUCCESS

Here are two brief visualizations to work with during the few minutes just before you begin your Short-term Task practice. If you are about to enter the grocery store, practice one or both of these visualizations while in your car at the store parking lot. Each of them takes about three minutes.

BRIEF VISUALS BEFORE TASK PRACTICE

1. Close your eyes and visualize yourself accomplishing your task easily and without discomfort. Repeat that positive image three or four times.
2. Close your eyes and visualize yourself moving through your task. Let yourself experience two or three episodes when you have some typical discomfort. Then rehearse what coping skills you want to use to take care of yourself during that discomfort.

Beginning the Practice

Now you are ready to enter the troubling situation. Remind yourself of each of your supportive statements. Take a gentle, slow Calming Breath after saying each one, giving yourself time to believe it.

Enter the situation with the expectation of responding naturally and easily to all that you encounter. Forget about yourself and pay attention to what you are presently perceiving with your senses: what you are seeing, hearing, touching, smelling, and maybe even what you are tasting.

Use any of your skills to manage your thoughts and your physical symptoms. Continue to encourage yourself and ask for any needed support from others.

At the end of chapter 16 I presented a set of steps called "Taking Control of the Moment of Panic." That design will help particularly when you suddenly notice symptoms of panic. With this chapter you are *planning* anxiety-provoking activities, so you will be expecting to experience symptoms. This allows you to respond to early difficulties before they build to a full-blown panic attack.

If you begin worried thoughts or if physical symptoms begin to bother you, use the two approaches below.

RESPONDING TO WORRIED THOUGHTS

The guidelines for handling worries during your task practice are simple: notice your worried thoughts, choose to stop them, then apply skills that support your decision. Which of these skills or combination of skills you use will depend on your Short-term Task, the nature of your worries, and what has helped in the past. Sometimes you will need to explore several options before coming up with the most successful combination.

RESPONDING TO UNCOMFORTABLE PHYSICAL SENSATIONS

As with your worries, the best approach to uncomfortable physical symptoms is a simple one. First, mentally "step back" and notice the sensations without making worried comments. Second, reassure yourself: "It's O.K. for these symptoms to exist right now. I can

RESPONDING TO WORRIES

Notice your worried thoughts.	"I'm working myself up."
↓	
Choose to stop them.	"These thoughts aren't helpful. I can let them go."
↓	
Take supportive action.	PRACTICE ANY OF THESE

PRACTICE ANY OF THESE

Supportive statements
Find something neutral or pleasant
   to do
Negative thought stopping
Postpone your worries
Sing your worries
Write your worries down
Take three Calming Breaths
Do Calming Counts
Move and loosen whole body
Turn attention elsewhere
Leave the situation and go to a
   "safe" place

handle these feelings." Third, ask yourself: "What can I do to support myself right now?"

I have previously discussed many of the supportive skills listed on this chart. Three new options are postponing your worries, singing them, and writing them down. Here is how to use them during your practice.

POSTPONING

An excellent tactic is to postpone your worries for a bit. When you notice yourself beginning to worry, mentally agree to pay attention to those worries. However, choose a specific later time when you will return to them.

How long can you postpone? Can you wait an hour? If you can't postpone for an hour, try a half hour. Try fifteen minutes. Five minutes. Whatever it takes, try to break the automatic process of worry. That's what postponing will do: let you take control over when and where you worry.

Continue to postpone as long as you can. When you feel incapable of postponing the worry any longer, then go ahead and address it. The key is to let at least some amount of time pass without worries dominating your thoughts during the practice.

Experiment with this technique a few times this week. Whatever your worries—whatever the unproductive noises are in your head—practice postponing them. In the process you will be practicing a skill that you can use in preparing for any new challenges panic offers you.

WRITE DOWN YOUR WORRIES

Another way to end your worries is to write them down. Carry a pencil and a small pad with you to your practice session. When you begin those noisy worries, write down your exact thoughts. Don't write down the theme, write down every single repetition of every single worried thought.

Now, what's the benefit here? When you worry, you tend to repeat the same content again and again, right? When you write down the worries, you recognize how repetitive and senseless they are. This perspective quiets the noise. After a while you will probably experience the task—of writing all the content verbatim—as a chore. That's how the writing will help you. After several extended writing sessions you are more likely to say, "OK, I'm worrying. Now I can either go through all the bother of writing these worthless thoughts, or I can just stop worrying right now."

SING A WORRIED TUNE

Another way to begin changing your noisy worries is to sing them. (Okay, stop laughing and let me explain.) Pick up a short phrase that summarizes your worry. Ignore its meaning for a while. Continue to repeat the words, but do so within a simple melody. Keep up this tune for several minutes. Whenever you feel you are less emotionally involved with these thoughts, let go of the tune and the words. Turn your attention elsewhere.

That sounds pretty silly, doesn't it? Here you are, suffering from very distressing thoughts, and I ask you to hum a few bars. But that's the idea. The process of singing your worries makes it difficult to simultaneously stay distressed. Yes, it's stupid. Yes, it sounds childish. Do it anyway!!

I don't expect that you will start singing this little tune and instantly feel happy. In fact, it will probably be hard to feel anything but anxiety when you start singing. But stick with it. And while you're singing, work to become detached from the content of your song. Remember, that's our goal.

Choose among the supportive actions listed, depending on the nature of your symptoms, the circumstances, and what has helped you in the past. Here are some examples.

- You can assure yourself that you can manage your task while experiencing these sensations. You then can turn your attention away from yourself and to the things around you. Involve yourself more actively in your surroundings (seek out a conversation or find something in your environment to study carefully) as a way to diminish your worried involvement in your body.
- You can use Calming Counts as a way to support your physical comfort.
- You can tell a supportive person about what you are feeling and what you want to do to take care of yourself. You can let that person support your efforts.
- You can leave the situation for a brief period as a way to increase your comfort and control, then return to continue your practice.
- You can leave the situation and not return at this time. As you continue to practice your skills, over time you will learn to remain in the scene.

As you study the chart you will notice how similar the actions are when your physical symptoms are your strongest concern. There is one primary difference. Can you see it?

As you can see, there is one distinct difference in how you

RESPONDING TO PHYSICAL SYMPTOMS

Notice your symptoms.   "I'm feeling uncomfortable."
        ↓
Accept them.   "That's O.K. I can handle this."
        ↓
Take supportive action.   PRACTICE ANY OF THESE

Natural breathing
Take three Calming Breaths
Calming Counts
Due-Controlled Brief Muscle
   Relaxation
Ten-Second Grip
Supportive statements
Paradoxically increase symptoms
Move and loosen whole body
Find something neutral or pleasant
   to do
Turn attention elsewhere
Leave the situation and go to a
   "safe" place

---

respond to worried thoughts and to physical sensations. As soon as you notice your worried thoughts, you *choose to stop them.* You reject the negative messages they are giving to your mind and body. The actions you take support that decision. On the other hand, when you notice your physical symptoms, you *choose to accept them.* Resisting your symptoms will only increase your discomfort.

This decision—to accept your symptoms before trying to modify them—is a pivotal one. We have talked about it in several chapters. Start to become curious about its value as you try it out during Short-term Task practice.

Ending the Practice

Now is the time to support yourself for all your efforts. At the same time, review your practice session objectively. Assess what worked and what didn't. Use that information to plan your next practice.

Remember that you are successful every time you decide to practice, regardless of how long you are able to stay in that situation. This is not a test of your ability to stop all sensations of discomfort. Nor is this a test of your progress. This, and every other thing you do, is an opportunity to practice your ability to support yourself. The more you practice supporting every effort and attempt, the stronger you will become and the more willing you will be to practice.

So LISTEN for any harsh self-criticisms or discouraged thoughts after your practice. ("I still get anxious. What's wrong with me! I'll never get better.")

REPLACE THEM with statements of support: "I'm working to change a lot of complex processes. I can't do it all at once. And I'm not trying to do it perfectly. One step at a time; I'm going to get there."

A FINAL NOTE

The trouble with our conscious mind is that it tries too hard.

Consider the performance of athletes. A professional athlete continually practices his drills and observes his techniques to improve his skill. But when it comes time to perform, the professional will stop paying attention to his body. Instead, he wants to trust his instincts, to trust his reflexes, to trust that all his practice has sunk in. He now looks outward, toward the game, toward the ball, toward the movements of other players. When he engages in the event he stops questioning or doubting his ability. He stops watching his style. In short, he asks his critical mind to quiet down so that his body can do its work without disturbance.

Watch and listen to a professional musician performing a concert. He will play with abandonment, often without benefit of sheet music. All the necessary skills and memories flow out of the musician without conscious effort. With effort, certainly, but not *conscious* effort. Professionals trust themselves at another level of being.

Too much conscious attention interferes with our performance, regardless of the task. The human body is the finest, most sophisticated multisensory teaching machine in existence. Our conscious mind is but a minor player. To achieve our best performance we must not allow our conscious mind to become excessively involved in the process. True concentration is effortless, but the hardest job during concentration is to quiet the conscious mind.

All the dozens of ways in which I have approached the problem of panic pivot around the principle of trusting your body. Although many of the practice tasks I suggest in this book involve conscious thinking about each step, your final objective is to do very little conscious work. After you master the basic skills, practice keeping your mind off your body while you think very simply and slowly.

You will evolve beyond technique, all in good time. Your final goal can be to respond automatically and reflexively during times of trouble. You will know you have arrived when, one day, your conscious mind says, "Hey, what happened? I just handled that situation smoothly, and I didn't even know I was doing it."

Part III

SPECIAL ISSUES

19

The Use of Medications

One of the most significant contributions of Western medicine has been the creation and uses of medications to reduce patients' suffering. In recent years, a growing number of medical researchers have been investigating the benefits of medication for individuals who experience panic and phobias. Current research efforts are focusing on all diagnostic categories: panic disorder and agoraphobia, simple phobias, obsessive-compulsive disorder, generalized anxiety disorder, and post-traumatic stress disorder.

The Food and Drug Administration has approved very few medications for use in the treatment of anxiety disorders. The FDA withholds approval until a medication has been proved to be safe and effective in extensive and well-controlled research studies that consistently establish its benefit. This government agency has sanctioned so few medications for two primary reasons. First, a clear and concise diagnosis of panic disorder, agoraphobia, and other anxiety disorders has eluded mental-health professionals for years. The American Psychiatric Association did not classify panic disorder as a distinct problem until its third edition of the *Diagnostic and Statistical Manual,* in 1980. Second, for years we underestimated the number of Americans suffering from these disorders. For this reason, scientists devoted fewer research projects to studying them. Now we know that the anxiety disorders are the number one mental-health problem in the country, ahead of depression and alcoholism. Because of this new knowledge, numerous major research efforts have begun and will continue throughout this decade.

The early years of research in any new area usually lack the coordinated efforts needed to clearly establish the facts. Each scientist is a pioneer, investigating territory never before explored. However, once patterns begin to unfold, we replicate study designs to verify benefits or limits of a specific medication. This period of replication is now under way.

In this chapter I identify several medications that the FDA has approved for use to treat a specific disorder. The edicts of the FDA primarily restrict the manufacturer of the medication from advertising the benefits of that drug for any particular disorder until the FDA approves it for that disorder. However, physicians are able to pre-scribe these medications for any disorder, on the basis of on their professional judgment of the risks and benefits to the patient, as long as the FDA approved the medications in the treatment of other disorders.

Current research suggests that several kinds of medications appear to help reduce symptoms in some individuals who experience anxiety disorders. I identify each of these and give details on each at the end of the chapter. Common brand names of each generic drug appear capitalized in parentheses. Other drugs are currently being investigated, but it is too early to determine their effectiveness. I will mention them, but details of their use are not yet available.*

COMMON MEDICATIONS FOR ANXIETY DISORDERS

Treatment with medications can help in six broad areas: panic attacks; obsessions and worries; general anxiety; simple phobias; social anxieties or phobias; and a combination of depression and anxiety or panic. In this section you will read about the medications that researchers indicate to be the most successful in treating each of these problems. Please know that new medications are continually being tested for anxiety problems. For the most current developments, consult with a psychiatrist who specializes in treatment of the anxiety disorders.

Panic Attacks

For panic attacks, the greatest benefit that medications can provide is to enhance the patient's motivation and accelerate progress

---

*The author gratefully acknowledges James Ballenger, M.D., for his review of this chapter.

toward facing panic and all of its repercussions. For a drug to help in this area, it must help in at least one of the two stages of panic. The first stage is anticipatory anxiety: all the uncomfortable physical symptoms and negative thoughts that rise up as you anticipate facing panic. The second stage is the symptoms of the panic attack itself. Both current research and clinical experience suggest that for some people certain medications may help reduce symptoms during one or both of these stages. If a medication can specifically block the panic attack itself, many patients no longer anticipate events with such anxiety and can overcome their phobias more quickly.

The primary medications used today for panic disorder are the *benzodiazepines,* several types of *antidepressants,* and the new *selective serotonin reuptake inhibitors (SSRIs),* sometimes in combination with these benzodiazepines.

The most common benzodiazepines for panic attacks are *alprazolam (Xanax)* and *clonazepam (Klonopin).* They both block panic attacks quicker than the antidepressants, often in a week or two. They also tend to have fewer side effects than the antidepressants. Both, however, can have withdrawal symptoms as you taper off them. Because alprazolam is quicker acting than clonazepam, its withdrawal effects can be stronger as well. In studies on panic disorder, 43 percent of patients on alprazolam improved after eight weeks on less than 4 mg per day, and 30 percent get better on 4 to 6 mg per day.

The quick-acting nature of alprazolam makes it an ideal medication to take as needed just before panic-provoking events. It takes about fifteen to twenty minutes to offer you its anxiety-reducing benefits. If you place it under your tongue to dissolve (called *sublingual medication*), it can offer benefits within five to eight minutes. Be ready for its bitter taste!

Clonazepam lasts longer in the body than alprazolam, meaning that you can take it just twice a day for a full twenty-four-hour coverage, while alprazolam requires four or five dosings for the same period. Clonazepam is also used as needed before a panic-provoking situation. Some investigators believe it is a better choice than alprazolam during those times because its primary effects are not as strong and also wear off more slowly. When you are practicing the skills of facing your fears, if you notice the effects of a medication, you may tend to attribute your successes more to the medication than to your own efforts. Medications should serve as helpers to your own courage and skills and not get all the credit for good results. Because clonazepam's effects can be less noticable, you will be more likely to say, "Hey, I did it!" instead of saying, "Boy, that drug really works well. Thank goodness it was there to save me!" However, some patients don't like how long the effects last.

There are a few early studies indicating the benefits of diazepam (Valium) and lorazepam (Ativan) for panic disorder. No reliable studies support the use of other minor tranquilizers such as oxazepam (Serax), chlordiazepoxide (Librium), or clorazepate (Tranxene), although these drugs may make the patient feel somewhat calmer.

Of the antidepressants, the tricyclic antidepressant drug *imipramine (Tofranil)* has the longest track record for treating panic attacks. Other tricyclic antidepressant drugs that can help control panic attacks are *desipramine (Norpramin* or *Pertofrane), nortriptyline (Aventyl* or *Pamelor), amitriptyline (Elavil), doxepin (Sinequan* or *Adapin)* and *clomipramine (Anafranil).* In studies of patients with panic disorder, 75 to 80 percent of those placed on an antidepressant significantly improve.

Monoamine oxidase inhibitors (MAOIs) are another family of antidepressants that manage the symptoms of panic. Research studies support extensive clinical experience that shows *phenelzine (Nardil)* as the preferred MAOI. *Tranylcypromine (Parnate)* is also sometimes effective.

Some of the new selective serotonin reuptake inhibitors (SSRIs) are helpful and offer fewer side effects than the tricyclic antidepressants. These include *fluoxetine (Prozac), fluvoxamine (Luvox), sertraline (Zoloft),* and *paroxetine (Paxil).* In studies of patients with panic disorder, 75 to 80 percent of those placed on an SSRI significantly improve. This rate is equal to the success rate of the tricyclic antidepressants that have proved helpful.

The antidepressants trazodone (Desyrel), amoxapine (Asendin), maprotiline (Ludiomil), and bupropion (Welbutrin) are not generally effective for panic disorder.

If a physician recommends a combination of a benzodiazepine and an antidepressant, two approaches are possible. One is to take the antidepressant daily and use a benzodiazepine as needed for increased periods of anxiety or panic. Another method is to use the benzodiazepine with the antidepressant during the first month or two of treatment. As the primary effects of the antidepressant begin, after four to eight weeks, the patient slowly tapers off the benzodiazepine.

Obsessions and Worries

In those suffering from obsessions and worries, medications can reduce the degree of intensity of the worries and their corresponding distress. Medications do not prevent obsessions from occurring. However, when the medication lessens the strength of the worries, the patient can use self-help skills to control them.

Currently, four SSRIs are helpful in treating obsessive-compulsive disorder (OCD): *fluoxetine (Prozac), fluvoxamine (Luvox), sertraline (Zoloft)* and *paroxetine (Paxil)*. The antidepressants *clomipramine (Anafranil)* and *venlafaxine (Effexor)* also help obsessions. The FDA approved Prozac, Luvox and Anafranil as medications beneficial for OCD. The anti-obsessional benefits of any of these medications may not be fully apparent until five to ten weeks after treatment starts.

Imipramine, and *alprazolam* and the mild tranquilizer *buspirone (BuSpar)* also show some indications of being useful for certain individuals. Some investigators have combined buspirone with clomipramine to successfully treat this problem. In addition, some patients with OCD may also have an underlying mood disorder and can benefit from the drug *lithium*.

About 20 percent of individuals with OCD also have tics, which are sudden, uncontrollable physical movements (such as eye blinking) or vocalizations (such as throat clearing). A combination of an SSRI and *haloperidol (Haldol)* can help with such tics and the OCD symptoms.

General Anxiety

For those with general anxiety, medications help reduce some of the symptoms of anxiety. The most commonly prescribed are *buspirone (BuSpar)* and several of the benzodiazepines, such as *diazepam (Valium), alprazolam (Xanax), lorazepam (Ativan), oxazepam (Serax),* and *chlordiazepoxide (Librium)*.

If the anxious patient is able to wait for the benefits of the medication for two to four weeks, buspirone is often a good first choice. However, if he or she needs a more immediate response, then the benzodiazepines may be more appropriate. There are current studies indicating that imipramine and the SSRIs may also be effective against general anxiety.

Simple Phobias

For those with simple phobias, medications can help to reduce the tensions associated with entering the fearful situation. A patient can take a low dose of a *benzodiazepine* about one hour before exposure to the phobic stimulus to help reduce anticipatory anxiety. If this is not sufficient, the physician can prescribe a higher dose for the next time. A chemically dependent patient who is not currently abusing drugs might benefit from one that is not attractive to drug abusers, such as *oxazaepam (Serax)* or *chlordiazepoxide (Librium)*. It is important to note that medications are *not* a successful primary treatment of simple phobias. The treatment of choice involves many of the steps you have read about in this book—learning skills of relaxation and gradually approaching the feared situation while applying those skills. Consider medications only as an option to assist you in your efforts.

Social Anxieties and Phobias

For social anxieties or phobias, medications can help to reduce the tensions associated with entering the fearful situation, can help bring a racing heart and sweaty palms under control, and reduce some shyness.

Physicians use several classes of medications that are beneficial, individually or in combination. The drugs with the longest history of use with social phobias are the beta adrenergic blocking agents, also known as *beta blockers*. The most commonly used are *propranolol (Inderal)* and *atenolol (Tenormin)*. The patient can take *propranolol* as needed or in dosages of 10 to 20 mg three to four times a day or *atenolol* in dosages of 25 to 100 mg once daily. Surprisingly, controlled research studies have not supported the widespread anecdotal reports of success with beta blockers. It's possible that their best use is for occasional mild social anxieties.

The high potency benzodiazepines *clonazepam* (1 to 4 mg per day) and *alprazolam* (1.5 to 6 mg per day) may also be effective. A combination of a beta blocker and low dosages of clonazepam or alprazolam could be best for some individuals.

Current research suggests that the *monoamine oxidase inhibitors (MAOIs),* especially *phenelzine,* are most highly effective medications for treating social phobias. In studies, about 70 percent of subjects improve significantly within four weeks. Occasionally, however, a social phobic can experience an exaggerated response to an MAOI and become *too* talkative, outgoing, or socially uninhibited. In that case the prescribing physician will lower the medication dosage or stop it altogether.

One approach to drug treatment that experts recommend for social fears is to begin by taking a medication only as needed. If patients are anxious only about specific events and if they experience primarily physical symptoms (sweating, racing heart, etc.), about one hour before the event they can take propranolol or atenolol. Propranolol seems to work better for occasional problems, while atenolol may work better for continued problems. If their symptoms are more cognitive (they worry about their performance or the judgment of others), then they can take alprazolam one hour before the event. If they have a mix of these symptoms then a combination of these medications may be more helpful. Benefits of these drugs should last about four hours.

If the social anxiety is more general, unpredictable, and widespread, patients may need to take one of these medications on a daily basis. If it is not helpful within two to three weeks, they can taper off the drug and switch to an MAOI such as phenelzine, at 45 to 90 mg per day. Keep in mind that an MAOI can take from four to six weeks to work.

A number of medications are currently under investigation and may also prove to be helpful. These include *fluoxetine (Prozac)* and other SSRIs.

Anxiety or Panic with Depression

For those suffering from a combination of depression and anxiety or panic, certain *antidepressant medications* can help reduce the depressive symptoms while simultaneously helping to control the panic attacks. The physician can prescribe one of the tricyclic antidepressants with sedating effects, such as *imipramine* or one of the MAOIs. It is also possible to combine the use of a tricyclic antidepressant with *buspirone* or the benzodiazepine *alprazolam*.

GUIDELINES FOR MEDICATION USE

If you would like to consider medication as a form of treatment for your anxiety symptoms, here are a few points that may make your decision easier.

Begin by Obtaining an Accurate Diagnosis

If you are having anxiety symptoms, follow the instructions outlined in chapter 2 to determine first if there is any physical cause. If your physician makes no physical diagnosis, he or she should refer you for an evaluation by a licensed mental-health professional who specializes in anxiety disorders. Once you receive a diagnosis, your options for medications will be clearer.

There Is No Magic Pill

Among clinicians who specialize in anxiety disorders, there is general agreement that medications can be beneficial for some anxious patients when used in conjunction with a treatment approach similar to the one outlined in this book—one that directs you toward altering your dysfunctional thoughts and encouraging your ability to face those situations that you fear. Although we base treatment on the specific problems and resources of each patient, the key to successful cure lies in each individual's sense of his personal ability to face the fearful situations and master his symptoms. All professional interventions, whether in the form of individual therapy, group therapy, medication, behavioral techniques, or practice exercises, should have but one purpose: to stabilize your belief that *you are able to exert personal control over your body and your life*.

Take medications within this context. Often medicines can be a beneficial *short-term* crutch to help while you heal yourself. They do not heal you any more than a cast heals a broken leg. The body heals itself of many problems, given the proper support. For some people, medications offer a good *long-term* support for a disorder that can be chronic and cyclical in nature. Without medications they seem to relapse into troubling symptoms.

Complex problems do not have simple solutions, although many people will look for a quick cure and a magic pill. If they can find a sympathetic physician, they will begin a regimen of medications as their only means of removing all discomfort. Unfortunately, reports in the media that present a limited analysis of a complex problem reinforce the belief that medications are the only answer. By deciding to believe that they have an uncontrollable physical disorder, some patients surrender themselves to anxiety and panic. And in the process, they lose self-esteem, determination, and the willingness to trust in the healing power of their bodies and minds. They remain dependent on medications, physicians, friends, and family as they continue to limit their personal freedom.

Don't Suffer Needlessly to Prove You Are "Strong"

Some people believe that medications are for "weak" people, and they don't want to be "dependent". These people tend to make three mistakes. They avoid taking medications at all, when medications could play an appropriate and significant part in their self-help program. They underdose the medication they are taking, falsely believing that "less is better." Or they prematurely decelerate from a medication that is currently helping them. Medications can be *effective,* and they can be *appropriate* for you, depending on your problem. There is a *specific dose that will be best* for you, that your physician will help identify. And there is justification for some people to remain on medication *even for years* if the side effects are not troubling them, they are not trying to get pregnant, and symptoms tend to return when they experiment with withdrawing from the medication.

Give Medication a Fair Trial

To evaluate the benefit of a medication, you must give it enough time to provide its therapeutic effect. Work with your physician, especially in the early weeks of your medication trial, to adjust the dose and to relieve any worries you might have. Most physicians will initiate any of these drugs at a low dose and then increase it slowly according to your response. You will need a trial of several weeks at full dose to determine the benefits.

Be Willing to Tolerate Some Side Effects of Medications

Side effects are unwanted psychological or physical changes that are typically not directly related to a medication's capability to treat a disorder. All medications have side effects. Rarely, they can be serious. Most will be minor symptoms that may be bothersome to you but do not require medical attention. These side effects may also diminish or end in a few days or weeks as your body adjusts to the medication. Before using one of these medications, ask your physician about the possible side effects: which can you expect, which might diminish over time, and which need his or her attention. Report any persistent or unexpected side effects to your prescribing physician.

I suggest that you educate yourself about the possible side effects, not because these medications are more powerful or more harmful than other drugs, but so that you can tolerate some of the minor symptoms. For instance, the symptoms of dry mouth, blurred near vision, constipation, and difficulty with urination are common side effects of a number of drugs, especially the tricyclic antidepressants. Often they diminish in a few weeks as your body adjusts, or when you reduce the dosage. In the meantime, your prescribing physician may suggest ways of relieving the discomfort. You can relieve a *dry mouth* by frequent rinsing or by sucking on hard candy or chewing gum (preferably sugarless). *Blurred vision* may clear up in a couple of weeks. If not, a new eyeglass prescription can help. You can counterbalance mild *constipation* by increasing your intake of bran, fluids (at least six glasses a day), and fresh fruits and vegetables. Laxatives may also help. To assist with *problems urinating*, your doctor may prescribe bethanecol (Urecholine).

Another possible side effect is *postural hypotension*, also called *orthostatic hypotension*. This is a lowering of the blood pressure as you stand up from a sitting or lying position, or after prolonged standing. This disequilibrium can cause sensations of dizziness or light-headedness, and sometimes fatigue, especially in the morning when you get out of bed. These are simply signs that your circulatory system needs a little more time to distribute blood equally throughout your body. You may also notice an increase in your heart rate (tachycardia or palpitations) to compensate for this brief hypotension. When this side effect is mild, doctors advise that you get out of bed more slowly in the morning, sitting at the side of the bed for a full minute before standing, and that you also take your time rising from a seated position during the day. If you feel dizzy, give your body a minute to adjust to the standing position. You may also benefit from increasing your salt and fluid intake and possibly even from wearing constrictive support hose.

Here are some ways to deal with a few other common side effects. Some medications have a *sedating effect,* making you drowsy. Physicians suggest that you take those close to bedtime if medically appropriate. On the other hand, if a drug causes you to have *difficulty sleeping,* they may suggest taking the medicine in the morning. As an alternative for either of these problems, you may need to lower the dose or change medications. For *increased sweating,* be sure you increase your fluid intake in warm weather to avoid dehydration. For *weight gain,* there are no simple answers, but watching your calorie and fat intake, and getting regular exercise, can help. Sexual side effects such as *inability to have an orgasm* often diminish within a few weeks. If not, your doctor may lower your dose or change to a different medication. Occasionally the drugs bethanecol (Urecholine), cyproheptadine (Periactin), buspirone (BuSpar) or amantadine (Symmetrel) can help with this problem. If the medication causes *increased sensitivity to the sun,* use suntan lotion with a sun protection factor of at least 15 whenever out in the sun.

How Long to Remain on Medication

It may take from three weeks to three months to establish the proper dosage of one of these medications. Most investigators suggest that a patient should taper off a medication after symptoms are under control. This could be from several weeks to twelve to eighteen months (or even not at all), depending on the conditions. Throughout this time you should actively face your anxiety-provoking situations, using the skills described in this book. As you taper off the medications you may experience some return of your symptoms. Be patient as your body adjusts to being medication-free, and continue to practice your skills. After about one month, you and your doctor will be able to assess how well you are handling the stresses of your life without medication. If needed, you can discuss a return to that medication or some alternative drug. If you and your doctor decide that long-term use of the medication is the best alternative for you, he or she will help you reduce the medicine to the lowest possible dose that controls the symptoms.

Taper These Medications Gradually

Once you have begun treatment with one of these medications, you should never abruptly discontinue your daily dose. Your prescribing physician will direct you in a safe withdrawal process, which may take several days to several months, depending on the condition.

Medications Are Optional

You always have a choice regarding the use of medication. Do not let anyone persuade you that you must take drugs as your only option to overcome an anxiety disorder or that they offer the only cure for anxiety symptoms. As you have read throughout this book, many forces come to bear on your anxiety. Symptoms can reflect any one of several different psychological disorders and a number of physical problems. Keep your mind open to all your options in resolving this difficulty. If you choose to use medications as part of your treatment, do so because of your values and beliefs and your trust in your physician. We know from research and clinical experience that these medications are of no benefit to some people and can make matters worse for others. If medications do not benefit you, continue to give your other options a fair trial.

Are You Dependent on Drugs or Alcohol?

About 24 percent of people with a long-standing anxiety disorder also have difficulty with drug or alcohol abuse. If you are having this kind of trouble, it is best to get treatment for your chemical dependency first. Consider participating in a long-term recovery program such as Alcoholics Anonymous (AA) or Narcotics Anonymous (NA). Stopping your drug or alcohol dependency will give you a much better chance of achieving your goals of recovering from your anxiety problems. It is also most important that you inform your prescribing physician that you are currently having trouble with drug abuse or if you have in the past. That will help your doctor determine which of your symptoms relate directly to anxiety, and will help him or her to choose the right medication for you. For instance, antidepressants, SSRIs or buspirone are usually better choices for anxious patients who have been chemically dependent because they do not lead to dependency or abuse.

MEDICATIONS FOR ANXIETY DISORDERS

BENZODIAZEPINES	USED IN TREATMENT OF
alprazolam (Xanax):	panic, generalized anxiety, phobias, social phobias
clonazepam (Klonopin):	panic, phobias, social phobia
diazepam (Valium):	generalized anxiety, panic, phobias
lorazepam (Ativan):	generalized anxiety, panic, phobias
oxazepam (Serax):	generalized anxiety, phobias
chlordiazepoxide (Librium):	generalized anxiety, phobias
BETA BLOCKERS	
propranolol (Inderal):	social phobia
atenolol (Tenormin):	social phobia
TRICYCLIC ANTIDEPRESSANTS	
imipramine (Tofranil):	panic, depression, generalized anxiety
desipramine (Norpramin, Pertofrane and others):	panic, depression
nortriptyline (Aventyl or Pamelor):	panic, depression

amitriptyline (Elavil):	panic, depression
doxepin (Sinequan or Adapin):	panic, depression
clomipramine (Anafranil):	panic, OCD, depression
venlafaxine (Effexor):	OCD, depression

MONOAMINE OXIDASE INHIBITORS (MAOIS)

phenelzine (Nardil):	panic, social phobia, depression
tranylcypromine (Parnate):	panic, depression

SELECTIVE SEROTONIN REUPTAKE INHIBITORS (SSRIS)

fluoxetine (Prozac):	OCD, depression, panic, social phobia
fluvoxamine (Luvox):	OCD, depression, panic, social phobia
sertraline (Zoloft):	OCD, depression, panic, social phobia
paroxetine (Paxil):	OCD, depression, panic, social phobia

MILD TRANQUILIZER

buspirone (BuSpar):	generalized anxiety, OCD

ANTICONVULSANT

Valproate (Depakote):	panic

MEDICATION PROFILES

Tricyclic Antidepressants (TCAs)

Physicians use tricyclic antidepressants in the treatment of severe depression or depression that occurs with anxiety. Several also have broad antiobsessional and antipanic effects.

Possible benefits. Often effective in reducing panic attacks and elevating depressed mood. Well researched. Usually a single daily dose. Some generics available, which reduces cost. Tolerance does not develop. Nonaddicting.

Possible disadvantages. Onset takes four to twelve weeks. Anticholinergic effects. Postural hypotension. Possible side effects initially (including insomnia, tremor, or both) may last up to the first two to three weeks of treatment. Weight gain can be as much as one pound per month with about 25 percent of patients gaining twenty pounds or more. Dangerous in overdose. Should not be used by patients with narrow-angle glaucoma or certain heart abnormalities. Men with an enlarged prostate should avoid certain antidepressants.

Possible side effects. The anticholinergic effects of dry mouth, blurred vision, constipation, and difficulty in urination; postural hypotension; tachycardia, loss of sex drive; erectile failure; increased sensitivity to the sun; weight gain; sedation (sleepiness); increased sweating. Some of these side effects will disappear with the passage of time or with a decrease in the dosage. Some people may experience side effects on dosages as low as 10 mg per day, such as jitteriness, irritation, unusual energy, and difficulty falling or staying asleep.

Dosages recommended by investigators. One third of panic-prone individuals become jittery and actually experience more anxiety symptoms for the first two to three weeks. For this reason, the medication trial should probably be initiated with a very low dose—as little as 10 to 25 milligrams (mg) per day of imipramine, for example. If uncomfortable side effects appear, one approach is to wait two to three weeks for them to diminish before increasing to the next higher dose. If the patient adjusts to the side effects, the physician increases the dosage every two or more days until the patient is taking the preferred dosage.

If daytime sedation or other side effects are bothersome to the patient, the physician may suggest taking the full dosage at night before bedtime.

Tapering. Your doctor may suggest that you begin to taper your TCA six months to a year after you have controlled your panic attacks. You can taper it gradually over a two- to three-week period as a way to avoid the flulike symptoms that commonly occur if you abruptly stop the medication; even more gradual tapering can help monitor for a relapse in panic attacks. If you stop this medication abruptly, withdrawal symptoms may begin in twenty-four hours, including nausea, tremor, headache, and insomnia. Few symptoms should be evident with a gradual decrease in dose. Panic attacks will not usually return immediately after you stop the medication, but may recur several weeks later.

Of this family, imipramine has been the focus of most of the panic treatment research.

IMIPRAMINE (TOFRANIL AND OTHERS)

Possible benefits. Blocks panic attacks in 70 percent of people. Nonaddicting. Tolerance doesn't develop. Helps depression. Continued improvement for several months. Because it is slowly metabolized by the body, you can take it once daily, usually at bedtime.

Possible disadvantages. Not very helpful for anticipatory anxiety. Response takes weeks or months. One quarter to one half of imipramine patients relapse after tapering off from the drug. Not recommended while breast-feeding and used only with physician consent while pregnant.

Possible side effects. See page 288. Initial use of imipramine occasionally causes an increase in anxiety that usually diminishes in several weeks. Anticholinergic effects are stronger than those of most other antidepressants. If they are bothersome to you, it may be possible to switch to a different TCA with less anticholinergic effects. Dizziness from a lowering of blood pressure is moderate. If postural hypotension troubles you, *nortriptyline* may work more effectively. Imipramine causes some jitteriness in about 20 to 25 percent of subjects, which usually lasts one to three weeks but can be often avoided by starting with as little as 10 mg before bed. The tendency toward weight gain is moderate. Some patients, especially males, experience reduced sex drive or responsiveness while taking this drug. Other side effects are palpitations (changes in heartbeat), sweating, and drowsiness. One third of patients are unable to tolerate side effects and must switch to another medication.

Dosages recommended by investigators. Once daily dosing. The best way to reduce the early anxiety symptoms with the start of imipramine is to begin with a very small dose, typically 10 mg at bedtime, and increase the dose 10 mg every day until you reach the dose of 50 mg per day. It can block panic in some patients with 50 mg per day, so maintaining this dose level for several days is a good strategy. If the dose is not effective, the physician can increase it 25 mg every third day, up to 100 mg. After one week, if panic continues, the dose can increase by 50 mg every third day. Although some patients require a smaller or larger dosage, the usual maintenance dosage is between 150 mg and 250 mg per day.

DESIPRAMINE (NORPRAMIN, PERTOFRANE, AND OTHERS)

Possible benefits. Helpful for depression as well as panic. Continued improvement for several months. Tolerance does not develop. Nonaddicting. Causes little or no drowsiness.

Possible disadvantages. Not much help for anticipatory anxiety. Response requires weeks or months. Use during pregnancy or breast-feeding only with physician's approval. Avoid alcohol completely. Increases sensitivity to sun.

Possible side effects. See page 288. Postural hypotension, memory impairment, jitteriness, tremor, insomnia (especially at start of treatment) and the anticholinergic effects of dry mouth, blurred vision, constipation, urinary retention. Insomnia and the tendency for weight gain are mild. Sedation is rare.

Dosages recommended by investigators. Once daily, 25–300 mg per day. Taper off gradually.

NORTRIPTYLINE (PAMELOR, AVENTYL)

Possible benefits. Helps depression as well as panic. Continued improvement for several months.

Possible disadvantages. Not much help for anticipatory anxiety. Response requires weeks or months. Often requires several blood tests over the first weeks to establish the proper level of the medication. Avoid use during first three months of pregnancy. Increases sensitivity to the sun.

Possible side effects. Less jitteriness than with imipramine; less postural hypotension than with other tricyclic antidepressants; light-headedness, mild sedation (sleepiness), weight gain, insomnia, impaired urination, and anticholinergic effects (20 percent experience dry mouth).

Dosages recommended by investigators. Once a day, starting at 10 to 25 mg. Therapeutic dose is typically between 50 and 75 mg per day, with some individuals requiring up to 150 mg, based on blood level. Taper slowly.

CLOMIPRAMINE (ANAFRANIL)

Possible benefits. Helps control obsessive-compulsive disorder by reducing the duration and intensity of these symptoms and the corresponding anxiety. May help as much as imipramine for panic attacks. Relieves depression.

Possible disadvantages. Strong side effects. Takes about four to six weeks to work. Patients with certain abnormal electrocardiograms, with narrow-angle glaucoma, or with an enlarged prostate should not take this medication. Avoid during last three months of pregnancy to prevent withdrawal symptoms in infant. Can be expensive.

Possible side effects. Like imipramine, you may experience more general anxiety the first few days up to three weeks. The most common side effects are headaches, drowsiness, dry mouth, constipation, and insomnia. Other common side effects are blurred vision, urinary retention, fatigue, weight gain, postural hypotension, nervousness, muscle twitching, decreased ability to have orgasm (42 percent of men), increased sweating, and sedation (sleepiness). Increases sensitivity to the sun. Elderly patients may experience confusion and memory impairment.

Dosages recommended by investigators. Ranging from 150 to 300 mg per day. Usually start at 25 mg for a few days. Increase by 25 mg every three to four days to 100 mg per day, usually taken in one dose. Raise the dose over the next few weeks to a maximum of 300 mg. Taking the dose at night can sometimes reduce the side effects. It takes four to six weeks to notice significant therapeutic benefits from clomipramine. The full range of benefits may take twelve weeks. Taper slowly, over three to four weeks or longer.

AMITRIPTYLINE (ELAVIL)

Possible benefits. Helpful for panic attacks and depression. Has less potential for insomnia. Is sometimes used when patients are having trouble sleeping, because of its sedating effects.

Possible disadvantages. Not much help for anticipatory anxiety. Response requires weeks or months. The sedating side effects can limit productivity and concentration during the day. Avoid during first three months of pregnancy and consult physician before using during the last six months and before breast-feeding. Increases sensitivity to sun.

Possible side effects. Strong anticholinergic effects and moderate levels of drowsiness, weight gain and dizziness.

Dosages recommended by investigators. Begin at 25 to 75 mg daily at bedtime and raise over two weeks to an average of 200 and maximum of 300 mg. Taper gradually.

DOXEPIN (SINEQUAN, ADAPIN)

Possible benefits. Helpful for panic attacks and depression.

Possible disadvantages. Not much help for anticipatory anxiety. Response requires weeks or months. The sedating side effects can limit productivity and concentration during the day. Therapeutic effects take several weeks. Consult your physician before using during pregnancy or breast-feeding.

Possible side effects. Anticholinergic effects, increased sensitivity to the sun, postural hypotension, weight gain, sleepiness, sweating.

Dosages recommended by investigators. Start at 25 to 75 mg per day and increase over one or two weeks to an average dose of 75 to 150 mg and a maximum dose of 300 mg. Typically taken in one dose at bedtime, but can be divided.

Other Cyclic Antidepressants

VENLAFAXINE (EFFEXOR)

Possible benefits. Helpful for obsessive-compulsive disorder and depression.

Possible disadvantages. Takes several weeks for primary effects to begin. Nausea and dizziness can be common side effects. Use during pregnancy or breast-feeding only after approval from your physician. Can be expensive.

Possible side effects. Anticholinergic effects, chills, dizziness, muscle tension, insomnia, headache, nausea, sleepiness, nervousness.

Dosages recommended by investigators. Start with 75 mg per day, divided into two or three doses. Increase by 75 mg every four or more days. Average maintenance dose is 150 mg per day, with a maximum dose of 300 mg per day. Take with food. Taper off slowly.

Selective Serotonin Reuptake Inhibitors (SSRIs)

A newer type of antidepressant medication was introduced into the United States in the 1980s, beginning with fluoxtine (Prozac). Serotonin reuptake blocking agents have a different chemical structure than the cyclic antidepressants and therefore produce different effects on the brain. Primarily they assist the brain in maintaining enough supply of the neurotransmitter serotonin. Researchers associate a deficiency of serotonin with depression and obsessive-compulsive disorder and implicate it in panic disorder and other psychological problems. These medications are called selective serotonin reuptake inhibitors, or SSRIs.

Possible benefits. SSRIs can be helpful for depression, panic disorder, social phobia, and obsessive-compulsive disorder. They are well-tolerated medications that are safe for medically ill or frail patients and are safe in overdose. There are no withdrawal effects unless the patient stops them abruptly, and no dependency develops. They generally do not promote weight gain.

Possible disadvantages. It takes four to six weeks to notice significant therapeutic benefits from the SSRIs. The full range of benefits can take twelve weeks. Patients often experience a temporary worsening of anxiety symptoms during the first two weeks of treatment. Abrupt discontinuation of the SSRIs could cause flulike symptoms. All the SSRIs can be expensive.

SSRIs cause sexual problems more than other antidepressants or benzodiazopines. In fact, this may be their principal limitation, occurring in as many as 35 to 40 percent of patients. It is unclear whether these problems are evident in one SSRI more than others. If these difficulties arise, your choices are to wait several weeks to determine if this side effect diminishes, to lower the dose, or to change to a different medication.

Possible side effects. Nausea, insomnia, headaches, sexual difficulties, initial agitation.

FLUOXETINE (PROZAC)

Possible benefits. Reduces depression, helps control obsessive-compulsive disorder. Blocks panic attacks. Current research suggests some benefits for social phobias. Few side effects. No dependency. A well-tolerated and safe medication.

Possible disadvantages. May cause anxiety or insomnia. Therapeutic response can take four to six weeks. It is best to be off Prozac for two menstrual cycles prior to attempting pregnancy. Do not use when breast-feeding.

Possible side effects. Nervousness and tremors, sweating, nausea, anxiety, diarrhea, difficulty falling asleep or frequent awakenings, difficulty achieving orgasm, decreased libido, headache, loss of appetite, postural hypotension, drowsiness or fatigue, upset stomach.

Dosages recommended by investigators. Prozac comes in 10 and 20 mg capsules and liquid oral solution that the patient usually takes in the morning. If you have a side effect of upset stomach, take it with food. Typically the initial dose is low, at 2.5 to 5 mg per day and is gradually raised to 20 mg per day. If there is no response to this dose after four to eight weeks, raise the dose by 20 mg a week until there is a response, to a maximum dose of 80 mg.

SERTRALINE (ZOLOFT)

Possible benefits. Useful for obsessive-compulsive disorder, panic disorder, and depression. Low level of nervousness or agitation as side effect.

Possible disadvantages. May cause anxiety or insomnia. Therapeutic response can take four to six weeks. Get your physician's approval before use during pregnancy or breast-feeding.

Possible side effects. Headache, dry mouth, sleepiness, dizziness, tremors, diarrhea, agitation, confusion, nausea, delayed ejaculation in men.

Dosages recommended by investigators. Start with 50 mg in morning or evening. Maximum dose is 200 mg. Taper off slowly.

PAROXETINE (PAXIL)

Possible benefits. Useful for obsessive-compulsive disorder, panic disorder, and depression.

Possible disadvantages. Therapeutic response can take four to six weeks. Discuss possible pregnancy or breast-feeding with your physician.

Possible side effects. Nausea, sleepiness, dry mouth, dizziness, insomnia, delayed ejaculation.

Dosages recommended by investigators. Start with 10 mg once a day. If no response after several weeks, can be increased 10 mg per week up to 60 mg. For OCD the minimum therapeutic dose is often 40 mg.

FLUVOXAMINE (LUVOX)

Possible benefits. Helpful for obsessive-compulsive disorder, depression.

Possible disadvantages. Therapeutic response can take four to six weeks. Avoid alcohol. Do not take during pregnancy or breast-feeding.

Possible side effects. Nausea, sleepiness, insomnia, dry mouth, headache, dizziness, delayed ejaculation.

Dosages recommended by investigators. Start at 50 mg at night. Increase to between 100 and 300 mg per day. Doses over 100 mg should be divided into morning and night, with larger dose at night. To reduce nausea, take with food.

Benzodiazepines (BZs)

Possible benefits. You can take benzodiazepines as a single-dose therapy or several times a day for months (or even years). Studies suggest that they are effective in reducing symptoms of anxiety in approximately 70 to 80 percent of patients. They are quick-acting. Tolerance does not develop in the antipanic or other therapeutic effects. Generics are available for many, which helps reduce cost. Overdose is not dangerous.

Possible side effects. Some patients experience the sedative effects of drowsiness or lethargy, decreased mental sharpness, slurring of speech and some decrease in coordination or unsteadiness of gait, less occupational efficiency or productivity, and, occasionally, headache. These may continue during the first few weeks, but tend to clear up, especially if you increase the dose gradually. Sexual side effects can arise. Some people experience low moods, irritability, or agitation. Rarely, a patient will experience disinhibition: they lose control of some of their impulses and do things they wouldn't ordinarily do, like increased arguing, driving the car recklessly, or shoplifting. BZs also increase the effects of alcohol. A patient taking a BZ should drink very little alcohol and should refrain from drinking within hours of driving a car.

If taken over long periods, the BZs can produce a loss of muscle coordination and some cognitive impairment, especially in the elderly.

DISADVANTAGES WITH BZs

There are two primary disadvantages with BZs. The first is *abuse potential*. Although it is rare for a person with an anxiety disorder to abuse a benzodiazepine, patients with a history of substance abuse report a more euphoric effect from the BZs than do control subjects. They also can use the BZs to help with sleep, to control anxiety produced by other drugs, or to reduce withdrawal symptoms from other drugs. Because of these concerns, it may not be in the best interest of patients who have both panic disorder and a current substance abuse problem to use the BZs for their anxiety.

The second disadvantage is that there can be *symptoms upon tapering off*. Studies indicate that 35 to 45 percent of patients are able to withdraw from the BZs without difficulty. With the others, three different problems can arise, withdrawal, relapse, and rebound, which can sometimes occur simultaneously.

Dependence and withdrawal symptoms. Physical dependence means that when a person stops taking a drug or reduces the dose quickly, he or she will experience symptoms of withdrawal. BZ withdrawal symptoms usually begin soon after reduction of the drug begins. They can be any of the following: confusion, diarrhea, blurred vision, heightened sensory perception, muscle cramping, reduced sensation of smell, muscle twitches, numbness or tingling, decreased appetite, and weight loss. These symptoms can be bothersome but are usually mild to moderate, almost never dangerous, and resolve over the period of a week or so.

At least 50 percent of patients experience some withdrawal symptoms when they stop taking a benzodiazepine, and almost all patients experience strong withdrawal symptoms if they stop the medication suddenly. Most experts now taper off quite slowly, often taking months to completely discontinue the benzodiazepine.

A higher dosage of a BZ, as well as longer use, can increase the intensity and frequency of the withdrawal symptoms. Short-acting drugs (Xanax, Serax, Ativan) are more likely to produce withdrawal reactions than longer-lasting BZs (Valium, Librium, Tranxene) if they are discontinued rapidly, although the difference is usually small if they are tapered off in an appropriately slow manner. Panic patients seem to be more susceptible to withdrawal symptoms than those with other anxiety disorders.

Relapse symptoms. Relapse means your original anxiety symptoms return after you reduce or stop the medication. Often in relapse the symptoms are not as severe or as frequent as they were before treatment began. Withdrawal symptoms start as the medication is reduced and end one to two weeks after stopping a medication. So if the symptoms persist four to six weeks after complete withdrawal, it probably indicates relapse.

Rebound symptoms. Rebound is the temporary return of greater anxiety symptoms after withdrawal from medication than you experienced before the medication. This usually occurs two to three days after a taper and is often caused by too big of a reduction of the drug at one time. It is possible that a rebound reaction can trigger a relapse reaction. Between 10 to 35 percent of patients will experience the rebound of anxiety symptoms, especially panic attacks, when they discontinue the BZs too rapidly.

A *slow tapering* of the medication is best. One approach is to remain at each new lower dose for two weeks before the next reduction. Tapering a BZ over a two- to four-month period can lead to significantly less withdrawal symptoms.

POSSIBLE SYMPTOMS OF WITHDRAWAL FROM BENZODIAZEPINES

Nervousness	Poor concentration
Insomnia	Confusion
Decreased appetite	Diarrhea
Blurred vision	Numbness or tingling
Headache	Lack of coordination
Perspiration	Lack of energy

Muscle aches, cramping, or twitching
Altered sensory perception (i.e., noises sound very loud, metallic taste, reduced sense of smell)

A third problem associated with BZs is connected with *alcohol use*. Alcohol will increase the drug's depressant effects on the brain and can result in excessive drowsiness or intoxication.

ALPRAZOLAM (XANAX)

Possible benefits. The FDA has approved alprazolam in the treatment of panic disorder, and several large-scale, placebo-controlled studies support its effectiveness. It is also helpful for generalized anxiety disorder. Is quick-acting so it can offer some relief within an hour. Has few side effects. Can be taken daily or only as needed. Both panic disorder patients and generalized anxiety disorder patients can start feeling better within a week. To block panic attacks, two to four weeks of treatment may be needed.

Possible disadvantages. See pages 301–2. About 10 to 20 percent of panic disorder patients fail to respond adequately to Xanax. Do not take if planning to get pregnant, while pregnant, or while breast-feeding. Be cautious in drinking alcohol, since it can lead to increased intoxication effects and drowsiness.

Possible side effects. See page 300. The principal side effect is sedation, but dizziness and postural hypotension, tachycardia, confusion, headache, insomnia, and depression also occur.

Dosages recommended by investigators. Alprazolam is usually started using .25 mg (1/4 mg) or .5 mg (1/2 mg) two to three times a day. This lower starting dose helps reduce the side effect of sedation (sleepiness) that can come during the first week or so of treatment. If taken after meals, side effects such as drowsiness can diminish, and the therapeutic effects can last longer. Your physician can increase this dosage by adding .5 mg to one of the three daily doses up to a maximum of 2 mg three times per day. From that level, you take any additional increases at bedtime or apply them equally during the day. The dosage range is 1 to 10 mg per day. A common recommendation is to take a new dose every four hours during the day. If anxiety symptoms return earlier than four hours, clonazepam (Klonopin) is sometimes added to the alprazolam.

Tapering. Generally physicians taper alprazolam at .25 mg every three days. Withdrawal and rebound symptoms can occur during taper. If you have been taking alprazolam for many months, it may be best that you gradually lower your dose over eight to twelve weeks. If you have difficulty with this regimen, your doctor may suggest that you switch to a longer-acting benzodiazepine, like clonazepam (Klonopin), or a barbiturate called phenobarbital (Luminal). An alternative is to add a medication to alprazolam that reduces some of the bothersome symptoms during the withdrawal period. These could be carbamazepine (Tegretol), propranolol, or clonidine (Catapres).

CLONAZEPAM (KLONOPIN)

Possible benefits. Useful for generalized anxiety disorder, panic disorder. Works quickly, reduces anticipatory anxiety. Controlled trials suggest it may be helpful for social phobia. Longer acting than alprazolam.

Possible disadvantages. See pages 301–2. Some patients develop depression while taking Klonopin. Best to avoid taking this drug during the first three months of pregnancy. Frequent use in later pregnancy can cause symptoms in the newborn. Avoid breast-feeding on this drug. Alcohol will increase the drug's depressant effects on the brain and can result in excessive drowsiness or intoxication.

Possible side effects. See page 300. Drowsiness occurs for 50 percent of patients, typically in the first two weeks. Fatigue, unsteadiness.

Dosages recommended by investigators. Twice a day, .25 to 2 mg.

LORAZEPAM (ATIVAN)

Possible benefits. Used for generalized anxiety, panic disorder. Few side effects.

Possible disadvantages. See pages 301–2. Do not take if planning to get pregnant, while pregnant, or while breast-feeding. Use alcohol with caution.

Possible side effects. See page 300. Drowsiness, dizziness, blurred vision, tachycardia, weakness, disinhibition (acting inappropriately grandiose or out of control).

Dosages recommended by investigators. Start with a .5 mg tablet per night on the first night. Increase to .5 mg twice a day. Can be increased .5 mg every two or three days or more. Dosing is usually three times a day. Maximum dose is 10 mg per day.

DIAZEPAM (VALIUM)

Possible benefits. Used for generalized anxiety disorder, panic disorder, and sometimes for a condition called night terrors that occurs in children.

Possible disadvantages. See pages 301–2. Avoid use during pregnancy and breast-feeding. Alcohol increases this drugs absorption and its depressant effects on the brain. Be cautious, and never drink alcohol if driving a car or operating dangerous equipment.

Possible side effects. See page 300. Drowsiness, fatigue, dizziness, blurred vision, tachycardia, loss of muscle coordination.

Dosages recommended by investigators. Between 5 and 20 mg daily. Valium is a long-acting benzodiazepine, so one or two doses can last the whole day. It is also fast-acting, so you can feel some relief within thirty minutes. You can divide the dose and take it in the morning and evening, or take it all at once.

CHLORDIAZEPOXIDE (LIBRIUM)

Possible benefits. Used for generalized anxiety.

Possible disadvantages. See pages 369–70. Do not take if planning to get pregnant, if pregnant, or breast-feeding. Use caution when drinking alcohol.

Possible side effects. See page 300. Postural hypotension, drowsiness, blurred vision, tachycardia, lack of muscle coordination, nausea.

Dosages recommended by investigators. Start with 5 to 25 mg two to four times per day and increase to average of 200 mg, as needed.

OXAZEPAM (SERAX)

Possible benefits. Used for generalized anxiety.

Possible disadvantages. See pages 301–2. May reduce blood pressure. Do not take if planning to get pregnant, if you are pregnant or if you are breast-feeding. Intensifies effects of alcohol.

Possible side effects. See page 300. Drowsiness, dizziness, postural hypotension, tachycardia.

Dosages recommended by investigators. The usual dose is 10 to 30 mg, three to four times per day.

Monoamine Oxidase Inhibitors

Monoamine oxidase inhibitors, commonly called MAOIs, are the other major antidepressant family. Phenelzine (Nardil) is the MAOI most researched for the treatment of panic. Another MAOI that may be effective against panic attacks is tranylcypromine (Parnate).

Possible benefits. Helpful in reducing panic attacks, elevating depressed mood, and increasing confidence. Can also help social phobias. Well studied. Tolerance does not develop. Nonaddicting.

Possible disadvantages. Dietary and medication restrictions are important and bothersome to some people. These include avoiding certain foods like aged cheese or meat and certain medications like cold remedies. Some agitation during first days. Requires weeks to months for full therapeutic effects. Not as helpful for anticipatory anxiety. Dangerous in overdose.

Dietary restrictions. Certain foods contain a substance called tyramine, which when combined with an MAOI can cause a "hypertensive crisis" that can produce dangerously high blood pressure, a severe headache, stiff neck, nausea, stroke, or even death.

The patient using an MAOI must be quite responsible, since this medication requires significant dietary restrictions. No cheese (except cottage, farmer, or cream cheese), sour cream, homemade yogurt, red wine, vermouth, liquors, beer, ale, sherry, cognac, Bovril or Marmite yeast extracts (baked goods prepared with yeast are O.K.), aged meats and fish, meat prepared with tenderizer, liver or liverwurst, overripe bananas, fava beans, Italian green beans, Chinese or English pea pods, or lima beans are to be eaten while on this medication.

Foods to eat in moderation include avocados, chocolate, figs, raisins and dates, soy sauce, caffeinated drinks, white wine, and distilled alcoholic beverages (whiskey, gin, vodka)

Medication restrictions. MAOIs have major interactions with many other drugs, including anesthetics, analgesics, other antidepressants, and anxiolytics. The patient using an MAOI should always consult the prescribing physician before taking any additional medications. This especially includes over-the-counter cold medicines (including nose drops or sprays), amphetamines, diet pills, tricyclic antidepressants, and certain antihistamines.

Possible side effects. Difficulty sleeping; increased appetite; sexual side effects, especially difficulty achieving orgasms for men and women; weight gain; dry mouth; sedation (sleepiness); and low blood pressure symptoms, particularly on standing up rapidly, which can lead to postural hypotension.

As with any antidepressant, some patients will experience "hypomania," which causes them to feel unusually "high" and full of energy, talkative and very self-confident, with little need for sleep and a high sex drive. Patients don't always recognize this as a problem, but it can certainly be irritating to those around them.

PHENELZINE (NARDIL)

Possible benefits. Useful for panic disorder as well as depression. In one study, using 45 to 90 mg per day, phenelzine produced significant panic symptom reduction in more than 75 percent of patients. Complete control of the panic attacks usually takes four to six weeks of treatment. Current research also suggests it can be beneficial for social phobia.

Possible disadvantages. See page 306. Use during pregnancy only with the approval of your physician. Avoid breast-feeding while on this drug.

Possible side effects. See pages 306–7. Weight gain, sometimes up to 20 pounds, and postural hypotension are common. Swelling around the ankles from fluid retention, headache, tremors, fatigue, constipation, dry mouth, loss of appetite, arrhythmias, difficulty having orgasm, insomnia or sleepiness. Decreased libido, inhibited orgasm and difficulty maintaining erection.

Dosages recommended by investigators. Each tablet of phenelzine is 15 mg. The initial dose is usually 15 mg or less and then gradually increased to 30 mg daily, in divided doses. Dosage is then three to six tablets per day, usually based on body weight. Most patients need a minimum of 45 mg daily. Maximum dose is usually 90 mg. You can take the entire dose at bedtime after one or two weeks unless you find this interferes with your sleep.

TRANYLCYPROMINE (PARNATE)

Possible benefits. Useful for panic attacks and depression. Very little anticholinergic or sedative effect. Little problem with weight gain.

Possible disadvantages. See page 306. Insomnia and postural hypotension can be persistent problems.

Possible side effects. Insomnia, postural hypotension, swelling around the ankles, some trouble having orgasm.

Dosages recommended by investigators. Starting dose is one to two 10 mg tablets. Increase the dose one tablet every three to four days. Maintenance dose is 30 to 60 mg in one or two doses in the morning or early afternoon.

Beta Blockers

Beta blockers can be helpful in the treatment of the physical symptoms of anxiety, especially social anxiety. Physicians prescribe them to control rapid heartbeat, shaking, trembling, and blushing in anxious situations.

Possible benefits. Very safe for most patients. Few side effects. Not habit-forming.

Possible disadvantages. Often social anxiety symptoms are so strong that beta blockers, while helpful, cannot reduce enough of the symptoms to provide relief. Because they can lower blood pressure and slow heart rate, people diagnosed with low blood pressure or heart conditions may not be able to take them. Not recommended for patients with asthma or any other respiratory illness that causes wheezing, or for patients with diabetes.

PROPRANOLOL (INDERAL)

Possible benefits. Used for short-term relief of social phobia. May reduce some peripheral symptoms of anxiety, such as tachycardia and sweating, and general tension, can help control symptoms of stage fright and public-speaking fears. Has few side effects.

Possible disadvantages. See above. Consult your physician before taking while pregnant or while breast-feeding. If taking daily, do not stop this drug abruptly.

Restrictions on use. Do not take propranolol if you suffer from chronic lung disease, asthma, diabetes, and certain heart diseases, or if you are severely depressed.

Possible side effects. Taken occasionally, propranolol has almost no side effects. Some people may feel a little light-headed, sleepy, short-term memory loss, unusually slow pulse, lethargy, insomnia, diarrhea, cold hands and feet, numbness and/or tingling of fingers and toes.

Dosages recommended by investigators. You can take a 20 to 40 mg dose of propranolol as needed about one hour before a stressful situation. If necessary, you can also combine it with imipramine or alprazolam without adverse effects.

ATENOLOL (TENORMIN)

Possible benefits. Used for social phobia. Atenolol is longer-acting than propranolol and generally has fewer side effects. It has less of a tendency to produce wheezing than other beta blockers. Once-a-day dosing is convenient.

Possible disadvantages. If taken daily, abrupt withdrawal can cause very high blood pressure. Use alcohol with caution, since alcohol can increase the sedative effect and exaggerate this drug's ability to lower blood pressure.

Possible side effects. Cold extremities, dizziness, and tiredness. Less frequent is a decrease in heart rate below fifty beats per minute, depression, and nightmares.

Dosages recommended by investigators. One 50 mg tablet a day for the first week. If there is no response, increase to two 50 mg tablets, taken together or divided. After two weeks of 100 mg the patient should notice a marked decrease in racing heart, trembling, blushing, and/or sweating in social situations.

Other Tranquilizers

BUSPIRONE (BUSPAR)

Possible benefits. Buspirone is helpful for generalized anxiety. The Food and Drug Administration has approved its use for anxiety with mild depressed mood. Early research indicates it also may help social phobias and can be used in combination with other medications for OCD. Buspirone is much less likely than the benzodiazepines to cause drowsiness and fatigue. A very safe medication, it is not habit-forming, and there are no withdrawal symptoms.

Possible disadvantages. Unlike the benzodiazepines, buspirone does not work right away. You can't take one as needed and expect to notice benefits. Avoid use during first three months of pregnancy. Consult physician regarding use in last six months of pregnancy or during breast-feeding.

Possible side effects. Few. Headache and dizziness can each occur in 3 to 12 percent of patients, but usually go away in a few days. Mild drowsiness is possible.

Dosages recommended by investigators. Five mg three times per day during the first week and 10 mg two to three times per day during Week 2. Symptom relief can begin as early as Week 1, with most symptom reduction by Week 4. Maximum dose is usually 60 mg. Subtle, progressive therapeutic effects, not dramatic effects. Others may notice improvement before the patient does.

Anticonvulsant

VALPROIC ACID (DEPAKOTE)

Valproic acid is an epilepsy medication that is now used for the treatment of panic attacks as well as other psychiatric problems.

Possible benefits. Treatment of panic disorder.

Possible disadvantages. Can cause bruising or bleeding when taken with aspirin. Can cause excessive sedation with alcohol and also with Klonipin or other benzodiazepines. Can cause liver problems. To monitor your liver function and your platelet count, your doctor may ask you to take a simple blood test every two months for the first six months and every three to four months after that. Avoid using during pregnancy and breast-feeding.

Possible side effects. Valproic acid is well tolerated. Nausea, vomiting, indigestion, headaches, confusion, and drowsiness sometimes occur but usually subside in a few weeks.

Dosages recommended by investigators. Comes in 250 and 500 mg capsules. Dose is primarily based on body weight.

20

The Fear of Being Seen: How to Face Social Anxieties

"I can't just start talking! He'll think I'm superficial!"
"If I sign my name, I'm sure my hands will shake and everyone
  will notice!"
"I'll go blank. We'll just stand there and stare at each other."
"I should be able to make a statement without stumbling over a
  word! What's wrong with me?"
"I'm so anxious! I know I'm coming across wrong."
"I'll never meet anyone. I'll be alone the rest of my life."

Everyone is capable of getting nervous when in a socially awkward situation. And many people worry about giving formal presentations. Some people, however, suffer more than the occasional
jitters. People who are socially anxious are excessively fearful that
others will criticize their public behavior. They worry that they will
appear inarticulate or stupid, or show embarrassing signs that they
are anxious or weak. It is this feared disapproval from others, and
not worry about a panic attack, that causes their distress.

Most people consider the term "performance" to mean some type
of formal presentation of our skills or knowledge. The socially anxious person is one who, can view the simplest of social interactions
as a performance. Even shaking someone's hand in a casual setting
can lead to performance anxiety and extensive, critical analysis
afterward. Their anxiety can cause them to forget their train of

thought, stumble over words, respond to questions with one word answers, or begin laughing at inappropriate moments.

Most people feel a certain degree of anxiety before performing in public, but once they begin their presentation, they gain composure. The socially anxious person seeks ways to avoid the risk whenever possible, feels significant anxiety long before the event, and continues experiencing anxiety and worry throughout the "performance." After the event, he analyzes his every move and negatively interprets the response of others, even if the "performance" was the simple act of eating a sandwich at a fast-food restaurant. (Throughout this chapter, I will use the term "performance" to mean this broad definition of *any* social contact.)

Almost all socially anxious people fear public speaking. The four other top-ranking fears are eating in public, signing one's name or writing in public, using public bathrooms, and being the center of attention. Some people only fear a few situations. Others, suffering from generalized social phobia, dread a broad number of situations where there is some chance of receiving disapproval. The chart on page 315 lists the common situations which socially anxious people can dread.

When facing a feared situation, the socially anxious person experiences many of the same worried thoughts and physical symptoms as those during a panic attack. However certain bodily symptoms—rapid heart rate, trembling voice, shaking hands, sweating and blushing—are more common and can be more distressing because they might be seen by others. Some people, when they become extremely anxious, will feel as if they can't move their body, like they are frozen in place (called *atonic immobility*).

BIOLOGY AND EXPERIENCE: THE POSSIBLE CONTRIBUTIONS TO SOCIAL FEARS

Researchers have not yet identified the exact causes of social anxieties. Biological scientists are actively studying the arenas of biochemical irregularities and genetic predispositions. Fascinating studies are exploring the social order and interactions of rhesus monkeys, the primates whose brains are most similar to humans. The current outcomes show a clear trend that approximately 20 percent of the rhesus population, both in captivity and in the wild, are "behaviorally inhibited," or socially avoidant. For instance, during mildly stressful times they will exhibit extreme anxiety responses while the rest of the monkey population responds normally. Researchers are now able to breed behaviorally inhibited young monkeys by matching up the right parents.

Substantial evidence with humans parallels this work with primates. Harvard psychologist Jerome Kagan's groundbreaking research supports his theory that inhibited children are born with a nervous system that is more easily stressed and excited—including the responses of increased heart rate and increased secretion of the stress hormone cortisol—when they are faced with changes in their social system. Looking at the available research, it appears that of all human personality traits, social shyness and inhibition have the most genetic involvement, and these traits are most likely to be passed from one generation to the next.

This means it is possible that some of us are preprogrammed to watch for others who are more "dominant" than us, to evaluate the possibility, however slight, of their rejection, and to act in any way needed to indicate our social submissiveness. If our more subtle gestures, such as avoiding eye contact, do not reassure us of our acceptance, then we will act out more primitive responses, by escaping, freezing, or avoiding contact altogether. These responses, when reflective of a biological predisposition, will occur instinctually, with little or no conscious thought.

In addition to the biological factors, childhood learnings can contribute to increasing or decreasing the likelihood of social anxieties in adolescence and adulthood. Kagan found that by age seven and a half the physiological differences began to narrow between children who were socially inhibited and those who were outgoing. You might say that as children have more time to get feedback about their degree of acceptance into their family, peer group, and community, they learn not to react so fearfully. They discover that they are a welcomed member of the group and others will tolerate their mistakes or weaknesses. Again, this result is matched in the primate population. Remember those rhesus monkeys who were bred to be the most behaviorally inhibited? If the scientists removed them from their natural mother and allowed mothers with stronger and more nurturing traits to raise them, these adolescent monkeys became some of the most socially outgoing!

This, of course, is great news. Even if you are biologically predisposed to develop social anxieties, your life experiences can influence your future comfort with people. You can learn how to loosen up the grip of fear.

The opposite is also true. Childhood experiences may reinforce social anxiety, hesitation, and avoidance in those who are already genetically vulnerable to such problems. From parents who are shy or reclusive, children can learn that the world is not so safe. These parents model avoidance as a means to cope with social anxieties. Any significant adults or peers can influence a vulnerable child in the direction of fear and intimidation. For instance, a third-grader "freezes" as she gets up in front of the class for a presentation, her teacher reprimands her, and later her classmates tease her. After a meal at the diner, a young boy's mother can chastise him, "You embarrassed me with your behavior," without informing him of his error or of proper restaurant etiquette. One client of mine was ridiculed by his mother for years at the family dinner table. By the time he entered seventh grade and attended his first school with a cafeteria, he felt too threatened to enter the lunch room. When he entered treatment in our clinic at the age of fifty-three he was on disability insurance from severe social phobia.

THE COMPLEX NATURE OF SOCIAL ANXIETIES AND PHOBIAS

Social anxieties often begin to surface in adolescence, although there is much variation. Some people describe themselves as shy and inhibited since early childhood; others develop the symptoms after one or more embarrassing events in adulthood. About twenty percent of the U.S. population suffers some degree of social anxiety, with 2 to 3 percent so significantly impaired that they fit the diagnosis of *social phobia* described in chapter 3. Over 80 percent of people with social phobia never seek professional help.

To obtain the comfort that you seek, you will need to persist in practicing various skills, using concentrated effort over several months. Certain characteristics of social anxieties, when combined, require that you use this degree of thoroughness. Here are seven of the most important aspects of recovery from social phobias.

ANXIETY-PROVOKING SOCIAL SITUATIONS

Acting, performing, or giving a talk in front of audience

Talking to people in authority

Job interview

Expressing opinions

Speaking up at a meeting

Expressing disagreement

Giving a report to a group

Responding to criticism

Eating in public places

Giving and receiving compliments

Drinking in public places

Asking for a date

Urinating in a public bathroom

Answering personal questions

Being the center of attention

Meeting strangers

Entering a room when others are already seated

Calling an unfamiliar person

Going to a party

Returning goods to a store

Giving a party

Making eye contact

Joining ongoing conversations

Resisting a high-pressure salesperson

Participating in small groups

Making mistakes in front of others

Bumping into someone you know

Taking a test

Talking with people you do not know very well

Writing while being observed

Initiating conversation with someone you are attracted to

Working while being observed

1. You Will Need to Work on Several Skills at Once.

As I discussed in chapter 18, you enhance your progress in master-ing anxiety when you follow several approaches to facing your fears. One approach is to break down your skills into manageable chunks of activities. As you accomplish early tasks, you can add complexity to your practices. A person with social anxieties who worries predominantly about the critical judgments of others will not typically have the chance to practice simple skills before she faces more complex situations. The skills needed to manage social interactions are inherently more sophisticated than those needed to sit in a crowded church, shop for groceries, or tolerate an elevator ride to the fifth floor. A person learning to face social fears must master the same type of tasks as someone with panic attacks. However, she often must cope with them while simultaneously interacting with others. It is this social interaction that adds signifi-cant complexity and therefore stress to the event. For instance, when giving a speech, she must practice tolerating uncomfortable physical symptoms, quieting her fearful thoughts, stopping herself from analyzing her every move, reducing her preoccupation with the reactions of her audience, *and* performing the complex skills needed to deliver a logical presentation.

2. You May Participate in Some Anxiety-Provoking Events Before You Feel Ready.

A similar principle for overcoming anxiety is to gradually face your feared situations as you learn your coping skills. It is best to begin with lower-grade fears and work your way to the more difficult events. When you have social anxiety, events that are high up on your list of threatening situations may take place before you have mastered your lower-level tasks. There are two primary ways that this occurs. First, you may need to participate in some events out of your ideal sequence simply because of your current responsibili-ties. For example, you are invited to a party for your close friend. Or you must meet with three managers about a new project. Or you are assigned an intern who must observe your work at the office. Any of these encounters can place you in an uncomfortable scene before you feel ready.

Second, distressing social encounters can pop up spontaneously and catch you unaware. Your boss may request a last-minute office meeting, you could be called on to give an informal report, an acquaintance might bump into you while you are eating lunch and ask to sit down. Suddenly you are thrust into a highly stressful event without planning your coping responses.

3. It's Not So Easy to Schedule Practice Sessions.

Frequent practice of your skills within a limited time period is another important principle for learning new behaviors. Some socially uncomfortable situations, however, don't occur on a routine schedule. If you want to practice formal presentations, job interviews, or taking exams, you may have to wait weeks or months for opportunities. Finding creative ways to simulate these events will be important additions to your practice. (I offer some suggestions on pages 330–31.)

4. Some Socially Uncomfortable Events Are Brief Contacts.

As I suggested in chapter 18, one of the goals of practice is to develop *habituation:* by remaining in anxiety-provoking situations for prolonged periods, your intense anxiety reaction gradually decreases. As you become less anxious, you can think more clearly and perform more comfortably. That's why I encouraged you to create practices that last forty-five to ninety minutes. However, a number of uncomfortable social contacts are brief, lasting seconds or a few minutes at most. Looking someone in the eye as you pass, saying hello in the hall at work, shaking hands, signing a credit card slip, answering a question in class, bumping into someone you know, asking someone for a date—all these events can instantly generate high distress but then end just as quickly.

Again, you may need to create simulations to practice these skills. For example, if you have difficulty writing in public, you can ask several friends to look over your shoulder while you sign your name fifty times.

5. Facing and Tolerating the Fearful Event Is Not Enough.

Phillip was a fifty-three-year-old engineer who came into treatment for his severe social phobia. His grave fears of writing and drawing in front of his colleagues cost him his job. He was sure that all who observed him would ridicule his shaking hands and "illegible" writing. By the time I saw him, he was on disability and couldn't publicly sign his name or lift a spoon, fork, or glass to his mouth unless he had previously taken two shot glasses of bourbon. One afternoon in treatment he took a giant step. I prearranged an agreement with the clerks in six stores, then Phillip entered each store, approached the clerk, asked if he could sign his name as the clerk watched, and then proceeded to do so. In the light of Phillip's severe limitations, this was a monumental task. I waited in the parking lot, and as he approached I asked if he had accomplished his goal. Phillip nodded, and when he reached my side, as he held out the writing tablet, his first sentence was "Look how shaky my writing was!"

This example illustrates that confronting the feared situation is necessary, but insufficient. Many people with social anxieties force themselves to interact with others in their feared situations. They will eat at restaurants, speak in a small group discussion, or answer questions when called on. But, like Phillip, they leave the scene and worry incessantly that they made a fool of themselves or will suffer dire consequences because of their humiliating actions. Along with entering your fearful arenas, you must specifically address your fear of others' judgments and your own harsh self-criticism.

6. You May Also Need to Develop Certain Social Skills.

Some people, in addition to feeling anxious about social interactions, are not confident of what behaviors are most socially appropriate. This is understandable if you have been socially withdrawn most of your life, or if your parents were also inhibited and failed to model interactional skills, or were critical of your social behaviors without instructing you in the correct actions. Such needed skills may include how to initiate conversation and pass time with others; body posture, facial expressions, and eye contact; formal presentation skills; grooming; and assertive communication.

7. Other Problems May Get in Your Way.

Studies of people with social phobia show that 70 percent also suffer from at least one other psychological problem. Sixty percent have another phobia and 45 percent have agoraphobia or panic disorder. Almost 40 percent experience some form of depression.

One study found that 70 percent meet the criteria for *avoidant personality disorder*. Avoidant traits include pervasive social anxiety, loneliness, low self-esteem, and the belief that others dislike you or will take advantage of you. In addition, people sometimes use alcohol as a means of coping with the social anxieties. Approximately 20 percent of those with social anxieties turn to alcohol in an attempt to self-medicate.

As this book illustrates, there are many ways in which you can help yourself overcome your social discomfort. In the following pages I will outline a positive approach based on the principles of this book. But if you think that your difficulties are more than you can manage while using the support of your family and friends, turn to a mental-health professional who specializes in the treatment of social phobias using cognitive-behavioral therapy. There is now a growing number of caring and competent specialists who treat these problems. Also, chapter 19 reviews the medications that specialists sometimes recommend to assist you during treatment.

HOW TO GET COMFORTABLE

When you do decide to help yourself become more comfortable socially, you will be able to use all the skills and understandings in part 2 of this book. Let me briefly remind you of these. Do not be misled by the fact that I describe them in only a few sentences. Most of these skills reflect the foundation upon which mental-health professionals treat all the anxiety disorders. You will learn their benefits within each chapter. My primary goal in this chapter is to *add to* these central skills so that you can apply them specifically to your needs regarding social anxiety. After you have read this chapter, return to the beginning of part 2 to start your self-help program. Refer to this chapter anytime you need to clarify your special concerns.

- It will be important to understand the body's anxiety reaction and how the mind plays a significant part in those symptoms. You will read about this in chapters 7, 8, and 9.

- Master the basics of relaxation and practice the breathing skills described in chapters 10 through 12.
- Study the value of the right attitude when facing symptoms (chapter 13) and the important principle of paradox (chapter 18).
- Learn how your mind tends to sabotage your goal of comfortable social interactions by generating worried, self-critical, or hopeless thoughts. Then study how to confront those negative thoughts and replace them with self-talk that supports your efforts. Chapters 14 through 16 will guide you through these most important skills.
- Chapter 18 will link all the skills together by outlining a step-by-step program for facing your actual feared situations. Use chapter 18 as your guide to putting all these skills and principles, including those within this chapter, into practice.

Challenge Your Negative Observers

While all the chapters in part 2 of the book are relevant to your success, the nature of social anxieties requires that you focus *primary* attention on your evaluations—of yourself, your behaviors, how you perceive that others judge you, and the imagined consequences of those judgments. Therefore, concentrate your efforts on the principles and skills presented in chapters 14 through 17. These pages introduce you to the destructive patterns of self-talk that I label the Negative Observers. The first steps toward change include recognizing and confronting those patterns. You will then need to develop a new way of rationally and respectfully addressing your intentions through the voice I call the Supportive Observer. As I will discuss later, you cannot improve by only facing feared events. (I am sure you already know this from experience.) You must also focus your resources on mentally vocalizing support for your desire to fit comfortably in to your community. This will require that you first challenge your current negative thinking.

LISTENING FOR THE NEGATIVE THOUGHTS

Worried, Critical, and Hopeless Observer comments flourish in the mind of the socially anxious person. When you listen closely to your own negative comments, you will probably notice that they differ from those of the Negative Observers described in chapter 14.

For instance, some statements may be a combination of Worried and Hopeless Observer comments. Instead of the typical "What if . . . ?" question of the Worried Observer, your comments may sound more like a statement of hopelessness. "*What if* I won't be able to answer their questions?" becomes "*I'm sure* I won't be able to answer their questions." "*What if* everyone notices that I'm sweaty and nervous?" becomes "*I'm sure* everyone will notice that I'm sweaty and nervous." Instead of being uncertain about the outcome, you declare that the negative outcome will, in fact, occur. This becomes a much stronger negative voice. You are certain it is reflective of the truth, and you then worry about the inevitable consequences. If you forge ahead into the feared situation, you are likely to be more frightened than others. This is because you are already predicting the dreaded failure and even calculating the dire costs you will pay in humiliation and rejection. Because you combine your worried thoughts with your hopeless comments, you are also more likely to avoid these situations instead of face them.

Here are more examples of the Worried-Hopeless Observer combination:

- I've got to quit this position, because I'll certainly keep failing.
- This will never work. Everyone will notice.
- I'll look like a fool.
- I won't be able to think of anything to say.
- I'll humiliate myself.
- I can't do it! I'm too nervous.
- I won't be able to get my point across.
- It'll be awful.
- I'll never find another job.
- I'll go blank. We'll just stand there and stare at each other.
- I'll be so nervous I won't be able to express myself.
- I'll never get better.
- I'm so anxious. I know I must be coming across wrong.

Many of your Critical Observer comments are typical, such as the following:

- I was so stupid.
- I stumbled over that word; I looked like a complete fool up there.
- I *always* get anxious!
- What's wrong with me? I'm just worthless.

Your Critical Observer also has two basic characteristics. First, you criticize yourself indirectly by fantasizing that other people are critical of you. If you are like many socially anxious people, this is a ruthless attack on your self-esteem because it goes to the core of your fears: that others will demean you or reject you. Here are some examples of others' statements you imagine:

- He's yawning. The entire audience is bored.
- She saw my hands shake when I was drinking. She knows how incompetent I am.
- He didn't like me because I didn't know what to talk about.
- She thinks I'm boring, stupid, obviously incapable.

A second characteristic is that your Critical Observer operates through a set of rules and expectations that are either impossible to meet or entirely unnecessary to adequate social performance. These often come in the form of "should" and "shouldn't" statements, and they place an inordinate amount of pressure on you to perform:

- I should have done that perfectly.
- I should be able to figure out what to say.
- Remember, never let them see you sweat!
- There are rules for how I should behave. I shouldn't be inappropriate.
- I shouldn't blink.
- I should always look people in the eye when I'm talking.
- I should be able to make a statement without mispronouncing my words.

To improve your comfort level in social situations you must first change your thoughts. There is little point of your entering fearful encounters and simply tolerating them. There is no learning in such an approach. So start with your thinking process—before, during and after any anxiety-producing social events. To take control of your thoughts, you need to identify your Negative Observers comments and to challenge them. The central focus of your attention will be on your distorted evaluation of your performance.

Listen for your self-talk in these four major areas.

1. *That you are likely to perform poorly*

- I'll never think of anything to say. My mind always goes blank.
- I'm sure my hands will shake, and they'll notice.
- I'm so nervous. I just know I'm going to mess up.
- I'm going to talk too much.

2. *That others will disapprove of your performance and their disapproval will be harsh*

- If I raise my hand and she calls on me, then everyone will know how nervous I am and they will reject me.
- I can't just start talking. He'll think I'm superficial.
- He'll never like me after he sees how I act.
- They will think I'm obviously incapable.

3. *That the consequences of their disapproval will be severe*

- He won't want to go out with me again.
- I'll never get this job.
- I'll never meet anyone, go on a date, get married.
- He'll fire me if I do that again.
- I'll be alone for the rest of my life.

4. *That your performance reflects your basic inadequacy and worthlessness*

- This proves that I'm a social incompetent.
- I'm so stupid!
- Who'd want to be with someone like me, anyway?
- I'm a born loser, a jerk, so boring.
- No one would ever want to go out with me.

HANDLING NEGATIVE THOUGHTS

We do not yet know to what degree social anxieties are biologically based problems. But let's assume that your social inhibitions *are* genetic—that you are preprogrammed to *automatically* think in this negative fashion. If this is true, it's not bad news. Please understand that most people suffering from any of the seven anxiety disorders discussed in chapter 3 who get the proper cognitive-behavioral treatment are able to improve. Thousands have recovered fully. So even though you may be biologically vulnerable to anxiety, you can change your future using psychological techniques. You don't have to live your life in pain and with the fear of humiliation.

If it is the nature of your disorder that your mind *automatically* generates fearful thoughts—without the benefits of logic or conscious reasoning—should you believe those thoughts? Certainly not! But when your *initial, spontaneous* thought is negative, your body tends to react to it instinctually, by generating symptoms of anxiety. As your anxious symptoms arise, you use them as a sign of how poorly you are going to perform. In essence, you say, "This proves that I'm going to fail."

It is very hard to perform while simultaneously listening to that critic or that hopeless worrier: that you are going to fail, that others will be harshly disapproving, that the consequences of their disapproval will be severe, and that all this shows how worthless you are. Your challenge is to stop taking those thoughts at face value. Recognize them as your automatic and impulsive Negative Observer comments. Even think of them as genetically preprogrammed if you want. *Just stop viewing them as reflective of reality!*

THE MOST POWERFUL QUESTION

You must listen for your negative thoughts, and you must disrupt them. But the last thing you want to do is to start arguing with yourself mentally, because your fearful thoughts will tend to win out, since they involve the strongest emotions. The most straightforward way to disrupt these thoughts is to say to yourself, "This is just my Negative Observer talking; I'm not going to listen." Then let those thoughts go and return to your Task. In chapter 16 I described this skill (page 232, "Stopping Negative Thoughts"):

1. Listen for your worried, self-critical, or hopeless thoughts.
2. Decide that you want to stop them. ("Are these thoughts helping me?")
3. Reinforce your decision through supportive comments ("I can let go of these thoughts.")
4. Mentally yell, "Stop!" (Snap rubber band on wrist.)
5. Begin the Calming Counts.

Of all these steps, the most important for you will be asking yourself "Are these thoughts helping me?" Keep in mind the goals of your practice: to learn to perform while you are anxious, to actively engage in your coping skills, to disrupt negative thoughts, and to participate in activities that you have been avoiding. When you question your thoughts, ask if they are helping you reach *these specific goals*.

Let's see an example of how this works. Let's say your goal is to support yourself as you give one of your first presentations to your office staff.

- You say to yourself, "This will never work. Everyone will notice." Is this thought helpful?
- You say to yourself, "I won't be able to get my point across." Is this thought helpful?
- You say to yourself, "What's wrong with me? I'm just worthless." Is this thought helpful?
- You say to yourself, "He's yawning. The entire audience is bored." Is this thought helpful?
- You say to yourself, "I should be able to make a statement without mispronouncing words." Is this thought helpful?

The central strategy that makes this intervention so powerful is that you are not disputing the accuracy of your thought. You are declaring that, regardless of its accuracy, it isn't helping you. It's hurting you. Some of these thoughts may be partly true. Perhaps a few people will see your hands shake or hear your voice crack. Maybe some audience members won't understand your point. A few others might have little interest in your topic and will feel bored. But if your goal is to support yourself before, during, and after your presentation, *none* of these negative comments further your goal. Don't analyze them, don't embellish them, don't argue with them. Notice them and let them go!

Once you let them go, offer yourself a supportive comment to keep you on track with your Task. The chart offers a few suggestions.

EXAMPLES OF SUPPORTIVE STATEMENTS

- I'll survive this.
- Remember to breathe.
- Most people will accept it if I make mistakes.
- I can handle disapproval.
- My self-esteem is not based on other people.
- It's O.K. to be nervous.
- I can handle these symptoms.
- There's no proof I'll fail.
- This is good practice.
- I've done this before.
- I know this topic.
- These people want me to succeed.
- There are many reasons for their behavior.

Sometimes your negative thoughts seem so powerful that you feel as though you can't disrupt them with a simple dismissal such as "This thought isn't helpful." Don't be surprised if you have such trouble for a while. I encourage you to persist in your efforts to master this skill even when you feel resistant to it. Don't give up on it! You are working to overcome a long-standing pattern, so repetition and a certain degree of tenacity will be important. This particular intervention will be your most powerful ally.

THE SECOND LEVEL OF CHALLENGE

There may be times when you need a different challenge to your negative thoughts. As I suggested earlier, your Worried Observer often gets tangled up with your Hopeless Observer, and together they lead you to feel certain about your inadequacies, and about how bad things are or will become. This second level of challenge is just as simple as the first. Its purpose is to confront your *certainty*. If you are like most socially anxious people, you have a great deal of conviction about negative assessments. Your mind quickly chooses some negative evaluation without considering any other options. That is what to question: your mind's automatic and rapid decision regarding a negative evaluation. The minimal goal is to open your mind to the possibility that you are not absolutely, incontestably, 100 percent, beyond doubt, sure of your conclusion.

It is not necessary that you take on a positive, optimistic view of yourself or your interaction. It is only important that you let yourself consider that there *are* other points of view. It's *possible* that something else could occur. It is *conceivable* that they are thinking something else about you. (Or not thinking about you at all!) Here are some examples of this challenge:

"No one would ever want to go out with me." ➡	"What evidence do I have?"
"If I raise my hand and she calls on me, then everyone will know how nervous I am, and they will reject me." ➡	"Do I know for certain that will happen?"
"He saw my hands shake when I was eating. He knows how incompetent I am." ➡	"Do I know that for certain?"
"I was so stupid." ➡	"Does labeling myself improve my performance?"
"I stumbled over that word; I looked like a complete fool up there." ➡	"Could there be a less harsh way to describe my behavior? Would I treat a friend this way?"
"I'll never find another job." ➡	"Am I a hundred percent sure?"

"It'll be awful."   ⟶   "What is the worst that could happen? How bad is that?"

"He's yawning. The entire ⟶ "Could there be any other audience is bored."   explanation?"

CHALLENGING NEGATIVE THOUGHTS

- Am I positive that this is true? What evidence do I have?
- Do I know for certain that will happen? Am I 100 percent sure?
- Does labeling myself improve my performance?
- Could there be a less harsh way of describing my behavior? Would I treat a friend this way?
- What is the worst that could happen? How bad is that?
- Could there be any other explanations?
- Is this my only opportunity?

By challenging your automatic negative thoughts, by loosening up your grip of certainty, you open the door to telling yourself, "This thought isn't helpful." You can then remind yourself of your positive goals: to learn to perform while you are anxious, to actively engage in your coping skills, to disrupt negative thoughts, and to engage in activities that you have been avoiding.

Practice Your Skills

Use chapter 18 to set your Long-term and Short-term Goals. Then create ways to practice facing your fears by designing your Short-term Tasks. Here are a few guidelines regarding your practice, to be added to those in chapter 18:

1. SET REALISTIC TASKS THAT HELP YOU PRACTICE THE CENTRAL SKILLS.

Can you tell where the flaws are in the following Tasks?

- Give my speech without anyone noticing my nervousness
- Sign my name smoothly, without my hand shaking

- Get someone to agree to go on a date
- Participate in a job interview without making a mistake

These objectives reflect more of the same negative attitude; they put unnecessary performance pressure on you through Critical Observer rules and regulations. These Task goals reflect the following types of beliefs:

- I should never let anyone see that I am nervous.
- I should perform perfectly.
- My self-worth should be based on what other people think.
- I should always be able to figure out what to say.

Beware of setting such unrealistic, self-defeating Tasks. At the same time, know that you are prone to establish such expectations *automatically*. That is why I encourage you to purposely stop and consciously review your expectations before and after any social encounter. By writing your intended purposes for any Task, and by reviewing them before and after the event, you can better catch yourself slipping into your Critical Observer rules. If your circumstances allow, review your expectations during the middle of your practice, to keep your thinking process on track.

2. Describe Your Tasks in Behavioral Terms.

Outline the specific actions you will take. State the number of times or the length of time you will engage in the behavior.

- Notice my Negative Observer comments during my next two conversations, and challenge them.
- Use three different supportive comments and work on believing them.
- Call three different stores to ask if an item is in stock.
- Make small talk of at least two exchanges with someone in line at the bank.
- Call one person, engage in small talk for at least three minutes, then ask her for a date.
- Purposely stumble over a word while ordering food at a restaurant.
- Compliment three people at work today.

- Raise my hand to ask or answer a question in three different classes this week.

3. Properly Assess Your Fear, Then Target Your Practice.

To become comfortable socially, you need to specifically address the fears that you dread. Think carefully about your true worries. For example:

- You may not be concerned about *giving* a speech. You worry about *sweating while* giving a speech.
- You may not feel apprehension about *ordering* food in a restaurant. You worry about *stumbling over a word* while ordering food.
- You may not be afraid of *signing* your name in public. You dread signing your name in public *while your hand shakes, causing your signature to appear irregular*.

What are your actual fears? Make sure that you design practices that get you closer and closer to managing the difficulties that you now avoid. Remember the principle I described in chapter 13, "Run toward the roar." By becoming courageous enough to provoke your dreaded symptoms or outcomes, you gain control over your fears. When you can no longer be blackmailed by your fears, then you become stronger and more comfortable. Don't simply practice entering the setting you fear, find ways to generate the behaviors that intimidate you.

4. Create Simulations, Role-Plays, and Other Structured Sessions for Skill Practice.

There are three reasons to set up simulated practices. First is that they provide a safer environment to practice your skills. You will then be more willing to experiment with new and different responses. Create role-plays with family members or friends to practice taking a job interview, using "small talk" at a party, asking someone for a date, talking to your boss or taking an exam. Enroll in an assertiveness training class in your community or local college. Join your local Toastmasters International for a supportive place to practice your speaking skills.

Second, during a simulation, you can set up certain responses from others that would be more difficult to create in "real life" settings. For instance, if you fear that others will interrupt you during your speech and criticize your main points, it is both impractical and self-defeating to mess up your actual presentation badly enough to receive such criticism. In this case, design a role-play with friends where the "audience" interrupts you with criticism.

Third, as I mentioned earlier, some socially uncomfortable events are brief contacts. Yet remaining in a distressing situation for extended periods is one of the best ways to improve your comfort. Therefore, it may be necessary to repeat a brief encounter several times during a single practice session. For instance, you might want to simulate calling someone on the phone to ask for a date. Since that Task may only take three minutes, plan to practice it with a friend as the "potential date" four or five times in a row. For this same reason, you may need to set up practice sessions in which you sign your name repeatedly while your friends gather around and look over your shoulder. Similar structured practice can help you become comfortable with looking someone in the eye as you pass, saying hello in the hall at work, shaking hands, answering a question in class, or bumping into someone you know.

5. Learn to Perform While Anxious.

You can read about this important principle in chapters 13 and 16. Learning to tolerate your anxiety symptoms should be one of your top goals. In any social setting, practice tolerating whatever anxiety you experience, to the best of your ability, using the coping skills you have learned. Try not to escape because of your discomfort. This is a learning opportunity for you consciously and it is a way for you to contribute to your body's unconscious habituation process. Don't just enter the feared situation, grit your teeth, and bear up. Actively engage in your coping skills. Over time, you will discover the paradoxical truth: the more you accept your uncomfortable symptoms, the less bothersome they'll be, and the greater the likelihood that they will diminish.

6. GIVE SPECIAL ATTENTION TO YOUR SELF-TALK.

Before, during and after your practice listen for your Negative Observer comments and disrupt them.

7. DO SOMETHING EVERY DAY TO CONFRONT YOUR FEARS.

Frequency is important. Find every opportunity to practice. Don't just wait for a natural time or setting. Purposely generate Tasks that put you face to face with the situations you fear, as a way to practice your skills.

8. USE IMAGERY TO REHEARSE YOUR SKILLS.

Most socially anxious people spend a great deal of their contemplation time fantasizing about how poorly they will perform. Put your powerful imagery skills to better use by seeing yourself perform successfully and by rehearsing the skills that will help you reach that goal. Use our audiotape series as a guide to this type of practice.

21
Achieving Comfortable Flight

Our job would be easier if we only had to address panic in its simplest form. But that is rarely the case in our complex world. As you learned in part 1, other psychological as well as physical disorders can complicate panic. And the underlying causes can vary according to genetic makeup, childhood experiences, and events in adulthood. Addressing panic sometimes means that we must take a number of additional variables into account.

The best example of this complexity—and its cost to our society—is the more than twenty-five million Americans who are either anxious or phobic about traveling on commercial airlines. One out of every six adults is afraid to fly. Some feel uncomfortable in tight spaces and only feel relaxed in wide-body aircraft. Some get nervous during takeoff, in cloudy weather, or while in choppy air. They cope by trying to distract themselves, by taking a few stiff drinks, or just toughing it out as white-knucklers. Others stop flying altogether. They take the train, drive, or just stay close to home.

The costs can be great. People turn down jobs and promotions, miss family gatherings, curtail vacations to exotic places, and waste days in travel that could take only hours by plane. Business travelers avoid six million flights a year because of their anxieties about flying. Because of their embarrassment, their fear usually goes undetected, but many jeopardize their jobs to avoid flying. According to the U.S. Travel Data Center, 36 percent of all airline flights are for business purposes. If the average cost of a one-way flight is $150, then one can calculate that airlines lose over $9 million each year because of fearful business flyers. The high cost to business and industry has yet to be calculated.

If you have trouble flying, many of the chapters in this book will be helpful to you. In this chapter you will learn about the multiple causes of fear of flying and the variety of issues that you may need to address as you decide to overcome this problem. I will suggest the best ways to handle your concerns about airline safety, then we will shift to the question of comfort. You will learn how to handle those anticipatory anxieties before a flight, to respond to symptoms while you are flying, and to relax more quickly and easily, so that you can enjoy your flights.

Even if you know planes are safe, you may have a hard time really believing it. Your worries might begin the moment you board a plane or as the plane enters turbulent, or choppy air. In those moments you may feel scared. We are going to talk about ways you can calm yourself down.

Do you have uncomfortable physical symptoms when you fly? Sweaty palms? Racing heart? Tense stomach? Do you worry that you won't be able to get rid of these feelings? Maybe you have no gripes with the airline industry. You believe planes are safe, and you want to fly comfortably. But when you fly, you feel trapped and out of control. You become claustrophobic, shaky, dizzy, or hot. Those symptoms make it hard for you to concentrate on anything else. You need to learn how to reverse those symptoms as they arise. I will offer suggestions about how to use this book and other resources to reach your goal of comfortable flying. I will summarize the best ways to use the skills you have been studying in this book—the ones that will give you the control you need to enjoy your flights now and in the years to come.

For thousands of people, flying has changed from an anxious time to the quickest, easiest way to travel. With patience and determination, you can overcome your troubles as well. If you want to enjoy flying, take this opportunity to learn how.

How Did Your Discomfort With Flying Begin?

Some people have gradually become uncomfortable flying, and no particular event seems to have caused their problem. We're not certain why people might grow increasingly fearful as the years go by. Perhaps it's an issue of age, since the fear of flying begins at twenty-seven years old on average. As we get older, many of us have a family we care about. If we are leaving our young children or a spouse behind when we fly, we may feel threatened or afraid that they'll be abandoned, that we will never see them again. It is those thoughts that may cause us to become more fearful. Or perhaps as we get older we pay more attention to the fragility of life, so that the older some people get, the more fearful they become. That fear can translate into a discomfort about flying.

You may not be able to pinpoint when your anxiety about flying began. Many people, though, can identify at least one of four different circumstances that contributed to their problems with flying. These are: remembering a bad flight, hearing scary stories about flying, taking a flight while feeling nervous or claustrophobic, or traveling during a personally stressful phase in their life. I will discuss each of these possibilities in the next few pages. See which ones seem to fit you.

1. You Had a Difficult Time During a Previous Flight.

The vast majority of people who become uncomfortable flying never experience actual danger on a flight. This is because danger is rare in commercial aviation. Yet they become frightened while flying, which causes them to worry about future flights.

How do you define a frightening experience? It is any experience that your *mind* decides is frightening. Realistically it might not be a problem; there may be no threat to your life or health. Yet if you feel scared, you will remember the experience as a dangerous one.

COMMON CAUSES OF FEAR OF FLYING

1. You had a difficult time during a previous flight
2. You reacted to stories you have heard
3. You developed other problems which increased your discomfort of flying
4. You had several months of stress prior to becoming uncomfortable

---

Let's say you're taking a commercial flight, and the ride is smooth and calm. Then you see the seat belt light turn on, and the captain announces, "Ladies and gentlemen, soon we will be approaching some choppy air. We would like everyone to return to their seats and fasten their seat belts." Simply hearing that there is going to be turbulence may make your heart race immediately. Even though the plane is safe, you end up feeling traumatized. Regardless of the real danger, you were frightened and felt out of control.

Whenever you think you are out of control, you will have fearful thoughts and your body will become tense. If that experience is frightening enough, you will become "conditioned" to it. This means that when you take flights in the future, you will begin to anticipate the possibility of turbulence again, and become anxious just thinking about it.

So if you have memories of past flights in which you felt uncomfortable and those memories come back to you easily, this can be at least partly responsible for your current discomfort.

2. You Reacted to Stories You Have Heard.

You can also develop discomfort simply by hearing about someone else's problem. We call this vicarious learning. You hear about another person's experience, and then imagine yourself having the same experience. We have clear examples of this phenomenon in the airline industry. Vicarious fears develop with every airplane accident we hear about. People imagine what it would have been like for them if they had been aboard that particular plane.

If your mind rehearses a traumatic event with imagery, your body will react to it almost as though it were happening in reality, and you will feel anxious. What if you then predict that it might occur when *you* next fly? ("Hey, it happened to that plane. That means it could happen to my plane!") You will likely get more anx-

---

HOW TO TURN STORIES INTO WORRY

Hear about ➡ Imagine it ➡ Get ➡ Worry
someone happening anxious about your
else's to you next flight
problem

ious and associate that anxiety with your next flight. It can be as simple as that.

Fearful fliers often look for data to reinforce their anxieties. They tend to ignore articles that talk about safety and how much the airline industry has improved in the past two decades. Instead, they seek out the articles discussing any possible danger or threat in the industry. This is a way people contribute to their own discomfort. They continue to gather evidence that supports their fearful position, while ignoring any data to the contrary.

3. You Developed Other Problems That Increased Your Discomfort of Flying.

Discomfort with flying can stem from a number of other fears: heights, crowds, closed-in spaces (claustrophobia), panic attacks, and feeling trapped or out of control.

Perhaps you are someone who has had panic attacks. Your first panic attack might have been in a sales meeting or just before giving a speech. Then, slowly but surely, the panic attacks started to occur elsewhere, such as in a car or on the subway, in a restaurant or a grocery store, in a church or in wide-open spaces.

WHAT PEOPLE FEAR ABOUT FLYING

Panic attacks	Weather
Closed-in spaces	Clouds
Heights	Turbulence
Crowds	Takeoffs
Stuffiness	Landings
Nausea	Flying over water
Being embarrassed	Traveling more than a certain length of time
Being trapped (door closing)	Trusting pilots
Being out of control	Trusting air traffic controllers
Crashing	Trusting airline industry
Dying	Trusting the mechanics
Being far away from loved ones	Trusting the integrity of the plane

Most people who have panic attacks need to believe that they can escape a fearful place easily, that they won't feel trapped or out of control. Well, planes don't sound too much like they fit that criterion! You board a plane, find your seat, and then sit back to watch other people board. A few minutes later you hear the announcements begin, and you realize that the door is about to close. What if you don't like feeling trapped, and the idea of the door closing makes you feel trapped? At this point you may experience a rush of sensations: racing heart; light-headedness or dizziness; cold, clammy hands; tingling in your fingers, toes and mouth; difficulty breathing; becoming very hot or claustrophobic. Coupled with all these physical symptoms, you may have the urge to rush off the plane, thinking, "I'm about to lose control, and I'm going to be trapped," "I'm going to go crazy," "I'll have a heart attack," "I can't tolerate these feelings," or, "I'll make a fool of myself." Thoughts such as these will obviously increase your panic.

Anytime you face your fears, such as claustrophobia, you may experience some symptoms of panic. If you have had uncomfortable symptoms on a recent flight, it wouldn't be surprising for you to start asking how well you will handle yourself on your next flight. Ironically, the more you worry about such problems, the greater the likelihood that they will occur. If you become worried enough, you may stop flying altogether as the only means you know to ensure your comfort.

4. You Had Several Months of Stress Prior to Becoming Uncomfortable.

Your first difficulties with flying might have come after a period of stress in your life. This frequently relates to people who have developed panic attacks. We know from research that people tend to have their first panic attack following six to eight months of stress. This stress often relates to the theme of loss, such as death in the family, long-standing illness of someone close to you, moving, changing jobs, divorce. Even some events that seem like gains, such as marriage or having a child, can precede the first panic attack. These positive events includes not only something that you gain, such as a partner or a son or daughter, but some sense of loss, such as your freedom, your ability to control your time, and your independence.

If you go through a very stressful period, it is as though your mind becomes more vulnerable and more fragile. Then, out of the clear blue, you have your first panic attack. If these panic attacks continue, then you will begin to fear places or situations in which you feel trapped or out of control. Airplanes can fit into that category, since you don't get to fly the plane and you can't get off whenever you want!

What did you learn about how your discomfort started? Did you notice several possible causes? Even more important than how your difficulty started is why it still exists. For instance, did any part of your discomfort come from concerns about the airline industry? If so, then you will want to pay attention to that issue in the section called "Learning how to fly comfortably." You cannot get the complete benefits of this chapter until you decide to trust the airline industry. As long as you believe that commercial aviation is inherently dangerous, then there are no techniques to make your flights comfortable. If your goal is to fly comfortably, you must add the goal of making peace with the airlines.

Then make sure you continue working with this chapter. Reassurance about airline safety alone may not be enough. If you have been worrying for a while, your worries may continue even when you get new data. You may need the skills of this chapter to help you translate your new trust in the industry into comfort on your future flights.

WHY DOES FEAR OF FLYING TAKE MORE EFFORT TO OVERCOME THAN OTHER ANXIETIES?

Even though one out of every six adult Americans is afraid of flying, a very small percentage of these people seek out help for their fears. For those who do confront their worries and symptoms, the task of getting more comfortable often takes significant encouragement and an extra dose of effort. Here are some of the reasons why:

1. You May Be Confronting Several Fears at Once.

When a person is phobic of elevators, she typically has only one fear, whether it is closed-in spaces, crowds, or heights. This simple phobia means that the task of getting better is not so complicated. Few people have only one fear regarding flying. There are two broad areas of concern. Some people have trouble believing that commercial air travel is safe. And, understandably, people dislike the anxious symptoms they feel when they fly. Within those two categories—as the chart on page 337 shows—are over two dozen fears. It's no wonder that many people don't even try to overcome so many obstacles to comfortable flying.

2. Your Perception of Risk May Work Against You.

Before we engage in a new or difficult activity, our minds automatically begin to assess the risk factors involved. Three criteria are common as we consider whether to move forward with action:

- Am I in control of the risk?
- Is it a big risk or many little ones?
- Is it familiar or unfamiliar?

Commercial flight doesn't score very well on this psychological assessment of risk. Let's contrast flying with traveling by automobile. First is, am I in control? People perceive that they have very little control of an airplane. They can't get off the plane and they aren't permitted in the cockpit. It *seems* much safer in a car because typically we can drive whenever we want and pull over whenever we feel like it. (By the way, that's why some people have trouble driving over bridges or in the left hand turn lane at a stoplight—they feel trapped by not being able to quickly pull off the road.) The second question is, will this be a big risk? In an automobile accident only a few people are injured or killed at the most. The mind perceives this as a small risk compared to the possibility of over one hundred people being killed in one airline accident. In addition, being on the ground while traveling *seems* less risky than traveling 35,000 feet in the air. Third, is this risk familiar? People think they have a general sense of how cars work. They know there is this engine that has pistons that produce energy that turn the wheels. We have been exposed to cars so frequently over so many years that we travel by car with little sense of risk. Flying, on the other hand, is an inherently unnatural event for humans and can seem quite mysterious. How do they put some many tons of

plane, people, and cargo into the air? How do they prevent colli-
sions? What if we run out of fuel, get a flat tire, run into a storm?
The complexity of commercial flight leads us to feel insecure, since
we are naturally more afraid of the unknown than the known.

None of these perceptions is reflective of reality! As you will read
in the next few pages, flying is indisputably the safest form of modern transportation. To reduce your anxieties about commercial
flight, you must challenge your *perceptions* of reality far more than
you need to address the actual risks of flying. As you realize this,
you will be well on your way to comfortable flight.

3. The Media Present a Lopsided View of Airline Accidents.

The media coverage of an airline accident can contribute to this
problem, too. We see or read about the same airline accident
repeatedly on the radio and TV and in newspaper articles. If there
has been a plane crash recently, it might be shown on the evening
news ten or fifteen times over the next three or four weeks. It
could come across our breakfast tables every morning for days
through the newspaper headlines. Seeing the traumatic event so
many times, we have ample opportunity to imagine ourselves on
that plane.

OBSTACLES TO ACHIEVING COMFORTABLE FLIGHT

- You may be confronting several fears at once.
- Your perception of risk may work against you.
- The media present a lopsided view of airline
  accidents.
- It is harder gradually to face your fears of flying.
- Repetition of practice is crucial, but it's costly.

Dr. Arnold Barnett, of the Massachusetts Institute of Technology,
compared the number of front-page stories in the *New York Times*
that addressed six major sources of death: AIDS, automobiles, cancer, homicide, suicide, and commercial jets. Over a period of a year,
stories about airline accidents far outnumbered stories about any of

the other five sources of death. In fact, when considering coverage on a per-death basis, the number of airline stories was sixty times the number of stories on AIDS, and over eight thousand times the number of stories about cancer, the nation's number two killer.

Airline accidents are certainly dramatic and newsworthy, and the media serves an important function of keeping the public eye on the industry's safety concerns. However, this kind of frequent reporting skews our sense of relative danger. We tend to associate greater exposure to a problem with our sense of how serious the problem is. It is not so much the number of people killed by a particular source that can produce our vicarious trauma. If that were true, few of us would feel safe enough to travel by car. But the greater the number of times our attention is drawn to the graphic image of those deaths, and the greater the number of times we imagine ourselves involved in that event, the stronger our chances of becoming uncomfortable.

4. It Is Harder to *Gradually* Face Your Fears of Flying.

We know from over twenty-five years of behavioral research that gradual exposure to fearful situations is a highly successful treatment. You can design a program for yourself that takes you through stages of exposure to components of flying: studying about the industry, visiting airports, talking with pilots, boarding stationary planes, practicing visualizations of comfortable flight. But the step between these practices and boarding a regular commercial flight is a large one. For those who have become phobic of flying and no longer travel by plane, this step requires significant courage.

5. Repetition of Practice Is Crucial, but with Flying It's Costly.

We also know that you continue to increase your comfort by continuing to practice facing your fears. If too much time passes between practices, the mind has a tendency to wander back to the fearful experiences and forget the successes. I recommend that my clients take at least one flight every three months to practice their skills during their first year after treatment. But with ticket prices for even short trips costing close to two hundred dollars, this can be so expensive that people fail to reinforce their gains through practice.

LEARNING HOW TO FLY COMFORTABLY

If you are afraid to fly, there are a number of steps you can take to overcome this fear. Your very first step needs to be motivation: facing anxiety is indeed uncomfortable, so you need to become determined to choose air travel as the easiest, quickest way to reach those far-away destinations. Is frequent flying a necessity in your profession? Do you have family and friends you want to visit more frequently? Do you want to take vacations abroad? These aims will help motivate you, because a strong desire to overcome your problem can guide you through any obstacles along the way.

In the rest of this chapter I will outline the six central tasks to flying comfortably. The first task—learning to trust the industry—specifically focuses on the issue of flying. The five other tasks all relate to the chapters in part 2 of this book. Once you have read this chapter, use it as a guide to study the central attitudes and skills presented in part 2.

Don't begin to judge whether these skills will help you until you've had a chance to practice them in real-life situations. Take small steps toward flying comfortably, such as visiting an airport, boarding a stationary plane, or taking a short flight as practice. These will be chances for you to try out some of these skills. The more you practice, the easier it will get. If you have patience, the world of commercial flight will soon be just the ticket for quick, easy, and comfortable travel.

LEARNING HOW TO FLY COMFORTABLY

1. Start by trusting the airline industry.
2. Accept your feelings.
3. Breathe!
4. Relax.
5. Take supportive actions.
6. Handle your worries.

1. Start by Trusting the Airline Industry.

Your first task is to settle all the worries you have regarding the airline industry. No self-help skills will assist you in your goal unless you choose to feel safe on commercial flights. The goal in this task is to reassure yourself whenever you feel anxious about taking a flight. This reassurance is not that you are going to be physically comfortable and relaxed, but that you are safe on the plane. Here is the communication to aim for: "My discomfort is not really about the plane being dangerous, this is about me having difficulty with not being in control [claustrophobia, panic attacks, being trapped]." Remember, you start here. Turn the issue back onto yourself, because you have far more control over yourself than you do over the plane. You have many skills and attitudes to apply to the problem of anxiety, and very little to apply to any problem of safety.

The good news is, you really *don't* need to worry about safety issues with flying. It is truly the safest mode of modern transportation. Furthermore, once you stop blaming the industry for your fears, you will instantly have significantly more psychological power to reduce your symptoms of anxiety.

So actively seek out information about air travel, including pilot training, aircraft construction and maintenance, the air traffic control system, the monitoring of weather systems, turbulence, and all the normal sights, sounds, and sensations that take place on a flight. There is much to learn if you choose to study this topic. Here are some examples:

- The cost and duration of training pilots with a major carrier are comparable to training a physician.
- Backup systems have been provided for virtually every system on the airplane so that if one system fails, another will take its place. For instance, a 747 has eighteen tires: four on each of the main landing struts and two on the nose wheel. Computers on the planes built this decade have two or three autopilots and generally three computers that are able to handle all necessary functions.
- Commercial aircraft average 12 hours of maintenance on the ground for every one hour spent in the air. Commonly scheduled maintenance checks while the plane is grounded include 12 person-hours daily; another 17 person-hours

every four or five days; 125 person-hours every thirty days; a 2,000 person-hour inspection (involving 110 people) once every twelve to eighteen months; and a major overhaul every four years, taking four to five weeks and requiring 22,000 person-hours of labor.

- Air traffic controllers go through rigorous training and internship that lasts three to four years. For every eight-hour shift, a controller is restricted to a maximum of five or six hours actively directing traffic, with several breaks throughout that time.
- Each plane flies right down the middle of a private highway in the sky that is ten miles wide. No other plane is allowed in that space.
- Standard industry policy is to avoid all thunderstorms by at least twenty nautical miles.
- We measure turbulence, or "chop," in terms of gravity: .4 g of force is rated "severe" and is rarely experienced during commercial flight. But federal regulations require planes to be able to fly without problems through at least 2 g's, and today's manufacturers build planes that are tested to withstand 6 to 7 g's of force. Mother Nature won't be creating any turbulence to match that.

On a flight, you may notice a number of "unusual" sounds and sensations that are actually normal and appropriate operations. For example:

- Cargo pallets are loaded while you are boarding the plane. You may feel the plane suddenly move in response to the pallets being positioned in the cargo bay.
- You may see "clouds" emerge from the air conditioning ducts on the lower wall next to your seat or in the ceiling ducts. It is not smoke, it just looks like it. Condensation occurs when the cold air from the air-conditioning system circulates into the hot, humid cabin. The cold air mixing with hot, moist air causes "clouds" of condensation.
- If you're sitting in the middle of the airplane, you'll probably encounter more sounds prior to takeoff and during the flight. All the flight controls and devices on the airplane are either electrically or hydraulically activated. Most of the

hydraulic pump system's actuators are located in the middle of the airplane in its belly, close to the landing gear. Therefore you may hear pumps that cycle on and off, which maintains a certain pressure. As the pressure slacks off, they pump it up again. You may also hear other pumps being activated to energize the hydraulic system operating the leading-edge devices and trailing-edge flaps, the main landing gear and nose wheel, the spoilers, and the speed brakes.

- Occasionally you might feel a light bumping of the tires during takeoff or landing. Don't worry; the plane doesn't have a flat tire! Down the center of the runway are reflectors that are slightly raised. If the pilot is exactly on the center line of the runway, the front nose wheel tires will ride directly on top of the reflectors. (Many pilots choose to move just a few inches to one side to avoid these bumps.)

We have developed a self-help program, *Achieving Comfortable Flight,* that provides you with a detailed understanding of the airline industry (See "Resources," page 367). Use that program as well as all other resources you can find to give you the facts you need. Once you have this information, you will be able to decide, "Do I trust the airline industry?" The facts should convince you that airline travel is one of our safest forms of transportation.

Even when you are reassured about the aviation industry, from time to time you may become concerned about some aspect of commercial flight. Imagine, for example, that some event has occurred that causes you to ask whether you should fly again. Perhaps the newspapers have reported some concerns about a particular airline in the industry. You begin to have questions about whether you should be flying on that carrier. Or maybe there has been a recent accident, and it has raised issues in your mind about safety. Or there have been threats of terrorist attacks. You will probably begin to worry anytime there has been a recent incident that calls into question your ability to feel safe on a flight.

When you have concerns like this, you need to slow down a little bit, think through exactly what those concerns are, and figure out what actions you need to take in light of these questions. It's not going to be helpful for you to simply ask over and over again in your mind, "Should I fly? Should I fly? Should I fly?" All that will do is stir you up and make you anxious. That's what worrying does: you keep defining the problem in your mind, you keep throwing the question up to the front of your consciousness, and you get anxious again and again.

What you need to do is put some of your creative intelligence to work to respond to the problem that you are worrying about, to answer these anxiety-provoking questions your mind asks. Whatever the issue is, set aside time devoted to looking at it. Define specifically what the problem is. For example, your definition of the problem might be, "There was an incident last month involving the airline I'm flying on Friday. That makes me question whether I should fly." Identify what that problem is, then sit down with paper and pencil, and write down all the components of the problem, everything that you feel concerned about.

Second, write down all possible solutions. Can you get more data about this? What do experts say is the probability of this problem recurring? What actions are being taken to solve this problem? How successful have those actions been, or will those actions be? Where can I gather information to help me answer these questions?

Third, go about the process of answering these questions. Turn to the FAA, the airline industry, consumer watch groups, and gather information as necessary.

Fourth, use that information to make your decision. If your conclusions, based on evidence and data, are that flying is unsafe and you shouldn't trust the industry, then by all means don't bother flying. Certainly, if you don't rationally believe it is safe to fly right now, you have the right to cancel your plans. Canceling will have consequences, of course. You may inconvenience yourself or others. But you are the one in control, and you get to decide what action is best for you.

If you feel it is necessary, postpone flying until you feel safe again. But make sure you are using information that is going to help you decide logically whether flying is safe. Don't simply respond to sensationalism and emotionalism. If you choose to make your decision on the basis of your emotions alone, your fears and anxiety are going to win out, because they are the most powerful of all your emotions in these situations, and they'll run the show.

Keep in mind that your fears may not be directly related to the safety of flying, even though your mind focuses on the safety issues. As I mentioned before, when you choose to learn to fly comfortably, you are confronting some common, basic fears that are built into all of us, such as fear of heights; of being closed in, crowded, or trapped; and of not being in control. It's no surprise so many people have trouble flying; when we fly we are challenging some primitive survival instincts. Be careful that you don't blame the industry for your discomfort when you actually need to be paying attention to issues unrelated to the industry.

Here's another example of how you may focus on the wrong concerns when you fly. Let's say you are about to fly to your family's home for the holidays. In the back of your mind you are worried about the health of one of your family members, but you are not consciously aware of that worry as you board the plane. You just notice that you are beginning to feel nervous.

Instead of realizing that you are nervous about your family member, you think you are scared of the plane. We call this *misattribution:* you attribute your discomfort to the process of flying instead of to your family. Then you focus all your worries on whether this flight will be safe. Since that's not the real problem at the moment, you will have a hard time calming yourself down by reassuring yourself about airline safety. If your discomfort continues despite your reassurances, you'll become more worked up. And that's the vicious circle we have talked about.

For this reason it's important for you to use logic and intellect as you respond to such worries. Take time to really think through all that could be influencing your worries. Then take action to learn more, and to think clearly about what you learn. Don't just dwell on your worries. Doing nothing is going to be the least successful avenue in solving this particular problem.

That's why I want to congratulate you on working with this book. You know you have been having some troubles, and you have decided to take a good long look at all that could be affecting you. Now you can make the leap from learning about your new choices to actually practicing them.

How Safe Is Commercial Flight?

Safety is a concern of everyone who flies or contemplates it. I can provide you with volumes of information about the attention to safety given by the airline industry. No other form of transportation is as scrutinized, investigated, and monitored as commercial aviation. Yet if you decide to hold on to the position that flying is dangerous, these reassuring safety facts are lost to you. Statistics and figures that prove airline transportation to be the safest way to travel relate to our logical, reasoning, rational mind. Worry about safety is an intrusion that seems to bypass those faculties of logic and to go directly to our emotions. And you will always find another article about some "near miss" or "the crowded skies" that will reinforce your belief.

Even if you hold the belief, "Statistics about flying don't help me," give yourself another chance to reexamine your judgment as you read through this section. After all, your goal is to feel as comfortable as possible when you fly, and there are some very comforting numbers here.

Most passengers who have knowledge of the commercial airline industry believe that flying is safe. But when something occurs that we don't understand, any of us can become quickly frightened. That's why I encourage you to study as much as you need to reassure yourself about the industry and to take some of the mystery out of commercial flight.

However, some small thing may occur on one of your flights that you haven't studied. If you become startled or frightened at that time, the statistics that I am about to present may come in handy. Airline accidents are extremely rare. When some unfamiliar noise or bump occurs, your response need not be, "Oh, no! What's wrong?!" Instead, it can be something like "I'm not sure what that sound was, but there's nothing to worry about." Feel free to press your overhead call button to page a flight attendant whenever you want to ask about unfamiliar sights or sounds. But you needn't jump to fearful conclusions.

Now you may notice something a little morbid about this section: most of these statistics have to do with death. This isn't the most pleasant of subjects, I know. But many people who are worried about flying concentrate on the fear that something will go wrong during the flight, and that the outcome of that error would be their own death. So let's put this possibility in perspective.

Dr. Arnold Barnett, of the Massachusetts Institute of Technology, has done extensive research in the field of commercial flight safety. He found that over the 20 years between 1975 and 1994, the death risk per flight was one in seven million. This statistic is the probability that someone who randomly selected one of the airline's flights over the twenty-year study period would be killed in route. That means that anytime you board a flight on a major carrier in this country, your chance of being in a fatal accident is one in seven million. It doesn't matter whether you fly once every three years or every day of the year. In fact, based on this incredible safety record, if you did fly every day of your life, probability indicates that it would take you 19,000 years before you would succumb to a fatal accident. Nineteen thousand years!

Perhaps you have occasionally taken the train for your travels, believing that it would be safer. Think again. On the basis of the number of train accidents over the past twenty years, your chances of dying on a transcontinental train journey are one in a million. Those are great odds, mind you. But flying coast to coast is ten times safer than making the trip by train.

How about driving, our typical form of transportation? Approximately 130 people are killed daily in auto accidents. That's every day—yesterday, today, and tomorrow, and 47,000 killed per year. In 1990, 500 million airline passengers were transported an average distance of eight hundred miles, through more than 7 million takeoffs and landings, in all kinds of weather conditions, with a loss of only 39 lives. During that same year the National Transportation Safety Board's report shows that over 46,000 people were killed in auto accidents. A sold-out 727 jet would have to crash every day of the week, with no survivors, to equal the highway deaths per year in this country.

The Airline Deregulation Act of 1978 permitted the airlines to be competitive both in the routes they flew and the fares they charged. When the price of air travel decreased, the number who flew increased. In 1977, 270 million passengers flew on U.S. scheduled airlines. In 1987 450 million flew. For passengers, that resulted in the frustration of crowded terminals and delayed boardings and takeoffs. But did deregulation cause safety to be compromised? Definitely not! Accident statistics provided by the National Transportation Safety Board show that despite a 50 percent *increase* in passengers during the ten years after deregulation, there was a 40 percent *decrease* in the number of fatal accidents and a 25 percent decrease in the number of fatalities, compared to the ten years before deregulation.

If you are going to worry about dying, there are many more

probable ways to die than on a commercial jet. Take a look at the chart below, which shows the chance of fatalities on a commercial flight compared to other causes of death in the United States. Notice that you are more likely to die from a bee sting than from a commercial flight. The number one killer in the United States is cardiovascular disease, with about 885,000 deaths per year. Each of us has about a 50 percent chance of dying of cardiovascular disease. Whenever we fly, we have a one seventy thousandth of one percent (.000014 percent) chance of dying!

ODDS OF DEATH

Death by	Your Odds
Cardiovascular disease	1 in 2
Smoking (by/before age 35)	1 in 600
Car trip, coast-to-coast	1 in 14,000
Bicycle accident	1 in 88,000
Tornado	1 in 450,000
Train, coast-to-coast	1 in 1 million
Lightning	1 in 1.9 million
Bee sting	1 in 5.5 million
U.S. commercial jet airline	1 in 7 million

(Sources: Natural History Museum of Los Angeles County, Massachusetts Institute of Technology, University of California at Berkeley)

How about accidental deaths? In the chart below you can compare the average number of airline fatalities per year (not including commuter airlines) from 1981 to 1994 with the most recent figures for other forms of accidental death. Again, you can see that flying is relatively insignificant compared to other causes of death.

NUMBERS OF ACCIDENTAL DEATHS PER YEAR BY CAUSE

100 on commercial flight
850 by electrical current
1,000 on a bicycle
1,452 by accidental gunfire
3,000 by complications to medical procedures
3,600 by inhaling or ingesting objects

5,000 by fire
5,000 by drowning
5,300 by accidental poisoning
8,000 as pedestrians
11,000 at work
12,000 by falls
22,500 at home
46,000 in auto accidents

(Sources: Bureau of Safety Statistics, National Transportation Safety Board)

I'm not trying to encourage you to become afraid of your bicycle or of walking down the stairs in your home. My most important point is that no one can anticipate all of your questions about flight safety and the airline industry. You may have specific questions about maintenance or security or pilot error that are not simple to address. I want to assure you that regardless of your worries, you are putting your life in the hands of an industry that has a tremendous record of dedicating its creative intelligence to your safety. And the Federal Aviation Administration, the air traffic controllers, the airline companies, the pilots, the flight attendants, the mechanics, the manufacturers are all striving to make every year safer than the year before within a highly professional industry.

Next time you begin to focus on the possibility of something going wrong on a plane, think about the probability instead. Then you will have little to worry about.

2. Accept Your Feelings.

All of the next five points are a summary of the primary themes covered in this book. I will review them briefly here, and again encourage you to reread part 2 for a more comprehensive understanding.

Whenever you begin to get anxious and panicky—before or during a flight—*accept* these symptoms. *Don't* fight or try to hold them back. If you struggle against your anxious feelings, you will cause an *increase* in the symptoms you are trying to reduce! Your heart will race more, your palms will sweat, you'll feel more light-headed and dizzy, your stomach will become more tense. When you notice your symptoms, tell yourself, "It's O.K. that I'm feeling this way. I expect to be nervous right now. I can handle this." Then work on *believing* those thoughts, not just repeating the words.

How Your Mind and Body Keep You Anxious

I assume that you are reading this chapter not because you have had one uncomfortable time on a plane, but several. Why do these anxious thoughts and feelings keep returning?

Let's assume that you have had some flight experience that you consider bad or traumatic. It may be a situation you were involved in, or it could be a vicarious experience of stories you have heard. In either case, let's also assume that this traumatic experience is fresh in your memory. Here is what occurs when you get uncomfortable again.

You think about flying. Perhaps you are out taking a walk in the park and hear a plane overhead. Or maybe you are reflecting on the possibility of taking a flight in a few weeks to go on vacation, or starting a new job that's going to require you to fly as part of your responsibilities. Anything that reminds you of flying can lead you to discomfort.

You remember a previous problem. Why would something as minor as hearing the sound of a plane cause you to feel tense? Any kind of stimulus such as this can trigger your negative memory, because your mind will retrieve the past relevant event that has the strongest emotion. As I mentioned earlier, when you remember that event, something interesting happens: your body responds to the imagery almost as if the event were happening again. In response, you get anxious.

You imagine the problem happening in the future. If you are thinking of the possibility of taking a flight soon, then your mind won't stop there. In the back of your mind, you will probably ask the question, "Can this happen to me in the future? How will I handle it?" To assess those questions, your mind will visually put you in that uncomfortable future scene.

HOW TO BECOME AN UNCOMFORTABLE FLIER

Think about flying.

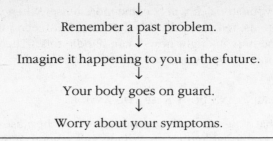

Remember a past problem.

Imagine it happening to you in the future.

Your body goes on guard.

Worry about your symptoms.

___

Your body goes on guard. Your body becomes directly involved in that experience and responds appropriately to the moment, only it will be responding to your imagery, not to reality. Even if you are taking a leisurely bath in the comfort of your own home, if you start seeing yourself on a plane, feeling claustrophobic, and not handling it well, then your body will give you symptoms of anxiety, just as I discussed in chapter 7, "The Anatomy of Panic." If you imagine yourself having trouble, your mind will send your body the message, "This is an emergency!" Your brain sends a signal to its hypothalamus, and the hypothalamus sends a signal to your adrenal glands, which are on top of your kidneys. Your adrenal glands secrete a hormone called epinephrine, which used to be called adrenaline. Epinephrine stimulates the production of specific physical changes: the eyes dilate to improve vision, the heart rate increases to circulate blood more quickly to vital organs, respiration increases to provide more oxygen to the rapidly circulating blood, the muscles tense in the arms and legs to help you move quickly and precisely.

This is your body's emergency response, gearing up to help you in a crisis, the same response that helps when you are about to fall or when your car goes into a skid in the rain or snow. We don't want to change your body's response; it is a valuable part of your survival skills. Instead, we want to stop your mind from sending your body the message "This is an emergency!" every time you think about being on a plane.

You worry about your symptoms. An interesting thing happens next. When your symptoms become strong and persist, you start to worry about them as well as the flight. You know you can't control the plane, and you know you can't get off whenever you want. And now you begin to think you can't control your body either!

How does your body respond when you say, "I don't feel in control"? Here is that same message again: "This is an emergency!" As soon as your body hears "emergency," it jumps to your rescue: "I'm here to protect you!" And it will secrete more epinephrine to prepare you for the "fight or flight" response.

As soon as that happens, you say, "Uh-oh, things are getting worse, I'm feeling even more terrible. This is really frightening." It becomes a vicious circle: you notice physical sensations, and you become frightened by them, which causes an increase in those physical symptoms. As they increase, it scares you even more.

Then either one of two things can happen. The first is that you continue to book the flight or to stay on the airplane, but you feel anxious and uncomfortable the whole time. This is why some people experience a tense stomach throughout an entire flight, even if the flight is smooth and routine. Your other choice is to escape. You say, "This is enough, I've had it, I can't tolerate it." And you walk off the plane before takeoff, or you cancel the flight that you booked.

Have you ever avoided a flight at the last minute because of your discomfort? What happens next? Let's say you are on a flight, and the door is closing before takeoff. Now your symptoms get very strong. You say, "Hey, I can't tolerate this. I am getting out of here!" And you walk off the plane. The door closes behind you, and the plane backs away from the gate.

Two things change. First, your symptoms will begin to diminish. Your breathing rate returns to normal, your heart rate starts to slow down, your blood pressure drops, and you begin to feel a sense of relief and comfort. In other words, your body reinforces your avoidance. Your body relaxes and tells you, "It was a smart decision to get off of that flight."

Second, you will tend to finish that picture of the flight in your mind. You say, "Thank goodness I got off the flight. What if I had stayed on the plane? My heart would have raced so strongly that I would have had a heart attack." Or, "My symptoms would have gotten so severe that I would have had a panic attack. I would have humiliated myself. We'd be thirty-one thousand feet in the air, and I'd be running down the aisle screaming."

The reduction of your physical symptoms, coupled with this image that things would have been awful if you had stayed on the plane, reinforces your decision to avoid flying, and the next time it might be much harder to face your discomfort.

How to Respond to Your Symptoms

I have explained what the protective "emergency" response is and why it occurs. I have also talked about what people tend to do when they experience the symptoms of this response. Now let's look at what to do differently so that you will become more comfortable.

I base almost all these next strategies on the important concept of paradox. Paradox means "the opposite of logic." In other words, when you begin to get anxious and panicky, your mind says, "You had better become scared of these symptoms. You had better run and escape from the situation." I encourage you, instead, to *accept* these symptoms, to not fight them. Chapter 17 describe this paradoxical approach in detail.

I'm not asking you to erase all of your fears and worries about flying. I'm suggesting that you respond to them differently once you notice them. It's all right if you are startled when you hear a noise or feel the plane bump. That's perfectly fine, and many people who fly will have that reaction. Once it occurs, how can you take care of yourself? Here is the beginning of what you do:

Notice your discomfort. Step back for a moment and comment on your discomfort. Keep it simple. Say to yourself, "I'm starting to work myself up." Or "I can feel myself getting more and more nervous right now." Or "I'm sitting here thinking how bad this flight could get, and I'm scaring myself."

Accept your discomfort. Your negative images are understandable: you are scared of the flight, so you worry about it. This causes your mind and body to brace for the worst possible outcome. That response is built into the brain as a genetic predisposition. When we are threatened, the mind and body shift to a survival stance, which is a natural, biologically based process. This is a fact. If you resist this fact, you only make matters worse for yourself.

So decide to accept this response, just as you would accept your startled response if someone made a sudden loud noise behind you. (I want to point out here that when you bring your attention to your symptoms, even in this manner when you are trying to help, you may become a little more nervous. Accept that added nervousness, too!) Find a statement that supports your acceptance. Say it in your mind, and let it help you. Try to believe what you are saying.

Two common statements that might reflect your acceptance are

"It's okay to be nervous."
"I can handle these feelings."

Acceptance is your initial position, your opening stance. You then *keep reminding yourself to accept your symptoms* as you begin to take action. There are a variety of simple techniques you can use to calm yourself down, but none of them work very well if you are saying to yourself, "This can't go on! I can't stand this! I've got to feel better now!" In other words, "This is an emergency!"

The rest of this chapter offers you specific actions you can take to become comfortable. Please keep in mind that accepting your symptoms will serve as the foundation of every other skill you learn. When you are having trouble applying new skills, think first about whether you are applying the principle of acceptance.

3. Breathe!

Medical research has proved that our breathing patterns influence our physical symptoms. Use straightforward and simple breathing skills to relieve your body's stresses and quiet your mind. They will help you to quickly clear unwanted thoughts and let you enjoy your flight with a quiet mind and a calm body. Study chapter 11 to learn how to use these skills. Here's a reminder of one, called the Calming Breath.

> *Completely exhale, then take a long deep breath. Hold your breath to the count of "three." Exhale very slowly, saying the word "relax" under your breath. Now rest for about fifteen seconds. Let your muscles go limp and warm, loosen your face and jaw muscles, and quiet your thoughts. Repeat that process two more times.*

4. Relax.

In several chapters I've already talked about relaxing your muscles. Why should you spend time learning how to relax? Because twenty-five years of research have shown that if you can loosen muscles in your body, your anxiety will reduce automatically. This is a great way to alleviate some of your symptoms! Instead of trying to quiet those noisy thoughts, you can loosen your muscles, and your thoughts will relax as well. Calming your body will help calm your mind.

Get Tense Before You Relax.

Many people give you the advice, "Just relax!" Sometimes you feel so tense that you can't "just relax." But remember the principle of paradox? These are the times to apply paradox by exaggerating your physical symptoms as a way to reduce them.

There are two different ways to apply this principle. You can reduce your tension by intensifying it before you begin to let it go, or you can encourage and invite certain physical symptoms instead of resisting them. Each of these ways enables you to reduce your uncomfortable physical symptoms.

These two approaches sound very much like the other kinds of paradox that I've talked about already. When you are growing increasingly anxious and tense on the plane, I suggest that you increase that tension, that you try to become even more tense. That goes against your basic nature, which is to resist tension. But when you apply this principle, you'll be surprised at the response you get from your body.

Keep in mind the body's physical reaction to fear. If you're like most people, every time you have a fearful thought, your body responds by becoming a little more tense. So why fight it? Because nobody wants to be tense.

But why fight it initially? In some cases you'll only be making yourself more tense. Instead, do the opposite. Go with your impulse to become tense, but do it *consciously, purposely, voluntarily*. Now you are taking control. You like to be in control, don't you? (Most people do.) So actually tighten your muscles before you loosen them, instead of simply trying to relax them.

One way is by using the Ten-Second Grip, described in chapter 14. Here's a review of it.

> *Grab the arm rests in your seat and squeeze them as hard as you can, making your lower and upper arms contract. Tense your stomach and leg muscles as well. Hold that for about ten seconds, while you continue to breathe. Then let go with a long, gentle Calming Breath. Repeat that two more times. Then shift around in your seat, shaking loose your arms, shoulders and legs and gently rolling your head a few times. Finish off by closing your eyes and breathing gently for about thirty seconds. Let your body feel warm, relaxed and heavy during that time.*

TRY TO INCREASE YOUR SYMPTOMS.

You may experience many other anxious symptoms besides physical tension. Your heart starts racing, you begin to get dizzy or lightheaded, perhaps you get a lump in your throat, you have a difficult time swallowing, some pain in your chest, numbness or tingling in your hands or feet or around your mouth, maybe shaking or nausea. All of these symptoms can make you even more frightened than you were when you began to have your fears, and we need to have a way to respond to them. Here is a summary of the paradoxical procedure from chapter 17 that you can apply to these symptoms. Review that chapter for details.

> Take a Calming Breath, then begin natural breathing. Don't fight your physical symptoms and don't run away. Observe your predominant physical symptom at this moment. Say to yourself, "I am going to take voluntary control of these symptoms. I would like to increase my heartbeat [other symptom]." Consciously attempt to increase that symptom. Now attempt to increase all the other symptoms you notice: "I would like to perspire more than this. Let me see if I can become very dizzy and make my legs turn into jelly, right now." Continue natural breathing, while you consciously and fully attempt to increase all your symptoms of panic. Do not get trapped in worried, critical, or hopeless comments ("This better start working soon! I certainly must be doing this wrong. It'll never work."

It's obvious that these are paradoxical instructions, because it seems somewhat crazy to say to yourself: "Here I am with shaky legs, feeling dizzy, like I'm about to faint. And now I'm supposed to try to make this worse!?" So it does take courage and a little faith. If you will practice during times of low-level anxiety, you will have another valuable skill on hand when a real worry sets in.

HELP YOUR BODY RELAX.

Remember that you don't have to be run by your discomfort. Take charge of your discomfort by taking action. If you have only a minute or two, take a single Calming Breath or do the Calming Counts, and release your tensions in the process. Practicing your breathing skills, using the Ten-Second Grip, paradoxically trying to increase your symptoms—these are all ways to reduce physical symptoms of tension. Use the formal relaxation skills discussed in chapter 12 to help train your body and mind to slow down and experience comfort. Practice them daily for several weeks.

There are other ways to manage your discomfort as well. For a summary of them, refer to the chart "Responding to Physical Symptoms" on page 274 of chapter 18.

GET INVOLVED!

Keep in mind, too, that you don't have to be totally relaxed to be in control. Sometimes you may need to try out your skills, let them help you reduce your tensions as much as possible, then accept that you may still have some leftover tension. Don't worry about that. The best thing to do at that point is to get involved with your surroundings. You may be surprised to discover that if you focus on that interesting person next to you, in a few minutes your tension isn't so bothersome.

I'm not suggesting that you neglect your discomfort. Too many people read the same paragraph in a novel over and over in an effort to distract themselves. That's not too helpful. Instead, pay attention to your physical discomfort, and choose some direct actions to increase your comfort. You might say, "It's O.K. that I'm feeling some tension now. This is my first transcontinental flight in eight years. I've reassured myself and practiced the skills. Now I'm going to get involved awhile with my novel. I'll check my symptoms in ten minutes."

5. Take Supportive Actions.

There are many other small changes you can make to increase your comfort.

- Start by reducing your caffeine and sugar intake on the day before and the day of your flight.
- Drink lots of water or fruit juices, even if you're not thirsty, to avoid dehydration from the dry plane air.
- Refrain from drinking alcohol before or during the flight.
- Pack a bag of pastimes for the flight: a good book, crossword puzzles, your favorite music and snacks, and so forth.

- Get to the airport early; don't rush. Watch planes take off for a while to get an idea of the motions you might expect.
- As you board the plane, greet the captain and look in the cockpit. Consider mentioning to the crew and the flight attendants that you sometimes get afraid on flights.
- At your seat, get comfortable; do some quieting exercises, talk to your neighbor. As others board, watch faces, notice relationships, greet people as they go by.
- During takeoff, wiggle your toes for those 30 to 50 seconds, or take three Calming Breaths.
- During the flight, ask the flight attendants about any sensations on the plane that bother you.
- Pull out your pastime bag and get occupied with a project.
- When the seat belt sign goes off, stand and stretch or take a walk.

In other words, get involved; don't sit and quietly concentrate on your worries while checking your watch. When you get anxious, review the major points of this chapter: remind yourself you can trust the airline industry, accept your feelings, handle your worries, breathe, relax, and again take new supportive actions.

6. Handle Your Worries.

Even after you decide to trust the airline industry, your mind may continue to scare you with "What if . . . ?" thoughts. ("What if something *does* go wrong!"; "What if people see that I'm nervous!"; or "What if I have a panic attack!") These worries are simply "noise"—distractions, ways to make you uncomfortable. You will want to get that noise out of your head, to clear your mind so that you can have more enjoyable flights. You will need some special skills to get rid of them, and I describe most of them in chapter 16 and 18. Here is a summary.

WORRIES AS "NOISE"

Let's say that even though there has been some recent incident in the airline industry, you are able to reassure yourself about the unlikely chance of this incident occurring again. If you continue to worry, you can say, "This is really 'noise.' I gathered the information I needed, and I trust the industry. So I am choosing to fly, and now I want to fly as comfortably as possible."

Making that decision is half the battle. You now need to address your worries head on, because worries don't usually dissolve in the face of logic. Now you must apply different skills to reduce the "noise" of your worries.

Before you do anything else, take a firm stand: "I am going to handle these worries that keep popping up again and again. They just start running in my mind and keep me awake at night. They are preventing me from flying comfortably." You cannot take half a stand here. You must fully commit yourself to confronting your worries as noise that you want to get rid of.

Then you have to plan for those moments when you begin worrying. What happens when those worries start? As you know from experience, you feel scared, tense, and have difficulty concentrating on anything besides your fears.

YOUR FIRST MOVE: ADDING SOME SUPPORT

It's probably becoming clear now that everything you say during these times will influence how you feel. The statements that increase your problems will be ones that start with "I can't . . ."—"I can't let people see me this way," "I can't be anxious right now," "I can't let this anxiety get any worse," or "I can't handle these feelings."

So let's find some statements that will support your comfort. We are looking for statements that give you the message "I can stop thinking those worried thoughts now."

When you are worried about your symptoms, the strongest kinds of supporting statements start with "It's O.K. . . ." and "I can . . ."— "It's O.K. to be nervous" and "I can handle these feelings." As I mentioned earlier, these statements reflect your willingness to accept your symptoms. They are permissive statements; they give you options. Those options make you feel less trapped. When you feel less trapped, you won't feel so uncomfortable.

There are many other statements that might feel supportive to you, such as "These feelings I am having are uncomfortable, but they're not dangerous." Other examples are "These negative thoughts aren't helping me. I can let them go"; "I can stop these worried thoughts now"; "This is only anxiety"; "I deserve to feel comfortable here."

If your worries include concerns about the flight, respond to the negative thoughts with positive ones that you can believe in. Here are some examples:

"These pilots are well-trained professionals whom I can trust."
"This plane is safe."
"Turbulence may feel uncomfortable, but it's not dangerous."
"This is not an emergency."

When you are worried, find statements that will help you let go of negative thoughts. Think about what you need to hear to reverse your worried thinking. Look for statements that allow you to say, "It's O.K. to relax now." But don't just mouth those words. Find statements you can believe in, then work on believing them.

Now we will build on this opening move with two techniques: thought stopping and postponing.

PUTTING A STOP TO YOUR WORRIES

Negative thought stopping is another handy tool to use as you start to worry. (Review negative thought stopping on page 232 of chapter 16.) Imagine sitting on the plane at cruising altitude. The captain announces that you will soon be entering some light turbulence. You think, "Oh, no, not turbulence! This plane can't take it!" If you want to get a grip on things, what do you do next?

- Notice that you are worrying: "I'm starting to work myself up."
- Decide if you want to stop it: "But I know that turbulence can't hurt this plane, even if it might spill a little of my coffee."
- Yell, "Stop!" in your mind. And snap a rubber band on your wrist, if you're wearing one.
- Then start Calming Counts or some other relaxation technique.

STALLING YOUR WORRIES

The postponing technique presented in chapter 18 is another useful tool. You need not allow your noisy worries to have free rein over your mind throughout each day. Here's a review of that skill.

Agree to pay attention to your worries instead of struggling to get rid of them. But choose your own specific time in the future to worry. Never let yourself worry on demand. As that designated time arrives, either start worrying again or consider postponing the worries to another specified time. Whenever possible, choose to postpone.

GET INVOLVED!

Thought stopping and postponing are good ways to disrupt the noise of your worries. But keep in mind that nature abhors a vacuum. If you quiet down your mind, it's going to start looking around for something to think about. Your worried thoughts are attractive, since they are full of emotions. And of course they were the last things you were thinking about.

So get involved! Refocus your attention toward other activities that will be interesting or enjoyable to you. If you are on the plane, you can strike up a conversation with the person next to you. There are many interesting people on a plane, going to lots of exciting places. Or you can start reading that good book you brought along, or get back to a business project in your briefcase. You can also take time for relaxation by listening to a tape. On most planes you can even call someone up on the phone and chat.

If you are worrying during the days before the flight, you can do all of these, plus you can take a drive, go for a walk, or get some other exercise. Whatever you choose, know that you, not your worries, are in charge. Take control of what you do and what you think. Purposely fill your time with activities you choose. That will help ensure that the worries don't creep back in so frequently or intensely.

USE VISUALIZATIONS FOR REHEARSAL

If you are like most of the people who are uncomfortable fliers, you have a great imagination. The only problem is, you turn your daydreams into nightmares by picturing terrible things happening to you up in the sky. You can easily visualize yourself feeling uncomfortable. You reinforce that by visualizing the last time you felt terrible on a flight. As I have said, these repetitive negative images may cause you to feel as uncomfortable on your next flight as you did on your last.

Our-self help program "Achieving Comfortable Flight" contains a series of prerecorded visualization exercises. Use them to counter these negative images and to prepare for comfortable flights in the future. It's now time to change all that. Chapter 20 contains a number of imagery practices you can adapt for your concerns. Review the entire chapter for suggestions. I recommend four specific visualization exercises to help you prepare for comfortable flight. I presented the first two in earlier chapters; the second two are specifically for this chapter. Written transcripts for all four are found at the end of the book, and prerecorded copies are available (See "Resources," page 367).

Generalized Relaxation and Imagery

Many anxious people benefit from first recognizing when their bodies are tense and then relaxing those tense muscle groups. If they can let go of the physical tension, they can lower their emotional anxiety at that moment. Generalized Relaxation and Imagery (GRI), first described in chapter 12, can teach you this skill through daily practice of formal relaxation. Cue-Controlled Deep Muscle Relaxation, also in chapter 12, offers you similar benefits.

Resources

We will send you information on self-help resources that support this book.

- The *Don't Panic* Audio Tape Series
  by R. Reid Wilson, Ph.D.

- The *Don't Panic* Self-Help Workbook
  by R. Reid Wilson, Ph.D.

- Achieving Comfortable Flight: Taking the Anxiety Out of Airline Travel
  by R. Reid Wilson, Ph.D. and Captain T. W. Cummings

- Stop Obsessing! How to Overcome Your Obsessions and Compulsions
  by Edna B. Foa, Ph.D and R. Reid Wilson, Ph.D.

> R. Reid Wilson, Ph.D.
> Pathway Systems
> P.O. Box 269
> Chapel Hill, NC 27514
> 1-800-394-2299

Index

Death:
  accidental, 351–352
  causes of, 341–342
  of loved ones, 77–80, 82–83
  odds of, 351
Decisions, 221–226
  during panic attacks, 234–239
  by Negative Observers, 222–224
  by Supportive Observer, 224–226,
    231
Deep Muscle Relaxation, *see* Cue-
  Controlled Deep Muscle
  Relaxation
Dental problems, 21
Depakote, 310
Depersonalization, 158
Depression, 93–97
  activities and, 95–96
  agoraphobia and, 82, 93
  alcoholism and, 99–100
  beliefs and, 95–97
  Hopeless Observer and, 200
  panic disorder and, 93–94, 284–285
  physical illness and, 95–97,
    106–107, 111
  polarity and, 243
  social anxieties and, 318
Desipramine, 295
Desyrel, 282
Diabetes mellitus, 90
Diagnosis of causes of panic attacks,
  12–13, 119, 279–280
Diaphragm, 155–157
Diaphragmatic breathing, 155–157,
  160–162
Diarrhea, 38
Diazepam, 282, 283, 301, 304–305
Digitalis, 30
Disruption of negative thoughts,
  324–326
Dizziness, 20–23, 158, 288, 289
"Don't just do something, stand
  there," 183
Doxepin, 297
Drug abuse, medications and, 284,
  290–291, 301–302

Drugs, *See* Medications
Dry mouth, 38
Dudley, Donald, 110
Dyspnea, 18–20

Ear, disorders of, 14, 20–22
Eating, premenstrual syndrome and,
  89
Effexor, 283, 297
Elavil, 296–297
Embolism:
  cerebral, 21, 22
  pulmonary, 14, 24, 26
Emergency Response, 135–139
  beliefs and, 143–144
  brain and, 142–145
  evolution and, 144
  to flying, 354–357
  hyperventilation and, 159, 161
  panic attacks compared with,
    137–138
  physical changes in, 137
Emotions:
  agoraphobia and, 71–75, 80–83
  breathing and, 155
  pulmonary disease and, 110–111
  repression of, 71–75, 80–83,
    110–111
Emphysema, 14, 19, 109
Endocrine disorders, 14, 24–26, 50
  *see also specific disorders and con-
    ditions*
Ephedrine, 30
Epilepsy, temporal lobe (TLE), 14, 27
Epinephrine, 30, 90, 354
Erection difficulties, 38
Events precipitating panic attacks, 6–8
Evolution, Emergency Response and,
  144
Exercise, physical, 89, 127–128,
  170–171
Exhalation, 156, 244–245, 357
Expectations:
  affirmations and, 178
  Critical Observer and, 329
Expression of values, 73–75

Perfectionism, agoraphobia and,
  62–66, 84–85
Performance:
  social anxiety and, 311–312, 323,
    331–332
  trust and, 275–276
Periactin, 289
Pericardial effusion, 18
Permission, overcoming panic through,
    178, 183, 226–230, 244–247
Pertofrane, 295
pH balance, 154, 157, 160
Phencyclidine (PCP), 24
Phenelzine, 282, 285, 307
Phenobarbital, 303
Pheochromocytoma, 14, 21, 24, 26
Phobias, 98, 128
  agoraphobia, see Agoraphobia
  claustrophobia, 334, 335–336, 337,
    338, 339, 344, 348
  medications for, 284–285
  social, see Social phobias
  specific, 40–43
  vicarious, 336–337, 341–342, 346,
    353
  see also Fears; Flying, fear of; Loss
    of control, fear of
Physical causes of panic attacks, 7, 9,
    11–26
  alcoholism, 14, 29, 51, 97–100,
    290–291, 300, 302, 319, 360
  aural disorders, 14, 20–22
  cardiovascular disorders, 13–20,
    22–23, 26–27, 101–107
  diagnosis of, 12–13, 119
  endocrine/hormonal disorders, 14,
    24–26, 90
  hematic disorders, 14, 26
  medications, 14, 29–30, 112
  neurological/muscular disorders,
    14, 19
  respiratory disorders, 14, 18–20,
    101, 107–113
  vascular disorders, 13–14, 22–23
  see also specific disorders and con-
    ditions

Physical exercise, 89, 127–128,
    170–171
Physical illness, reaction to, 13, 15,
    16–17, 105–107, 126–128, 153,
    189–191
Physical responses:
  acceptance of, 274
  to anxiety, list of possible, 38–39
  to Calming Response, 148–149
  to Emergency Response, 137
  to fear of flying, 334, 354–359
  to hyperventilation, 158–160
  to panic attacks, 5–6, 17, 137–138,
    247–251, 270–271, 274
  to social anxieties, 312, 319, 324
Pilot training, 344
Planning short-term tasks, 266–270
Pleural effusion, 19
Pneumoconiosis, 19
Pneumothorax, 19
Polarity, 241–243
Poor concentration, 39
Post-myocardial infarction patients,
    14, 16–17, 105–107
  agoraphobia in, 127–128
  depression in, 106–107
Postponing worries, 271–272, 363–364
Post-traumatic stress disorder (PTSD),
    45–47
Postural (orthostatic) hypotension, 13,
    21, 22, 288–289
Power, balance of, 241–243
Practicing, testing vs., 185–187
Practicing with anxiety, 265–275
  beginning, 270–274
  ending, 274–275
  how long to, 267–268
  preparing for, 266–270
  simulations and role-playing in,
    330–331
  social anxieties and, 317, 328–332
  with fear of flying, 342, 343, 360
Predicting, see Forecasting the future
Prednisone, 30, 112
Preferences, 221
Pregnancy, 14